Advance Praise for *Ending Redlining*

"Josh Silver is the nation's preeminent expert on the CRA, including its regulatory and legislative evolution over the last forty-five years. He documents both the strengths and serious limitations of the law, and makes bold recommendations for how to make it more effective and to bring it in line with contemporary financial markets."

–Dan Immergluck, professor of urban studies at Georgia State University and author of *Red-Hot City: Housing, Race, and Exclusion in Twenty-First Century Atlanta*

"*Ending Redlining* is a vital resource in helping to strengthen the CRA in tangible ways to revitalize neighborhoods, combat discrimination, and spur growth among all segments of the economy."

–Stephen Cross, director of compliance and consumer affairs, FDIC, 1999-2001, and deputy comptroller for compliance management, OCC, 1991-1999

"Whether you work for a lender, a community organization, or as a fair lending consultant, you need to read Josh Silver's new and comprehensive book about the CRA, a law that works best if it is used as a bottom-up model of community development."

–Marva Williams, PhD, senior consultant, CDFI Friendly America

"This important book provides a comprehensive and honest look at how well the CRA has lived up to its promise of 'ending redlining.' Without the reforms Silver advocates, including that banks be evaluated on their efforts to promote integrated communities, the CRA cannot fulfill this promise. Silver helps us understand the law's history and impact thus far, while helping us to imagine a more effective future for the CRA."

–Leah Rothstein, co-author of *Just Action: How to Challenge Segregation Enacted Under the Color of Law*

"Josh Silver shows how community benefits agreements and updating CRA are win-wins for our communities and the sustainability of the financial institutions residing there."

–Scott McKee, senior vice president, director of corporate social responsibility, First Merchants Bank

Ending Redlining
through a
Community-Centered Reform
of the
Community Reinvestment Act

Armin Lear Press, Inc.
215 W Riverside Drive, #4362
Estes Park, CO 80517

Ending Redlining
through a
Community-Centered Reform
of the
Community Reinvestment Act

Josh Silver

Foreword by Gregory D. Squires

ARMINLEAR

To my loving family – Kathy, Michelle, and Daphne, the cat.

To my professional colleagues in the reinvestment arena working to make our country fairer and more equitable.

Contents

Foreword

If Gale Cincotta was the "Mother of the Community Reinvestment Act," as her admirers affectionately called her, then Josh Silver is at least a first cousin. To mix metaphors, Josh is both "Mr. Inside" and "Mr. Outside" when it comes to CRA. He has advised regulatory agencies and testified before Congressional committees on the evolution of legislative and regulatory initiatives as part of the policymaking infrastructure that has implemented the law. At the same time, he has provided research assistance, organizing advice, and other guidance to advocacy groups who have challenged policymakers and the industry they supervise in utilizing the CRA to advance revitalization of traditionally underserved communities. In addition, as a middleman of sorts he has been an integral part of teams that have negotiated community benefits agreements directly with financial service providers. Throughout the book he points to many victories that would not have been achieved absent the CRA, many in which he was a key player.

This book provides encyclopedic analyses of many of the controversies surrounding the CRA, from the legislative debates leading up to passage of the statute in 1977 through subsequent and current debates over passage (and sometimes rejection) of various proposals for reform in efforts to modernize the law. Much of the book focuses on the role of the National Community Reinvestment Coalition (NCRC) where Josh has "lived" for over 25 years. He is an advocate. But he offers careful, nuanced analyses of the many perspectives that have shaped the debate. And while an advocate, he astutely recognizes the importance of the CRA, the need for compromise, and the limits of this law.

At the same time, while no one law can achieve the vision of CRA, in the conclusion Josh points to "CRA-inspired synergies among legal requirements, public policy, and private-sector actors" that are essential to address a wide range of issues including climate change, living wage requirements, health care, and many more. So CRA offers many lessons for financial service industries, their regulators, and the communities they serve. But these lessons apply to many other actors as well.

Perhaps the most important message of this book, reiterated throughout, is the vital role of community organizations and the voice of local communities. But this points to the greatest threat to the letter and spirit of this law as well. Lenders and their lobbyists are commonly well heeled. They will always be around, paid well and granted influence. And they will be focused on the narrow interests of their employers and clients. Community organizations are almost always looking for resources, particularly funding. Burnout is very real among underpaid organizers. Demands on advocacy groups seem to grow. Foundation priorities change. Public officials who support community reinvestment leave office and are often replaced by those with a very different agenda. The future is uncertain.

Community reinvestment has long been an arena of contested terrain. This is not likely to change soon, as this book makes so clear. The challenges are many. Josh Silver is one figure who provides reason for optimism that there are bright lights ahead and they are not all trains coming the other way.

—Gregory D. Squires, Research Professor and Professor Emeritus in the Department of Sociology at George Washington University

Introduction

Where you live often determines your life chances, and lending discrimination places residents of communities of color at significant disadvantages. Recent research by Raj Chetty and his colleagues reveal that "All else equal, low-income boys who grow up in such areas (areas with lower income) earn about 35 percent less on average than otherwise similar low-income children who grow up in the best areas for mobility. For girls, the gap is closer to 25 percent." The research found that neighborhoods with large populations of lower income and African American residents in some of the largest cities such as Chicago, Atlanta, and Milwaukee in our country have some of the "worst odds."[1]

The fair lending and civil rights organization where I worked for almost 30 years, the National Community Reinvestment Coalition (NCRC), has produced similar research detailed in Chapter 1 revealing stark disparities in health outcomes as well as economic outcomes depending on a person's neighborhood.[2]

Tragically, these outcomes did not happen by chance. They are the product of systemic discrimination. Racism drove the development of housing segregation and separation of the races, immigrants, and religious minorities into distinct neighborhoods. White neighborhoods had the advantages of superior schools, health care, and job opportunities while people of color were cornered into neighborhoods lacking these opportunities. Initially, jurisdictions such as Louisville and Baltimore passed laws that prohibited African Americans from purchasing homes in desirable neighborhoods. After the Supreme Court struck down these laws, real estate and other powerful economic brokers developed racial covenants that prohibited Whites from selling to African Americans, Jews, and other immigrant populations deemed to present destabilizing influences on neighborhoods. Chicago real estate interests were among the pioneers of racial covenants.[3] But they were not the only pioneers. Baltimore's Mayor who embarked on a similar path in the early twentieth century declared, "Blacks should be quarantined in isolated slums in order to reduce the incidence of civil disturbance, to prevent the spread of communicable disease into the nearby White neighborhoods, and to protect property values among the White majority."[4]

Eventually, the Supreme Court in Shelley v. Kraemer invalidated judicial enforcement of racial covenants.[5] However, these instruments were not the only devices used to perpetuate segregation. In the 1930s, reflective of the racism in our country, the Roosevelt administration further developed the practice of redlining. Its Great Depression recovery efforts included programs to rescue homeowners from the brink of foreclosures and to create government back-stops for home lending that facilitated the rise of the White middle class. As the next chapter will describe, federal agencies developed maps of urban neighborhoods across the country advising lending institutions where to lend and what neighborhoods to avoid.[6] Tragically, the maps deemed African American neighborhoods the riskiest and as a result few loans were made in these neighborhoods in the ensuing decades.[7] Without access to private lending and capital, most of these neighborhoods withered economically and imperiled residents' health and quality of life.[8] As discussed in more detail in the next chapter, lending discrimination was one of the multiple causes of neighborhood declines; other contributors were discriminatory real estate practices, discrimination in labor markets, and inferior schools. As a result of all these forces, Whites entered the middle class while discrimination shut the doors to opportunity for too many African Americans during the twentieth century.

If the public and private sectors created disadvantage based on place, could a law effectively require federal agencies to enforce a mandate that lending institutions engage community residents and reinvest in redlined neighborhoods? During the civil rights movement, neighborhood activists pushed an agenda of integration and allowing people of color to move into predominantly White neighborhoods to improve their life chances. Many scholars and practitioners have written about these efforts.[9] Less seems to have been written about efforts to reinvest in neighborhoods where the government and the private sector had previously shut off access to credit.[10] Can efforts to reinvest in neighborhoods succeed in improving the lives of victims of discrimination and complement integration strategies? Can the victims of discrimination be empowered to be part of reinvestment strategies and programs in their communities? This book is aimed at providing at least partial answers and recommending ways to improve the Community Reinvestment Act (CRA), the main law intended to eradicate redlining.

Neighborhood activists led by Gale Cincotta and National People's Action (NPA) in Chicago sought to combat discrimination that contributed to segregation and economically devasted communities. They worked with Senator William Proxmire to pass a data disclosure law in 1975 called the Home Mortgage Disclosure Act (HMDA) that they used to document redlining and bank refusal to lend in communities of color and White ethnic neighborhoods becoming more segregated in Chicago. Citing data driven evidence of redlining, Proxmire then seized the opportunities presented by new Democratic majorities in the House and Senate to pass CRA in 1977.[11] Even though CRA passed on its first attempt, its passage was a squeaker by thin margins as Chapter 4 will describe. It required the legislative acumen of Proxmire and the dogged persistence of advocates to build national support for the law in 1977 and in subsequent decades when it came under attack.[12]

Consistent with the grassroots advocacy motivating its passage, CRA is one of the relatively few federal laws that is grounded in a democratic philosophy. It involves community residents in remediating discrimination and disinvestment by requiring banks to respond to credit needs. Under CRA, federal agencies assess and rate banks' records of meeting community credit needs and then consider banks' CRA performance when deciding whether to approve bank mergers and other bank applications.[13] Federal agencies solicit the input of the public and community-based organizations when conducting CRA exams and considering merger applications as Chapter 3 describes in detail. The law's premise is that democratic participation and input will help make the economy more equitable and efficient as banks utilize the expertise and first-hand knowledge of community residents regarding needs and opportunities in their neighborhoods. Labor law is a close analogy to CRA. Just like CRA, labor law creates a role for labor unions and workers to have input into working conditions and production processes in industries across America.

In their recent book, *The Anti-Oligarchy Constitution*, law professors Fishkin and Forbath describe a "democracy-of-opportunity" tradition in American history. This tradition believes that democracy thrives only if oligarchy (a concentration of economic and political power) is diminished, a broad middle-class grows and flourishes, and society is inclusive in offering people of all races, ethnicities, and genders opportunities for a decent standard of living. They assert that the Constitution demands that our society strive for these three preconditions of democracy. CRA fits into this tradition by seeking to empower a sizable segment of society that was disenfranchised and include them in the middle class by increasing their access to credit and capital.[14]

CRA also combats the destructive tendencies of the financial industry by increasing its accountability to communities. In his book, *The Great Divide*, the economist Joseph Stiglitz asserts that the financial sector has contributed to inequality by appropriating wealth of modest income Americans. He states, "While some of the wealth of those in the financial sector comes at the expense of wealthy people...much of it comes from siphoning money from the bottom of the economic pyramid. This is true of the billions generated through abusive credit card practices and predatory and discriminatory lending."[15] By increasing public accountability, CRA pushes banks back into the business of providing responsible loans and thereby building community wealth. In the years of de-regulation leading up to the Great Recession of 2008, banks, particularly their investment arms, were fixated on financial speculation and concealing the harms of abusive lending, which contributed significantly to inequality and to the financial crisis as Stiglitz maintains.[16]

Has CRA been effective?

Fighting discrimination provides opportunities for wealth building that not only benefits victims of discrimination but also the national economy. The American dream of homeownership or small business ownership could not be realized by creditworthy residents of neighborhoods unfairly rejected for loans due to their skin color or where they lived. If CRA eliminated or at least reduced discrimination based on place, would increases in bank lending promote wealth building opportunities on a wide scale? If so, could the nation's economic success be boosted if significant segments of neighborhoods that were economically depressed become vibrant and offer quality life chances for their residents?

As CRA turns 50 in 2027, stakeholders need to assess its history, its successes, and consider needed improvements so that its vital objectives can be better realized. Chapter 2 provides an overview of CRA and describes how federal bank agencies (the Federal Reserve Board, the Federal Deposit Insurance Corporation, and the Office of the Comptroller of the Currency) rate banks' lending, investments, and services in low- and moderate-income (LMI) communities and take these ratings into account when considering bank requests to merge or open new branches. Federal agency bank CRA exams are available to the public. The public is encouraged to comment on bank performance when agencies are completing exams or considering merger applications.

The public accountability mechanisms of CRA have encouraged banks to increase their lending and investments in LMI communities. For example, the National Community Reinvestment Coalition (NCRC) estimated that banks have made more than $2.8 trillion in home loans in LMI communities or to LMI borrowers from 2009 through 2020.[17] Despite these successes and the benefits CRA has bestowed on banks and communities, the law has been controversial, including allegations of undue market interference as Chapters 2, 4, and 6 will review.

While economists and academics have conducted various quantitative studies confirming CRA's effectiveness as reviewed in detail in Chapter 2, there are fewer up-to-date analyses that comprehensively review CRA's practice (the process of CRA exams and merger applications) and whether CRA practice conforms with the legislation's intent to rectify the economic disenfranchisement of redlined communities. In other words, has CRA practice succeeded in putting communities front and center to stimulate meaningful reinvestment that results in vibrant communities? Has CRA practice empowered community stakeholders to have a significant role in revitalizing their communities? To shed light on how successful CRA practice is, it is necessary to review the legislative and regulatory history of CRA to identify the objectives of Congress and whether the bank agencies have developed a regulation and examination regime that faithfully implements these objectives. The book will also include insights about CRA's successes and frustrations from interviews with local leaders of community-based organizations and banks serving a diversity of modest income and communities of color across the country.

CRA has a complex mission to measure bank responsiveness to local needs that vary across the country. Although the statute itself is just a few pages, the CRA regulation is lengthy and a CRA exam of a large bank can take up hundreds of pages. Banks complain about the regulatory burdens and costs of CRA exams. Community advocates, on the other hand, point out that almost 100 percent of banks pass their CRA exams (see Chapter 2 for a review of the distribution of ratings over CRA's history) and that the law therefore has not realized its potential to increase lending and investment in traditionally underserved communities. The challenge for the federal bank agencies is whether they can make CRA exams both more efficient and rigorous. Can some of the verbiage in exams be reduced? At the same time, can more penetrating analyses of the numbers and charts in CRA exams effectively identify geographical areas where banks are serving modest income communities well and other areas in which banks performance must improve. Can exams be made effective for both banks and community groups to use in a way to identify unmet credit needs and design programs and approaches that best meet these needs?

A pass rate of almost 100 percent would indicate to casual observers that banks are doing great in terms of meeting credit and capital needs.[18] Neighborhoods across America should be thriving. But we know that this is not the case. Deficiencies in bank lending and investment are not the sole reasons for impoverished and struggling neighborhoods. As this book points out, discrimination against communities of color and people of color occurs in many sectors including education and at work. A perfect CRA will not therefore completely remedy inequalities and inequities across neighborhoods. However, a better CRA can provide the credit and capital needed to successfully revitalize more neighborhoods.

A better CRA does not seek to fail hundreds of banks and reduce the pass rate to something like 50 percent. Rather, the grading system needs to be more nuanced and identify more banks that are performing at a B- or C level. If a bank is judged as barely passing, it will want to improve its CRA performance by making more loans and investments in traditionally underserved neighborhoods. Banks are quite sensitive to their public reputations so a lackluster CRA rating, even if it is a passing rating, will likely motivate many of them to improve their performance. This book will offer suggestions about how to make the rating system more reflective of variations in performance and therefore be more effective at stimulating bank improvements. The book will also make the case that all concerned stakeholders must do better research to document how or if public input has positively influenced bank reinvestment performance.

CRA exams need to elevate the voice of communities

Better CRA evaluations, however, are not a panacea. A more effective CRA also needs to put community voices at the center of CRA. The current CRA regulation requires that CRA examiners consider public comment when they are conducting CRA exams and rating banks. However, the current CRA exams mostly engage community-based organizations and stakeholders in a perfunctory manner that does not provide many insights into how banks are meeting needs as Chapter 3 will describe.

CRA exams will summarize community views and often use boilerplate language to report that a metropolitan area or rural county needs more affordable housing or job creation. However, almost all underserved neighborhoods will need more affordable housing or job creation. Chapter 3 will make the case that CRA examiners could do a better job at probing for specific needs that some examined banks will be meeting but others are not.

For example, some geographical areas might need more housing for an elderly population to age-in place. Adaptations such as improved walkways leading up to the housing or alterations within bathrooms or stairways might be particularly important. Some banks might be better at responding to these needs than others; the better performers should be awarded better scores on subtests in some geographical areas or overall CRA ratings.

In other cases, preventing displacement of people of color and modest income residents in gentrifying areas are major issues in both larger metropolitan areas and smaller cities.[19] CRA exams currently do an uneven job at identifying these demographic trends, utilizing community concerns about displacement, and assessing banks' responsiveness to these trends.

CRA exams should also do a better job in addressing the large scale sociological and environmental issues of our times. Congress passed CRA in response to redlining and discrimination against communities of color. However, the CRA statute passed in 1977 addressed the needs of low- and moderate-income communities and omitted mention of communities of color as explained in Chapter 4. Congress amended the law a few times thereafter to indirectly address racial inequities such as offering incentives for banks to provide financial assistance to minority-owned banks and women-owned banks.[20] However, Congress opted against an explicit addition of race to the CRA statute. This book will probe into the reasons for this omission and contemplate whether direct or indirect approaches can be effective in addressing racial lending inequities identified by community organizations.

The paucity of traditional banks in communities of color provided an opportunity for unscrupulous and high-cost lenders (often called subprime lenders) to flood communities of color with abusive loans in the late 1990s and into the 2000s.[21] Widespread irresponsible lending was a primary cause of the collapse of the global economy in 2007 and 2008.[22] Better protections for communities of color may have safeguarded all of us. If CRA had done a better job in addressing a dearth of responsible credit in communities of color, it is possible that the crisis may have been averted or at least reduced in its severity. Perhaps there would have been fewer subprime lenders peddling abusive loans if CRA had motivated traditional banks to have been more present in communities of color. Since the Great Recession, the tragic murder of George Floyd and rising racial inequalities in the wake of the COVID pandemic compel a reconsideration of CRA and race.

A lack of sufficient attention to community voices may have blinded CRA exams to overflows of irresponsible lending in communities of color. Community-based organizations used whatever means they could to call alarm to the rise of risky lending – the bully pulpit, Congressional hearings, comments to the bank agencies on CRA policy as well as exams and media interviews.[23] As described in Chapter 2, banks were not the main perpetrators of irresponsible lending.[24] Yet, some banks acquired and operated subprime mortgage companies and used regulatory loopholes to omit consideration of these companies on CRA exams.[25] In addition, as delinquencies and foreclosures increased in communities, CRA exams could have probed whether banks offered foreclosure prevention counseling or helped borrowers refinance into affordable loans. CRA exams did not do so on a regular basis despite requests from advocates.

Climate change is another monumental challenge that is an existential threat to all of us. Just as with racial inequity, CRA by itself will not eliminate global warming. Society will have to marshal an extraordinary policy and economic response to global warming. However, CRA is currently an under-utilized tool to address climate change which disproportionately impacts communities of color.[26] In response to grassroots advocacy, the federal agencies are attempting to bolster CRA incentives for banks to finance climate remediation, resiliency, and adaptation. This book will provide an early assessment of the likelihood of climate remediation success in this update to CRA.

Community voice must not only be a major component of CRA exams; community involvement must be part of the entire CRA process. Since redlining entailed the lack of service in modest income neighborhoods and communities of color, some banks over the years became ignorant of how to serve these communities. Meanwhile, the communities organized, articulated their needs, and formed community-based organizations to address housing inadequacy, food insecurity, environmental hazards, and a host of other problems. These community-based nonprofit organizations are a base of extensive knowledge of community needs and how to address them. Accordingly, banks must continue to seek partnerships with these organizations if they are to successfully serve overlooked communities. Today, banks engage with a variety of non-profit community-based organizations. They help finance affordable housing production, small business development, and the creation of community-based health care centers and other facilities. They partner with community-based organizations to provide financial counseling, homeownership counseling and small business technical assistance. Yet, the partnership building, in some cases, can be episodic and not continuous. This book will examine ways in which to promote durable partnerships between banks and community organizations.

The future of CRA must include more rigorous application to banks and expanding CRA's coverage to non-bank financial institutions

When banks apply to acquire or merge with other banks, the CRA statute requires federal bank agencies to consider the CRA records of banks. The agencies review the most recent exams of the banks and consider public comments. They are also required to consider the public benefits of mergers and assess whether these benefits exceed harms such as less competition or branch closures after the mergers.[27] As the book will describe particularly in chapters 2 and 3, the receptiveness of the agencies to public comment and input waxes and wanes depending on the leadership of the agencies.

Community-based organizations seek to avoid the harmful impacts of mergers by negotiating community benefits agreements (CBAs) with banks as detailed in Chapter 3. CBAs commit banks to specified future levels of loans, investments, and services.[28] CBAs promote increases in bank reinvestment activity and prevent reduced access to bank lending and services that can occur after mergers when banks re-structure themselves. Recommendations offered by the book will include how to enhance consideration of CBAs as part of merger applications and CRA exams and how to prevent any misuse or mischaracterization of CBAs. CBAs have similarities to labor union contracts in empowering economically disenfranchised segments of the population.

Since CRA's passage in 1977, Congress has not substantially updated the law. It has made additions that the book reviews but these do not address significant structural and technological changes in the banking industry. Likewise, the federal bank agencies have made some changes to their regulation implementing the CRA law over the years, but these changes often fell short in keeping up to date with industry transformation. For example, while several banks still make most of their loans through branches, a significant number offer large number of loans either through the internet or via loan officers or brokers that are not located in bank branches.[29] At the same time, the numbers of banks have dropped dramatically over the last few decades and the nation has half a dozen banks with more than $1 trillion each in assets.[30] CRA requirements must consider the rise of virtual banking and the massive size of the largest banks. As this book was being written, the federal bank agencies updated their CRA regulations in the fall of 2023. The book will provide an early assessment regarding the extent to which the agencies succeeded in tackling the significant changes in the banking industry to improve CRA's effectiveness in increasing reinvestment. A related set of policy issues is whether and how CRA requirements can and should be extended to non-bank financial institutions that are increasingly offering loans and other bank products or are merging with banks.

During 2025, the prospects of strengthening CRA will be undoubtedly influenced by the results of the recent presidential election. Thus, a book reviewing CRA's history – where it has been and where it was going – will contribute to the dialogue that will occur as the new administration and Congress undertake policy initiatives.

Organization and perspective of the book

The book is organized in the following chapters:

"Chapter 1: Redlining: The Practices that Contributed to Community Decline" explains how redlining was combined with other discriminatory practices to harm communities of color and modest income neighborhoods. It describes the stunted life chances of residents in redlined communities. The chapter will conclude on a positive note and illustrate how CRA can jump start revitalization in a neighborhood, providing opportunities and wealth building for residents.

"Chapter 2: Unraveling Redlining: How the CRA Works" reviews the nuts and bolts of CRA and will be especially useful for readers that are not familiar with CRA. It then considers academic and stakeholder studies of CRA's effectiveness. It concludes with some major observations and recommendations that respond to the weaknesses and strengths of CRA as identified by the literature and observations from CRA practitioners.

"Chapter 3: Reinvestment: Leveraging the CRA at the Community Level" includes interviews of stakeholders and case studies of how community-based organizations have been involved in commenting on CRA exams and merger applications to increase bank lending and investment in the neighborhoods they serve. In addition, it describes how banks, community groups, and local public agencies use CRA regularly to design loan and investment programs and products. The chapter ends with recommendations about how to increase public input on CRA exams and merger applications as well as how to improve regular communication with the federal bank agencies.

"Chapter 4: Breakthrough! CRA Squeaks through Congress" revisits the history of how the much-heralded antidote to redlining nearly did not happen at all. During three days of public hearings, proponents and opponents aired their differences, culminating in a law that squeaked through Congress but that nonetheless created a sound foundation for implementing regulations and congressional amendments in the future. This chapter also reviews early implementation efforts during the administrations of Jimmy Carter, Ronald Reagan, and George H. W. Bush.

"Chapter 5: Revisions: Clinton-Era Regulatory Reforms an Incomplete Advance" explores a period in which implementation of the law was improved, but not enough. In response to calls from community-based organizations and banks to improve CRA exams and an executive order from President Clinton, the federal agencies undertook an arduous multi-year process that featured two proposed rules and resulted in a new CRA examination regime that was durable over a period of several years. The agencies deferred on some critical reforms, which would have made CRA more effective, but they established a solid foundation from which to build during subsequent rulemakings.

"Chapter 6: Rollback: Congress Weakens the CRA" shows how the law was weakened by not updating it. The financial industry pushed Congress to pass a major law in 1999 that fostered the merging of banks, insurance companies, and securities firms. In the shuffle, CRA got lost and was not updated to apply to all parts of the new financial conglomerates. While CRA still applied to banks, it did not apply to insurance companies and securities firms that were now bank affiliates in many cases. Lawmakers in subsequent sessions of Congress introduced important bills that were not passed but that provided a blueprint of how to update CRA to account for changes in the financial industry.

"Chapter 7: A Lawsuit and a Regulatory Reversal" reviews regulatory changes made in the mid-2000s during the George W. Bush administration that streamlined CRA according to proponents of the changes but that weakened CRA implementation according to those that opposed the changes. The chapter then explains how the Office of the Comptroller of the Currency (OCC), one of the three regulatory agencies that oversees the CRA, changed its CRA regulation during the administration of Donald Trump, prompting a lawsuit by community organizations.

"Chapter 8: Will a Promise of Progress Endure?" describes the OCC reversal of its rule after the arrival of the Joe Biden administration. Subsequently, the three federal bank agencies proposed and finalized major changes in the CRA regulations, which will likely increase bank reinvestment but missed the mark in some important respects. The interagency final rule in 2023 is the most significant change in CRA regulations since 1995. It should not have taken 28 years for this change; the chapter explores the need and feasibility for more frequent updates to the CRA regulation. On the heels of the regulatory reform, bank trade associations sued the agencies, seeking to overturn the new regulations. As this book goes to press, the future is unclear regarding this important update to CRA because of the lawsuit and the recent election.

"Chapter 9: Next Steps for CRA: Recommendations for Lasting Impact" reviews the strengths and shortcomings of CRA from the perspective of empowering communities and leveraging reinvestment in the form of safe and sound loans and investments. Proposed reforms describe revisions to CRA as applied to banks and other industries that should be covered by a CRA-like requirement.

The chapters contain references to NCRC, its research, and its advocacy. Part of this is because I worked there for almost 30 years, so I take advantage of the knowledge I gained at NCRC about CRA and how advocates use this critical law. In addition, NCRC is a leading coalition of local community organizations across the country using CRA in rural and urban settings. According to NCRC's webpage, "Today our members include more than 700 nonprofit community development and finance organizations; community organizing and civil rights groups; minority and women-owned business associations; national, state and local housing, economic development, education, media, arts, healthcare and investment organizations; state and local government agencies; faith-based institutions; and committed, hopeful individuals from across the nation."[31] The book gains from the richness of the experiences of this diverse group of local organizations.

I speak from the perspective of community-based organizations because that is who I have worked with for decades and many of their leaders are my heroes who have done great things in their neighborhoods with few resources. Thus, some of my grassroots readers will be cheering as the pages go by; other community leaders will wish that I was tougher in some places. Some bankers will not like what I say but others will react in ways that range from grudging respect to agreement with various points. Regulatory officials and members of Congress will also react in various ways to my points. I have met and collaborated with thoughtful and devoted people in the lending industry as well as policymakers. I call it as I see it throughout the book. I offer some compromises. I hope this book increases consensus for the eminent commonsense of this vital law that empowers communities, helps build wealth, and makes capitalism work better and more fairly. At the same time, this law cannot be regarded as a panacea and expectations must be realistic in that CRA must be paired with other restorative policies and efforts to make our country a better place for all.

1

Redlining: The Practices that Contributed to Community Decline

Mural of Freddie Gray in his former neighborhood

Source: Anacostia Community Museum, Smithsonian Institution

Abraham Lincoln stated that the "leading object" of government is "to elevate the condition of men – to lift artificial weights from all shoulders – to clear the paths of laudable pursuit for all- to afford all, an unfettered start, and a fair chance, in the race of life."[32] Yet, our country has not achieved this aspiration as illustrated by the life of Freddie Gray.

In mid-April 2015, a young man named Freddie Gray was hanging out in a Baltimore neighborhood called Sandtown-Winchester. Police became suspicious because Gray was in an area known for drug dealing. Gray ran and the police chased. They put him in a van and drove to the police station. When Gray got out of the van, he appeared to have a serious spinal injury. Within a week, Gray died from his injuries. He was a 25-year-old African American male. It was a tragic death that should never have occurred. As Derek Hyra discusses in *Slow and Sudden Violence*, decades of disinvestment and discrimination across communities of color like Gray's exacerbates police brutality and subsequent unrest as occurred in Baltimore.[33]

Police tactics were questioned. Criminal trials exonerated six of the involved officers.[34] The Gray family settled with the City of Baltimore for $6.4 million.[35] The millions of dollars of settlement money was inadequate compensation, especially considering that this tragedy should have been avoided. The policing may not have been a factor in Gray's death had he been raised in a neighborhood that gave him more of a chance to lead a decent quality of life. If the public and private sector had invested in the neighborhood over decades instead of discriminating against it, it is possible that Freddie Gray would be alive today and enjoying a full life of opportunities.

Gray was raised in public housing that had dangerous levels of lead and peeling paint. By his second birthday, Gray had concentrations of lead in his body that was seven times the concentration that results in brain damage. Dan Levy, an assistant professor of pediatrics at Johns Hopkins University, stated "The fact that Mr. Gray had these high levels of lead in all likelihood affected his ability to think and to self-regulate and profoundly affected his cognitive ability to process information."[36] It seemed like Gray had two strikes against him when he encountered police that day: being a Black male *and* an individual who had a serious mental deficiency dealing with a high stress situation.

If only his housing had been safe and affordable instead of giving Gray lead poisoning. If only his cognitive abilities were not impaired by lead poisoning, perhaps Gray may have been able to better deal with the police that day or may never have been in that situation. If only the public and private sectors had invested in decent housing in the Sandtown-Winchester neighborhood.[37]

In addition to the housing, the Sandtown-Winchester neighborhood presents economic and sociological disadvantages that do not empower youth and help them climb life's ladder of success. The census tract encompassing the Gilmor Homes, one of the residences for Gray's family, had a poverty rate of 40 percent.[38] According to Washington Post articles, the larger 72 block area which is almost 100 percent African American, had an unemployment rate of 25 percent and more residents in state prisons than other neighborhoods in Baltimore.[39]

The origins of redlining

Gray's neighborhood is a victim of redlining, an insidious form of discrimination invented decades ago by the federal government working with the private sector. In the midst of the Great Depression and in a genuine effort to uplift the dispossessed through the New Deal and a program to rescue families from foreclosure, the Roosevelt administration nevertheless promoted redlining and exacerbated segregation. Within the administration, there were civil rights figures including Eleanor Roosevelt but the overwhelming racism within federal agencies and in society at large guided the Home Owners' Loan Corporation (HOLC). Redlining is the practice of refusing to lend and serve communities of color and modest income neighborhoods. As this chapter will describe, the federal government initially encouraged redlining, but this form of discrimination continued long after the federal government stopped publishing maps and underwriting criteria that encouraged it.

As a federal agency, HOLC sponsored the creation of maps that classified city neighborhoods by the risk they posed to lending institutions. Neighborhoods were color coded – green for the most desirable neighborhoods while red classified the most hazardous ones, which is the classification that Gray's Sandtown-Winchester received. The classifications were guided by some objective criteria such as the quality of the housing stock but a heavily weighted factor, if not the predominant factor, was the racial composition of the neighborhoods.[40] HOLC was not a lender that originated home purchase loans. Instead, it purchased delinquent loans from private sector lenders, refinanced them, and improved loan terms and conditions so that most of the delinquent borrowers would not end up in foreclosure. It ceased operations in 1951.[41] Its racist attitudes and the production of its maps reflected the discriminatory practices of the lending industry of that era. Despite the production of the maps, HOLC did not deny refinance loans to African American borrowers that were delinquent on their home purchase loans.[42] HOLC developed its maps and risk assessment system so that it could estimate how the loans it purchased would perform and which ones were likely to become delinquent.[43]

A significant presence of African Americans or an in-migration of African Americans usually resulted in a HOLC map classification of "hazardous." A presence of other "undesirables" such as Jews or other recent Eastern or Southern European immigrants often propelled a neighborhood into the red category.

These classifications mirrored the maps created by the Federal Housing Administration (FHA). There is a discussion and some disagreement among historians about the extent to which the HOLC maps influenced the FHA, but it was the leading thought leaders and private sector practitioners that put together the HOLC maps and the FHA approach to lending.[44] HOLC maps classified areas as risky that biased lending institutions were avoiding, according to Immergluck.[45] Under the leadership of Homer Hoyt and Frederick Babcock, the FHA created maps and underwriting manuals that relied upon fallacious racist assumptions of risk.[46] Recent research, including NCRC's, uses HOLC maps because the FHA destroyed most of its maps in response to a lawsuit against the agency in 1969.[47]

Redlining reflects systemic discrimination and exacerbates disadvantages

In the post-World War II years, FHA-guaranteed lending standardized industry underwriting with redlining as a central feature. Under guaranteed lending, the private sector lender is reimbursed by the FHA if losses are incurred on the loan due to delinquency and foreclosure. FHA-guaranteed lending was a major factor contributing to segregated White suburbs and a White middle class of homeowners. In addition to the racist assumptions about risk and avoidance of communities of color in FHA underwriting, the FHA favored newly constructed and suburban single-family developments over higher density multifamily developments and mixed use (residential and commercial) developments disproportionately located in cities. For example, Immergluck cited research showing that 91 percent of FHA loans in the St. Louis area between 1935 and 1939 were for homes in the suburbs. Similar patterns occurred in the New Jersey and the Washington, D.C. metropolitan area.[48] Fishback, Rose, Snowden, and Storrs document similar trends using county deed records and census data. In Greensboro, North Carolina, they found that one FHA-guaranteed loan was issued to an African American while African Americans totaled 1,300 homeowners in the city in 1940.[49]

Across the country, African Americans were systematically excluded. Conley and Kirp, Dwyer, and Rosenthal document that from 1930 to 1960, lenders issued about 1 percent of their mortgage loans to African Americans across the entire country.[50] The FHA and the private sector suburban development it subsidized was a major factor shutting African Americans out of the American Dream of homeownership and equity accumulation. They were too often confined to the economically and socially disadvantaged neighborhoods that stunted life chances of Freddie Gray and too many of his contemporaries.

Assisted by underwriting practices promoted by the federal government, lending institutions engaged in widespread levels of redlining over the decades. Before the advent of the internet, redlining was the practice of banks receiving deposits from neighborhoods and refusing to lend to those neighborhoods, which were often minority and working-class communities. Today, even though lending institutions no longer use HOLC or FHA maps as tools of discrimination, the traditional form of redlining still occurs in which banks are not reinvesting in disadvantaged neighborhoods where they have branches or are avoiding these neighborhoods altogether by not lending or placing branches in them. Redlining also has a digital component. A bank with significant internet-based lending can still opt to avoid predominantly minority neighborhoods. Redlining has been dramatically illustrated by mapping whereby loans are represented as dots on a map and minority neighborhoods in a city or county have significantly fewer dots or loans on the map.

Far from disappearing, lending discrimination is an enduring characteristic in the marketplace and needs to be constantly combated by enforcement efforts. Using home loan data, one of the early statistical studies by the Federal Reserve Bank of Boston in 1992 confirmed that even after controlling for borrower and neighborhood characteristics, people of color nevertheless confronted significantly higher denial rates than Whites. In underwriting and making decisions on loan applications, lenders consider what is known as the three Cs – character, capacity, and collateral.[51] The first two refer to borrower characteristics. These include credit history regarding the likelihood the borrower will repay and the borrower's income and wealth that help determine the ability of the borrower to afford the loan. Collateral refers to the house's value and its condition. The characteristics of the neighborhood also affect the house's value as collateral for the lender. The 1992 study was one of the first to combine demographic data with private sector and nonpublic data concerning the three Cs.

Before controlling for borrower and neighborhood characteristics, people of color faced denial rates about 2.7 times higher than Whites in the Boston metropolitan area. After adding borrower and neighborhood characteristics such as credit history, expense-to-income ratios, debt- to-income ratios, and whether the property was single or multi-unit into the regression equations, the difference in denial rates narrowed but was still 1.6 times higher for minority applicants.[52] In other words, even after considering variables commonly used in underwriting, minorities were still more likely to be denied loans. This suggests the possibilities of discrimination or at the very least, differential treatment of similarly situated applicants.

Unfortunately, redlining continues today. Since 2021, the Department of Justice (DOJ) has secured ten settlements totaling $107 million in compensation and lender outreach and lending programs offered to redlined neighborhoods. One of these settlements involved Ameris Bank and its redlining of communities of color in Jacksonville, Florida. Ameris operated 18 branches in the Jacksonville metropolitan area but not one of them was in a majority African American or Hispanic neighborhood. In addition, lender peers of Ameris generated applications from people of color at three times the rate of Ameris from 2016 through 2021. Some of the neighborhoods that Ameris redlined were deemed hazardous by HOLC eight decades ago. The maps accompanying the DOJ complaint are stark showing a dearth of loans in predominantly minority neighborhoods to the north and west and a lack of marketing by mail in these neighborhoods. In contrast, the White neighborhoods to the south and east have high volumes of applications and loans.[53]

The extent of virtual redlining has not been studied and investigated to the same extent as redlining by lenders with branches and offices. Yet, there is evidence that racial disparities in the virtual marketplace exist. Friedline and Chen used proprietary and publicly available data to compare access to online and mobile banking among Whites and people of color. They used a variety of variables to control for a wide range of characteristics that could influence virtual access to banking. At the zip code level, these included the percentage of people with a college education, median net worth, percent of owner-occupied housing units, percent of people with a checking account, bank branches per 1,000 people, unemployment rate, percent of people with high-speed internet access, and percent of people with smartphones.[54]

The authors predicted the percentage of people with access to online and mobile banking using various combinations of the socio-economic variables. Their equations produced the most negative impacts on access to online and mobile banking in the case of African Americans. For every percentage point increase for African Americans at a zip code level, there was a 12 percent decrease in online banking, and a 3 percent decrease in mobile banking. The results were mixed for Native Americans and Latinos, showing negative associations in some of the equations but not in others.[55] Further research should investigate these racial and ethnic differences and whether the findings hold up for sub-categories of Hispanics (those from different countries) and Native Americans (those from different tribes or regions of the country).

For the purposes of this book, it is most important to note the real possibility of virtual redlining and the need to nip it in the bud and prevent its spread. A few years ago, a virtual student lender applied for a bank charter. Writing on behalf of NCRC, I opposed the charter application because the lender was proposing to offer more expensive credit cards to lower income people without a compelling explanation based on differences in risk of delinquency or default and without guidelines as to when consumers could graduate to the less expensive credit card options.[56] A high-volume online lender offering products that differ by cost or other characteristics could significantly multiply unfairness to a group of borrowers and/ or neighborhoods in the marketplace in the absence of guardrails ensuring fair lending protections.

To further investigate the health and socioeconomic impacts of HOLC- and FHA-inspired redlining practiced over the decades, the National Community Reinvestment Coalition (NCRC) studied the fate of the urban neighborhoods classified into the various HOLC risk categories. HOLC by itself did not cause perverse socioeconomic outcomes but the racist theories of HOLC and the FHA exacerbated redlining practices. By denying loans to entire neighborhoods, redlining contributes to segregation since Whites will leave redlined neighborhoods while people of color were prevented from doing so in the decades prior to the civil rights laws. In the NCRC study, Richardson and his co-authors state that:

"Race- and place-based discrimination, both past and present, have created and actively maintained racial residential segregation. Racial residential segregation has systematically shaped characteristics of the built environment that may increase susceptibility...to health conditions. Racial residential segregation may impact health through poor housing conditions, disparity in educational and employment opportunities, inadequate transportation infrastructure, access to healthcare and economic instability." In addition, "Governmental policies and social structures of the time buttressed residential segregation, with mortgage and insurance redlining establishing neighborhood trajectories of investment and disinvestment."[57]

In other words, redlining was not the only culprit in creating disadvantage across social and economic dimensions. It combined with government policies, other segregationist practices such as racial covenants, and vigilante violence to create distressed neighborhoods.[58] For decades, systemic or structural discrimination across several markets and institutions victimized redlined neighborhoods. While this book will describe disadvantage across several socioeconomic dimensions in redlined neighborhoods, it is beyond the scope of the book to describe in an econometric or statistical fashion the extent of the contribution of each of the causes of disadvantage ranging from lender redlining to racial covenants and discrimination in the labor markets. Redlining, at first exacerbated by the federal government and then intensified by private sector lenders, was a significant contributor to disadvantage. Therefore, this book will focus on redlining and CRA, its antidote.

NCRC's study on the current condition of neighborhoods in cities where the risk of neighborhoods were classified by HOLC found that:

- 91% of the HOLC areas classified as "best" are middle and upper income today, while 74% of the areas classified as "hazardous" are low- and moderate-income (LMI) today.

- By race, 85% of the "best" areas are predominantly White today while 63% of the "hazardous" areas are majority-minority.[59]

- The average poverty rate increased from 14.3% in tracts in the lowest quartile of historic redlining score to 28.1% in tracts in the highest quartile of historic redlining score.[60]

NCRC also found statistically significant associations between greater redlining and pre-existing conditions for heightened risk of serious health conditions like asthma, diabetes, hypertension, high cholesterol, kidney disease, obesity, and stroke. All of these conditions made the "hazardous HOLC communities" more susceptible to COVID during the pandemic.

On average, life expectancy was lower by 3.6 years in redlined communities than those that were higher graded by the HOLC.[61] In addition to health risk factors, the Center for American Progress found that underserved tracts with high percentages of people of color were also more likely to confront environmental hazards.[62]

Neighborhoods classified as hazardous by HOLC were more likely decades later to be underserved by lending institutions than those that were not. Mitchell and Silver categorized census tracts into quintiles based on home loans per housing units and small business loans per operating businesses. Quintile 1 tracts were 20 percent of the tracts with the lowest number of loans per housing units and businesses while Quintile 5 tracts were the 20 percent of tracts with the highest number of loans per housing units and small businesses. We found that Quintile 1 tracts had an average of 2.8 home loans per 100 housing units in 2017. In contrast, Quintile 5 tracts had an average of 5.3 loans per 100 housing units, about twice the amount on a per housing unit basis. Similar disparities were observed for small business lending. In addition, Quintile 1 tracts had the highest numbers of redlined tracts (definitely declining or hazardous as classified by HOLC) at 1,850 tracts while Quintiles 5 had 468 tracts that had poor HOLC classifications. While some tracts were able to overcome their unfavorable HOLC classifications, considerably more were not able to do so decades later.

Quintile 1 tracts were on average, 56.8 percent minority, in contrast to Quintile 5 tracts that were, on average, 28.7 percent minority. In addition, a much greater percentage of Quintile 1 residents were low- and moderate-income than Quintile 5 residents; poverty and unemployment rates were also considerably higher in Quintile 1 than 5.[63] While redlining did not cause all of these disadvantages, low levels of lending tend to be associated with other poor economic outcomes. Structural discrimination practiced by several institutions and in numerous markets created neighborhoods where residents had stark differences in quality of life.

Considering Freddie Gray's hometown, Baltimore was one of the 239 cities that HOLC surveyed and for which it developed maps.[64] Sandtown-Winchester was one of the areas coded red or high risk (darker gray shades in map below).

HOLC Map of Baltimore: the legacy of redlining sanctioned by the federal government created disadvantages decades later for communities of color. The gray shade for the neighborhoods surrounding downtown would be red on the HOLC maps indicating African American neighborhoods the HOLC deemed risky for lending.

Source: The Digital Scholarship Lab and the National Community Reinvestment Coalition, "Not Even Past: Social Vulnerability and the Legacy of Redlining," *American Panorama*, ed. Robert K. Nelson and Edward L. Ayers

Sandtown-Winchester is west or to the left of downtown, which is shaded white. The Sandtown-Winchester area was called D4 as seen in the blow-up below.

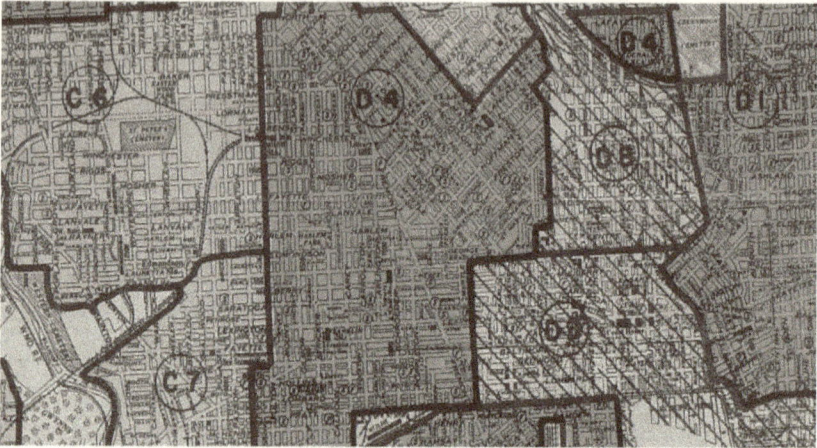

Blow-up of Baltimore HOLC Map showing the Sandtown-Winchester area.

In notes that are publicly available today, the HOLC surveyors remarked that detrimental influences in the area included, "considerable vandalism, obsolescence and high Negro concentration." The disadvantage continues more than eight decades later. As part of the NCRC report, the University of Richmond's Digital Scholarship Lab also showed the following about Sandtown-Winchester compared to other Baltimore neighborhoods.[65]

- Life expectancy: 69.2 years – one of lowest among neighborhoods; 62.6 years is lowest and 86.2 years is highest.

- Asthma – 13% of residents or one of highest rates in Baltimore neighborhoods; 15.6% is the highest.

- Diabetes – 18.2% of residents, which is one of highest; 25.9% is the highest.

- High blood pressure – 46% of residents; 56.7% is the highest.

- Obesity – 48.5% of residents; 55.3% is the highest.

- Mental health problems – 19.5% of residents; 26.5% is the highest.

When all of this is added up together, Sandtown-Winchester is one of the neighborhoods least equipped to be able to withstand adverse events. Social scientists have constructed a Social Vulnerability Index (SVI) which measures a community's ability to withstand and respond to natural or human disasters. The SVI has a scale of 0 to 1, with one being the most vulnerable to disasters.[66] Sandtown-Winchester's SVA index is .922, which indicates extreme vulnerability. This was manifested in that awful day in April of 2015 leading to Gray's death.

Sadly, the impact on a neighborhood's prospects was not confined to Baltimore. One of the centers of the civil rights struggle was the City of Birmingham, Alabama. Even predominantly African American communities in Birmingham did not escape the disadvantages created by the HOLC maps. An example is a community called Smithfield Court.

Here is what the appraiser creating the HOLC map said about that community:[67]

- Located in this area is Smithfield Court, a few low-cost slum clearance projects containing 544 units. This area is generally considered real African American property in Birmingham.

- Locations of property within this area justifies policy of selling rather than holding. Vandalism. Difficulty of rental collections.

- City jail in area. Heavy traffic. Pan-American Petroleum Refinery in northwest portion presents fire hazard. Birmingham Gas Co. in area. Obnoxious odors, noises and dirt. Fertilizer plant in area. Three main line railroads.

The disadvantage continues today. Here are the current socio-economic statistics for the community:

- Percent people of color - 94%
- Life expectancy – 69 years
- Poverty rate - 34%
- Rate of serious health ailments: asthma – 13%,
- High blood pressure – 56%

This contributes to a SVI index of .864 for Smithfield.

Recently, a new study found that public and private sector entities continued to place facilities such as oil rigs in HOLC "hazardous areas" that exacerbated the disadvantage of the redlined areas.[68] It seems like once disadvantaged, forever disadvantaged. Note that the refinery and jail were recorded by the appraiser in the Smithfield community above.

National responses to redlining: fair lending laws and CRA

Systemic racism and redlining not only exacerbated urban decline but also tore at the fabric of the nation. Social unrest and riots prompted President Lyndon Baines Johnson to commission the Kerner report, which in an oft quoted conclusion stated unequivocally:

> Our nation is moving toward two societies, one black, one white – separate and unequal. What white Americans have never fully understood – but what the Negro can never forget – is that white society is deeply implicated in the ghetto. White institutions created it, white institutions maintain it, and white society condones it.[69]

After the Kerner Commission report, the Johnson Administration worked with Congress to pass the 1968 Housing and Urban Development Act (HUD Act).[70] The act retooled the FHA program to focus on lending in urban areas and promote homeownership for African Americans. Despite its well-intentioned goal, the HUD Act embedded racist notions of risk. Policymakers believed that lending institutions needed to be goaded into lending in African American neighborhoods they believed posed undue risk by offering loan guarantees. Under FHA guarantees, the federal government would assume losses associated with borrower defaults. At the same time, the retooled FHA program relied on mortgage-backed securities (MBS). Lending institutions, predominantly mortgage companies (which, although they make loans like banks, are not federally insured since they do not accept deposits) would bundle their inner-city loans into MBS and sell them via FHA secondary market entities such as Ginnie Mae to institutional investors including pension funds and insurance companies. Real estate agents would collect a commission on home sales and mortgage companies would collect fees on making the loans.[71]

This combination of fee-based income and the federal government assuming losses on the loans led to a proliferation of high cost and unscrupulous lending in redlined inner-city neighborhoods. By the late 1960s, more than half of FHA lending was in urban communities.[72] In neighborhoods undergoing racial transition from predominantly White to African American, panic peddling real estate agents would entice Whites to sell low and then raise home prices, financed by FHA loans, to unsuspecting African Americans. Neighborhoods became unstable and unkempt with rapid property flipping of housing that increasingly stood vacant and fell into disrepair.[73] By the mid-1970s, HUD owned 74,000 foreclosed homes across the country at a cost of more than $20 million a month.[74] Tragically, neighborhoods that were starved of credit for decades suddenly experienced an influx of harmful and predatory credit. As future chapters will describe, this would not be the last time this occurred in communities of color.

Led by Gale Cincotta, a nascent national interracial coalition of advocates, the National People's Action on Housing (subsequently shortened to National People's Action (NPA)), tried to maintain integration in racially changing neighborhoods and complained that some traditional savings and loans (S&Ls) would no longer make conventional, non-FHA loans in these neighborhoods.[75] Other S&L's joined mortgage companies in a frenzy of obtaining easy investor money for making FHA loans with high interest rates and fees.[76] Traditional lenders engaged in a new round of redlining due to perceptions of rising risk levels, which had nothing to do with the skin color of the newcomers and more to do with unscrupulous institutions taking advantage of disenfranchised and vulnerable populations. Decades later, conservative thinkers would point to ill-equipped government interference in the housing market as the cause of neighborhood misfortune in the wake of the subprime lending fiasco. But this is a half-truth. In this case, the retooled FHA program failed because it continued to feed a false racist theory of risk and did not adequately monitor the incentives it was creating for various institutions in the housing market.

One of the Kerner report's major recommendations was an emphasis on integration. In 1968, Congress passed the Fair Housing Act making it illegal to discriminate in the sale or rental of housing.[77] In 1974, Congress passed the Equal Credit Opportunity Act outlawing discrimination in the provision of credit.[78] As valuable as these new laws were, they were passive in that they prevented discrimination if a person of color or a woman approached a home seller or lending institution. But the laws did not impose an affirmative obligation on lenders to market to and lend in all communities.

In 1975, Senator William Proxmire and other sympathetic members of Congress enlisted NPA in advocating for the passage of the Home Mortgage Disclosure Act (HMDA). Before HMDA, NPA pointed out to lawmakers that documenting redlining was arduous and time-consuming requiring neighborhood advocates to visit county courthouses and retrieve deed records. HMDA simplified this research by requiring lending institutions to disclose their lending activity by census tract.[79] NPA advocates across the country used the new data to document that banks and S&Ls would take deposits from inner city residents but make most of their conventional, non-FHA loans in predominantly White suburban areas.[80]

As Ken McLean, Senate Banking Committee staffer recalls, "Cincotta blew the whistle on that. Her first push was to make banks disclose where they were making their mortgage loans. Her theory was…if people knew that banks were systematically siphoning money out of these older neighborhoods and investing it all in the suburbs and letting these older communities wither on the vine, people would be up in arms and wouldn't make deposits anymore. So then she came to Congress and talked to Proxmire about a national bill, which eventually became the Home Mortgage Disclosure Act."[81]

Even after passage of HMDA, a law was needed that imposed an obligation on the private sector to affirmatively meet community needs, including the need for credit. Gale Cincotta, NPA, Proxmire, and his staff devised the Community Reinvestment Act, on the heels of HMDA, as a further means to empower community organizations to leverage reinvestment using the regulatory process involving bank mergers and branch applications. In an oral history project, McLean stated:

"And the idea (behind CRA) was that banks should be encouraged to serve local needs in their communities…if the bank was investing all of its money in the lily-white suburbs and doing nothing in its own neighborhood, maybe when they wanted to apply for a branch, they wouldn't get it. It sort of gave community groups a seat at the table, because they could go to a bank and sort of pressure the bank into making loan commitments in these older neighborhoods. And if they didn't make them, the community groups would raise all kind of hell and petition the regulators to deny the banks the next time that they went forward with an application for a new branch, or whatever, it could be denied. So it gave local groups a lot of leverage. It empowered them and made them real players on the local scene, which was the whole idea."[82]

Robert Kuttner, renowned author and former Banking Committee staffer, emphasized the importance of the affirmative obligation this way, "If we can normalize the credit flow to neighborhoods, then we're not going to be preyed upon by blockbusters. If you get normal (conventional) credit flowing to these neighborhoods, then you don't get all this sketchy stuff (such as contract sales in which the seller can foreclose if the borrower even misses one payment)."[83] [84]

Sponsored by Senator William Proxmire, the Community Reinvestment Act (CRA) of 1977 imposes an affirmative obligation on banks to meet the needs of all communities in which the bank is chartered to serve.[85] Federal bank agencies periodically conduct exams in which they measure banks' lending, investment, and service to communities and then rate or grade banks' performance. CRA exams are public. HMDA data is an important data source for CRA exams.[86]

CRA is akin to a report card for banks. Banks depend on their reputations to succeed. A poor CRA rating is a blow to their reputation. It is this public accountability that has motivated banks to increase their activity in formerly redlined communities. The next chapter will describe in more detail how CRA works and the extent of its success in revitalizing overlooked communities and neighborhoods victimized by discrimination. Partnerships between banks and community-based organizations inspired by CRA have improved lives and turned around neighborhoods. The tragedy of Freddie Gray and countless other stunted lives possibly could have been averted if CRA and fair lending laws had been enacted in earlier decades and had been rigorously enforced.

Examples of CRA-led Reinvestment in Washington DC

CRA is an antidote to disinvestment and its associated ills as illustrated in local areas around the country. For example, in Washington DC, Manna Inc., a nonprofit housing developer and counseling agency, has been rehabilitating and constructing affordable housing and providing homeownership opportunities for LMI residents of Washington DC since the early 1980s. Most of their rehabilitation and new construction projects include CRA-eligible bank financing. Several new homeowners in the Manna houses also received mortgages from banks. In 2014, I coauthored a study that quantified the benefits of homeownership for the Manna homeowners.[87] We conducted a survey involving 706 Manna homeowners and used public deed records to determine the status of their mortgages. First, we determined that Manna's homeownership is sustainable. Since 2004, no homeowners had experienced foreclosures, and from 1995 through 2012, the foreclosure rate for Manna's homeowners was lower than the citywide rate.[88] Extensive Manna homeownership counseling and preparation succeeded in creating successful ownership opportunities for populations that had not previously been homeowners and whose parents and grandparents were not homeowners.

The equity accumulation was also impressive. The study calculated that the median equity gain was about $171,000. In addition, for those homeowners with the longest tenure of at least 15 years, the median equity accumulation was over $576,000.[89] The benefits of this equity accumulation cannot be over-estimated. It can help parents fund college education for their children, it can enable parents to pass along inheritances to their children, and it can help homeowners start businesses. Most of Manna's clients are single parent African American females. CRA thus helped start a process of multi-generational wealth accumulation for an economically disenfranchised population that had been denied these opportunities due to redlining.

CRA's wealth-building impacts is an important antidote to racial wealth inequality as suggested by sociologist Dalton Conley as asserted by his pathbreaking study "Being Black, Living in the Red." Using longitudinal survey data of families' income and wealth, Dalton found that the wealth of Black parents had the largest positive impact on the wealth levels of their adult children and was even more powerful than the impacts of the educational or income levels of the parents or their children.[90] By providing homeownership and wealth building for hundreds of African Americans parents, Manna, with an assist by CRA, is pursuing the strategy recommended by Dalton. Dalton emphasizes that only an aggressive and "progressive wealth-based policy will redress the issue."[91] The issue he is referring to is the wealth gap. This book will help illuminate how CRA can promote homeownership, small business ownership, and family bank savings accounts to address it.

In addition, Manna's homeownership program helped jump start revitalization in formerly redlined neighborhoods. For example, Manna started in the Shaw neighborhood, a historic African American neighborhood which in the 1970s and 1980s became economically depressed and overrun with drugs.[92] Now, Shaw is a thriving neighborhood with a new set of economic pressures associated with gentrification. Manna helped preserve integration by preventing displacement and providing homeownership opportunities for at least 60 LMI households and rental housing for several more including 35 tenants at the historic Whitelaw.[93] Other neighborhoods with a concentration of Manna homeowners include Adams Morgan, Columbia Heights, Lanier Heights, Southeast Washington, Skyland, Barry Farm, Douglas, Buena Vista, Fairlawn, Hillcrest and Dupont Park.[94] Shown on the inside front cover of the book is a FHA map from around 1940 that coded several neighborhoods indicating "risky" neighborhoods with concentrations of African Americans (while the FHA destroyed most of its maps as stated above, a few somehow survived).[95] Many of these neighborhoods subsequently benefited from Manna's affordable housing and homeownership that received a boost from CRA.

Sabrina Walls at her condo called Oramenta Gardens in Anacostia, a neighborhood in the Southeast section of the District of Columbia

Source: Silver and Walls

One of these neighborhoods is in Southeast DC in an area called Anacostia and contains a mixed-income Manna development called Oramenta Gardens. This development sits on a refurbished block lined with trees and adjacent housing stock in good condition. One of the Manna homeowners is Sabrina Walls, a single African American female parent with a 15-year-old son. Before encountering Manna, Sabrina was heavily in debt. With determination, she spent five years in Manna's homeownership counseling programs, repairing her credit, and building up savings. In the spring of 2021, she moved into a condominium unit and now relishes the sense of security homeownership provides. Her mortgage payments are now less than her previous rental payments. Her financial burden is reduced, "she is not stressed out about whether she has enough to pay the bills next month," and she has "wiggle room to save money and enjoy life more."[96]

Her son enjoys the stability of their new home and no longer has to move from apartment to apartment. Previously, they even had to move back to Sabrina's mom's home for a while. He can now say, "this is home and he knows we are going to be here. We are not going anywhere. So he was really excited."

The condo is in a development with 11 other units. Oramenta residents have developed camaraderie with each other by serving on the condo board and establishing ties with the condo across the street. Walls stated that the neighbors conduct informal clean-ups and look out for each other, performing tasks like jump-starting cars or helping to carry bulky items.

Reflecting on the benefits of homeownership Walls maintained, "Homeownership is achievable, if you work at it, and get into a program that gives you a plan or blueprint."

Manna's homeownership counseling establishes "accountability – did you save money; you got to be honest with yourself."[97] Walls found a community-based infrastructure in the form of Manna that helped a determined individual find a path and hew to it. Manna, in turn, has received bank support motivated by CRA. While bank support fluctuates and is not enough at times, Manna would have significantly reduced capacity to offer the life building and wealth creating services it offers if CRA was not a federal law. Indirectly, by supporting community infrastructure, CRA saves lives and improves their quality.

Conclusion

Decades of systemic discrimination and redlining created neighborhoods with daunting disadvantages and dashed lives as exemplified by the tragic death of Freddie Gray. However, since CRA and the fair lending laws have been implemented for about 50 years, why have the disadvantages not disappeared? Bob Dickerson, an African American civic leader in Birmingham, remarked that the "The accountability ought to be on the communities' condition, status, and look. I could take you on a ride through Birmingham and you tell me if there could be a bank with an Outstanding CRA rating. I don't know how you can figure that out. It doesn't add up. Communities don't look a whole lot different than they did 45 years ago."[98]

I understand Dickerson's comments and share the same frustration. The issue, however, is whether CRA by itself could ever succeed in turning around the multitude of underserved communities across the country. The full force of discrimination is of a scale that has not been counteracted with the same magnitude by corrective civil rights laws. It is not just redlining that has disadvantaged communities of color. After slavery, Jim Crow laws proliferated in the South but Jim Crow also found its way north. Segregation and disadvantage in the North as well as the South were enforced by racial covenants preventing the sale of homes and homeownership opportunities for people of color throughout the country.[99] Restrictive zoning reinforced segregation.

KKK violence displaced African Americans from their own vibrant communities and relegated them to less desirable neighborhoods. The fury against school integration and busing provides more visible evidence of the systematic discrimination encountered by people of color. It is not just the lending marketplace that discriminated against African Americans and people of color. The discrimination is pervasive and across the board including the education system, the labor market, and countless other spheres of life.

A set of civil rights laws including CRA enacted about 50 years ago and which have been enforced in an episodic and inconsistent manner cannot eradicate the massive disadvantages exacerbated by several decades of redlining and other systemic discrimination. As well as documenting CRA successes, future chapters will discuss loopholes in the CRA regulation that diminish the effectiveness of CRA exams. Moreover, only a subset of the financial industry is covered by CRA. As necessary as it is to require banks to serve all communities, the resources of this subset of financial institutions, though substantial, are probably not enough to succeed in revitalizing most of the disadvantaged neighborhoods. Moreover, although the public sector has directed resources towards community development, these programs most likely pale against the subsidization of White suburbs and the destruction of inner-city neighborhoods by highways and other large-scale infrastructure. NPA advocates were correct in their assessment in the 1970s that CRA could not substitute for public sector programs and needed to be complemented by funding from the federal government, state and local governments.[100] However, they were fighting an uphill battle, and it remains unclear whether substantially more public sector resources would turn around many more neighborhoods without significantly more financing from the financial sector.

At the same time, we cannot despair. Even with current limitations, CRA has helped the nonprofit sector and financial institutions turn around neighborhoods. The story of Manna's affordable housing development offers hope. Manna was determined, prescient, and lucky to some extent because it reached neighborhoods in the District of Columbia before market forces started the process of gentrification and displacement in some cases. Manna's efforts helped sizable numbers of people of color with modest incomes benefit from large scale development in the District of Columbia that was often spurred by the publicly funded expansion of the local transit system and subway. In other neighborhoods not yet experiencing gentrification, Manna has likewise jump-started revitalization. For instance, Ward 8 is a part of the District of Columbia that is predominantly African American and has high rates of poverty. The report I co-authored estimated that as of 2014, Manna's homeowners constituted about 1 in 179 homeowners in that Ward, which is a large area.[101] If Ward 8 grows economically in future years, it is in no small part due to the work of Manna. Yet, success is not assured as the private and public sectors need to provide significant financing over a span of several years, informed and guided by input from community residents to assure benefits accrue equitably to longtime residents as well as more recent arrivals to the neighborhoods.

The story of CRA is complicated. Even now, it has scored significant successes, but it cannot by itself and in its present form eradicate all blight, poverty, and disadvantaged neighborhoods. Such expectations will set it up for failure and unfair criticism. Instead, the task going forward is to see how loopholes in CRA can be closed, how to expand its reach, and how public sector financing of affordable housing and economic development (including infrastructure) can be paired most effectively with CRA-leveraged financing. In addition, a major theme of this chapter is that redlining has disproportionately impacted African American neighborhoods and other communities of color. Yet, the CRA statute remains focused on incomes, directing banks to serve low- and moderate-income communities but not explicitly communities of color. How and whether this can change will be the subject of future chapters.

As a country, we are a long way from lifting the "artificial weights" from "all shoulders" since our society imposed those weights mostly on people of color but also on other segments of the population. A stronger CRA is just one of the tools, but an important one, needed to give everyone a fair chance in Lincoln's race of life. The task for the rest of this book is to explore how to bolster CRA.

2
Unraveling Redlining: How the CRA Works

"As we try to shake off the financial crisis, here's a bright idea. Take a law that has led to the writing of an enormous amount of bad mortgages and expand it. Then take enforcement away from bank examiners and give it to housing activists." - **Peter Schweizer in Forbes**[102]

"Some critics of the CRA contend that by encouraging banking institutions to help meet the credit needs of lower-income borrowers and areas, the law pushed banking institutions to undertake high-risk mortgage lending. We have not yet seen empirical evidence to support these claims, nor has it been our experience in implementing the law over the past 30 years that the CRA has contributed to the erosion of safe and sound lending practice." - **Former Federal Reserve Governor Randall Kroszner**[103]

In the wake of the financial crisis, some conservative thinkers tried to blame CRA by asserting that the law coerced banks to make unsafe and unsound loans to low- and moderate-income (LMI) borrowers so that they could pass their CRA exams. In response, policymakers and economists, including some at the federal bank agencies, conducted a slew of studies described below finding that CRA was true to its legal mandate requiring banks to make safe and sound loans. This is just one example of how CRA has been blamed for everything from poor lending to the global financial crisis. Implicit in the criticism is an assertion that CRA is all powerful and ever present. In fact, while CRA has been a valuable tool in the struggle to revitalize neighborhoods, it is not as powerful as its foes imply to cause a global meltdown. This chapter will take a sober look at CRA, first describing the law and how the statute is currently implemented via regulations and examinations. The chapter will then review the extensive literature on the strengths and weaknesses of CRA.

The CRA statute

Enacted in 1977, CRA decreed that depository institutions (banks and thrifts) "serve the convenience and needs of the communities in which they are chartered to do business."[104] The statement of purpose indicated that community needs entail loans (credit services) as well as deposits. The next part of the law's opening $§ 2901$(a) (3), stipulated that meeting needs is not a one-time activity but that depository institutions have a "continuing and affirmative obligation to help meet the credit needs of the local communities in which they are chartered." The final part of $§ 2901$(b) required the federal financial supervisory agencies to conduct exams in order to encourage depository institutions to meet local community needs consistent with the safe and sound operation of such institutions.

A following section, *§ 2903*, established that the federal agencies must conduct exams of depository institutions' record of serving their entire communities, including LMI neighborhoods. The agencies shall then consider the performance of the depository institutions (banks and thrifts) in meeting the needs of their communities when depository institutions apply for permission to obtain charters and deposit insurance, open branches, and merge with or acquire other depository institutions.[105]

A section on examination requirements, *§ 2906*, mandated that the federal agencies prepare written evaluations describing the factors used to evaluate depository institutions' performance and the data supporting the ratings assigned to the banks' performance of meeting community needs. One of four possible ratings can be assigned to bank performance: Outstanding, Satisfactory, Needs-to-Improve, and Substantial Noncompliance.[106] In the case of depository institutions with branches in more than one state, the evaluation is to examine and rate performance in each state in which a depository institution maintains a branch.[107] Within each state, the evaluation is to evaluate and rate performance in each metropolitan area in which a depository institution has a branch and in the non-metropolitan areas (rural counties) of the state if a depository institution has one or more branches there.[108]

CRA regulations and exams

As the statute directed, the federal supervisory agencies developed and revised regulations over the decades that described examination criteria and identified credit, service, and investment activities that would be considered favorably on exams. Prior to 2023, the regulations implemented by the Federal Reserve Board, the Federal Deposit Insurance Corporation (FDIC), and the Office of the Comptroller of the Currency (OCC) were based on revisions adopted in 1995 with subsequent modifications that refined aspects of the regulation but did not change the core of the 1995 revisions. The regulations established exams for various categories of banks and thrifts with the most detailed and comprehensive exams for "large" banks defined as possessing assets above $1.564 billion. The asset levels adjust annually based on inflation.[109]

Large banks have three component tests or subtests: a lending test, an investment test, and a service test.[110] The lending test has the most weight, counting 50 percent towards the final rating. It assesses a bank's performance at issuing retail loans (most commonly home and small business loans) to LMI borrowers and in LMI communities, the record of offering flexible and innovative loans, and the level of community development lending (larger scale loans such as those for construction of multi-family rental housing).[111,112] The investment test assesses the quality and quantity of a depository institution's community development investments ranging from grants for community-based nonprofit organizations, Low Income Housing Tax Credits, to equity investments in funds that finance small business development.[113,114] Finally, the service test scrutinizes a depository institution's record of branching in LMI tracts, the range of services and products offered at those branches, and the provision of community development services including housing counseling and service on the board of nonprofit organizations engaged in neighborhood development.[115,116] The investment and service test are each worth 25 percent of the rating (up to 12 points can be awarded under the lending test for Outstanding performance as opposed to 6 points each for the investment and service test, indicating that the lending test has double the weight of the investment or service tests).[117]

Intermediate small banks (ISB) have assets ranging from $391 million to $1.564 billion as of 2024.[118] Their test is streamlined compared to the large bank test and has two components, the lending test and the community development test. The lending test includes an evaluation of the distribution of retail lending to borrowers and communities of different income levels.[119] The community development test combines aspects of the large bank investment test and the service test. It assesses the ISB's record of community development financing (loans and investments) and community development services.[120]

Continuing the theme of less comprehensive tests as depository institutions become smaller, the small bank exam for institutions with assets under $391 million consists largely of the lending test.[121] Like the exams of the other banks, the small bank exam is required to consider comments from the general public on the CRA performance of the institution.[122] Finally, wholesale and limited purpose CRA exams consist of a community development test for banks that are not traditional retail banks and offer a narrow product line or do not serve retail customers.[123]

Another exam option for banks of any asset size is the strategic plan. In lieu of the regular exam, a bank can develop a plan with measurable goals for the subtests that would have applied to them.[124] Under strategic plans, depository institutions are required to engage members of the public in developing the plans and federal agencies are required to consider the extent of public input when evaluating the plan's goals.[125]

Under any of the exam types, evidence of discrimination and other violations of consumer protection law can lower a rating depending on the extent and nature of the violations.[126] Per the statute, the federal agencies make CRA exams publicly available.

Members of the public can access them on agency websites or the website of the Federal Financial Institution Examination Council (FFIEC).[127]

CRA exams use a considerable amount of data that is displayed on tables and charts on the exam. In addition, banks are to provide this data to the public upon request. Alternatively, the public can visit federal agency websites to obtain the data. The data includes the Home Mortgage Disclosure Act (HMDA) on home lending and CRA data on small business and farm lending.[128] The public availability of data increases the accountability of institutions for their CRA performance by enabling members of the public to conduct their own data analyses and offer views of their data analyses to CRA examiners from the federal agencies as examiners are conducting the evaluations.

The CRA statute does not specify an exam frequency except in the case of small banks with assets of less than $250 million. These banks have the least frequent exams (the statute identifies banks with up to $250 million in assets as the subset of small banks with the least frequent exams. In contrast, for purposes of determining the type of exam applying to smaller banks, the CRA regulation adjusts the asset level for small banks and ISB banks annually based on inflation as described above). For small banks with assets under $250 million, *§ 2908* specified that exams are to occur once every five years for those banks whose most recent rating was Outstanding, once every four years for those whose most recent rating was Satisfactory. For small banks with the two failed ratings of Needs to Improve and Substantial Noncompliance, the statute provides the agencies with discretion regarding exam frequency.[129]

After the change to the CRA statute regarding small bank exam schedules made by the Gramm Leach Bliley Act of 1999,

NCRC asserted that less frequent exams for small banks would reduce accountability and banks' performance in lending to and serving LMI populations.[130] Industry stakeholders had maintained that frequency reductions were necessary in order to reduce cost and burdens for small banks. However, the federal agencies had calculated that the exams "impose a modest information collection burden on small institutions – an average of 10 burden hours per institution per year."[131] Furthermore, smaller banks disproportionately serve rural communities and smaller metropolitan areas, which generally have fewer community organizations holding banks accountable for their CRA performance. The smaller banks are also less likely to submit merger applications and undergo public scrutiny during the application process.[132] The exam therefore becomes the paramount accountability mechanism, suggesting that frequency reductions are harmful in this context.

This tension between rigor and frequency of exams, on the one hand, and burden reduction, on the other, is present at several aspects of CRA policymaking and will be revisited throughout this book. The challenge for the agencies is to create a rigorous exam regime that minimizes unnecessary costs.

Although the statute does not mandate exam frequency for most banks, the federal agencies strive to examine banks above $250 million in assets on a two- to three-year cycle. A NCRC paper of the exam characteristics of the top 100 banks by asset size found that about 65 percent of the exams were conducted during this time period.[133] It is important to maintain a two-to-three-year cycle because less frequent examination schedules like those for small banks allow banks to relax their efforts to serve LMI populations in the early years of the cycle and to increase their efforts during the later years. An exam schedule of once every five years, for example, encourages a bank to reduce effort during the first three or four years and then intensify their effort months before the exam starts. In contrast, an exam schedule of once every two or three years does not permit relaxation since each year of the shorter time period is likely to be examined with equal rigor by the agencies.

Two additional aspects of CRA exams with significant implications are assessment areas and affiliates. Assessment areas are geographical areas on CRA exams and generally are those areas in which a bank has branches and deposit-taking ATMs.[134] In future chapters, the book investigates how and whether assessment areas can evolve to also include areas where banks lend or take deposits although they do not have branches. Finally, a bank at its option can include an affiliate that lends or offers other products and services.[135] This optional treatment introduces possibilities of exam manipulation and selectively including or excluding affiliates based on their CRA and fair lending record.

Per the statute, the regulation requires the federal agencies to consider CRA performance when evaluating applications for new branches or mergers between depository institutions. In the case of applications for new charters and deposit insurance, an applicant shall describe how it will meet its CRA objectives. The agencies are required to consider the input of members of the public when considering applications. The agencies have the discretion of approving applications, denying them or conditioning approval on specific actions an applicant must take including steps to improve its CRA performance.[136] As well as considering past CRA performance, bank merger law requires agencies to consider the future public benefits of mergers. Amending the Federal Deposit Insurance Act, the Bank Merger Act mandates that a federal agency shall not approve anticompetitive mergers:

…unless it finds that the anticompetitive effects of the proposed transaction are clearly outweighed in the public interest by the probable effect of the transaction in meeting the convenience and needs of the community to be served.

In every case, the responsible agency shall take into consideration the financial and managerial resources and future prospects of the existing and proposed institutions, the convenience and needs of the community to be served, and the risk to the stability of the United States banking or financial system.[137]

While all the factors listed in the quote are vital, for our purposes, the emphasis on the depository institution's future ability to meet convenience and needs is the most relevant in that the agencies must assess if the merged banks will be able to serve the convenience and needs of communities. The mandate is two parts. The first part of the law allows for an anti-competitive merger only if the public interest is served and the probable effect on meeting convenience and needs is positive. The second part stipulates that in every merger, the agencies are to consider the impact on the banks' abilities to meet convenience and needs.

Review of CRA ratings

Since the CRA ratings became public in 1990, the federal agencies have conducted more than 76,000 exams. From 1990 through 2022, the overall ratings distribution is Outstanding for 14.3 percent of the exams, Satisfactory for 82.2 percent of the exams, Needs-to-Improve for 3.2 percent of the exams, and Substantial Noncompliance for .3 percent of the exams. The earliest years exhibited the highest failure rates of Needs-to-Improve and Substantial Noncompliance.

In 1990, almost 10 percent of banks failed and by 1994 just over 5 percent failed. Since 1994, the aggregate failure rate has been about 2 percent as shown below.[138]

The rapid decrease in failure rates could be due to banks' understanding the expectations of the federal agencies after the first few years. Alternatively, the agencies could have become more lenient. Stephen Cross, a former senior compliance official at both the OCC and FDIC, stated, "In the early 1990's, about 10% of national banks supervised by the OCC were rated Needs-to-Improve or Substantial Noncompliance. By 1995 that number had fallen by about half. Meanwhile at the FDIC, the number of banks rated Needs-to-Improve or Substantial Noncompliance temporarily rose around the year 2000 only to fall within a few years. It's all about who is doing the examinations and the guidance they have been given. If you are not really committed to the principles of the CRA or if you believe everyone is doing a good job, the number of banks rated less than Satisfactory will decline. A 10% failure rate will fall to (say) 1%. At the end of the day, it all comes down to implementation."[139]

Perhaps failure rates fell both because banks got better at reinvesting and agencies were inconsistent in their grading, depending on who was leading or staffing the agencies. In addition to a failure rate which is likely to be too low, another clear shortcoming of the ratings is the lack of distinctions for the vast majority of banks. As stated above, about 82% have received a rating of Satisfactory. From 2002 through 2022, the percentage was closer to 90%. This huge swath of Satisfactory ratings blurs distinctions among a considerable number of banks, many of whom could be performing at a relatively high level (though not in an Outstanding manner) and several of whom could be performing at a mediocre level in a manner that is barely passing their exams. A ratings system that is inflated or that does not meaningfully reveal distinctions among bank performance reduces the incentive for banks to serve LMI borrowers and communities continually and affirmatively as they are legally required to do so.

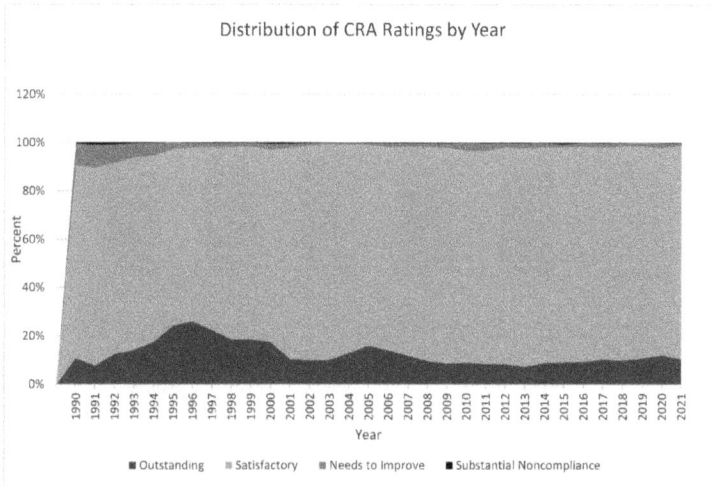

Distribution of CRA Ratings by Year

CRA ratings by type of CRA exam reveals that large banks have higher percentages of Outstanding ratings than either small banks or intermediate small banks (ISB). Since 2012, CRA exams for large banks gave them a rating of Outstanding 20 percent of the time as opposed to 6 percent for small banks and 8.6 percent for ISB banks. The failure rates are similar across all three categories of CRA exams, meaning that the main difference is the frequency of Outstanding ratings. Evidence will be presented below suggesting that large bank exams should be more rigorous since smaller banks tend to exhibit better performance on the lending test. The strategic plan and wholesale and limited purpose exams have high percentages of Outstanding ratings (almost 50 percent for strategic plans and 43 percent for wholesale and limited purpose).[140] This high incidence of Outstanding ratings reflects imperfections in those exams that CRA reform sought to address as will be discussed in Chapter 8. For example, several banks under those types of exams were not evaluated for considerable volumes of retail lending in which they engage.

CRA Ratings 2012-2022 by Type of Exam

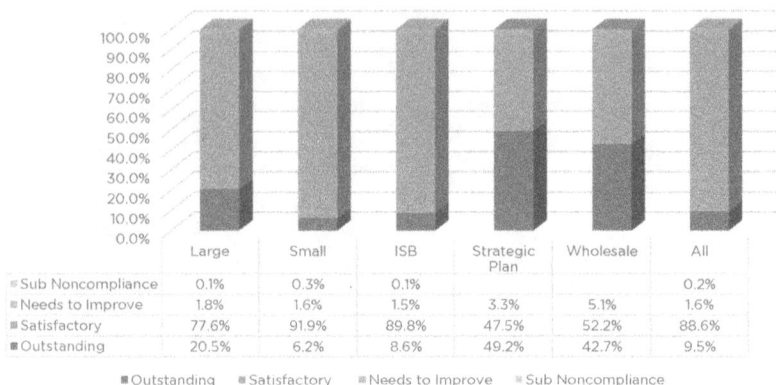

	Large	Small	ISB	Strategic Plan	Wholesale	All
Sub Noncompliance	0.1%	0.3%	0.1%			0.2%
Needs to Improve	1.8%	1.6%	1.5%	3.3%	5.1%	1.6%
Satisfactory	77.6%	91.9%	89.8%	47.5%	52.2%	88.6%
Outstanding	20.5%	6.2%	8.6%	49.2%	42.7%	9.5%

Outstanding ■ Satisfactory ■ Needs to Improve ■ Sub Noncompliance

Over the years, community organizations have proposed several reforms to the ratings system. One option is to add a fifth rating. The current subtests such as the lending test already have five ratings with the Satisfactory rating being split into two separate ratings of High Satisfactory and Low Satisfactory. Five ratings would reveal more distinctions among performance by assigning substantial numbers of banks with the overall rating of Satisfactory into Low and High Satisfactory categories. Unfortunately, the agencies have not adopted this suggestion, citing the statute that only lists four ratings. However, this change would be supported by a variety of stakeholders ranging from community advocates to some banks which seek more distinctions among the ratings.[141] Another option would be to develop a point system as recommended by NCRC from 1 to 100 or some other range that logically corresponds to the ratings categories.[142] The point system could also effectively identify Low and High Satisfactory performers. For instance, if the Satisfactory category had a range of 20 points from 70 to 90, the top 10 points from 80 to 90 could be reserved for High Satisfactory performers and the bottom 10 points from 70 to 79 would be for the Low Satisfactory performers. Outstanding ratings would correspond to a range of 90 to 100 points; below 70 points would correspond to the failing ratings of Needs to Improve and Substantial Noncompliance (Chapter 8 discusses how the agencies incorporated a similar point system).

As described below, CRA has motivated increases in loans, investments, and services above the levels that banks would provide without CRA. However, the issue of CRA ratings reform remains a substantial one. If CRA ratings created more transparency regarding performance, the level of loans, investments, and services would be higher, and possibly considerably higher, in traditionally underserved communities. Banks are nonetheless motivated by the current ratings system due to a variety of motivations. Despite the top-heavy nature of banking with half a dozen institutions with trillions of dollars of assets, more than 4,700 banks and thrifts remain in this country that compete vigorously with each other and with mortgage companies and credit unions for customers.[143] Some will seek every advantage in this competition including an enhanced public reputation associated with an Outstanding rating signifying commendable service to all communities. Moreover, banks compete for state and municipal deposits. When seeking this business, some would rather approach elected officials with an Outstanding rating and record of serving all constituents of the elected officials.

In addition, some industry stakeholders have suggested that banks aim for Outstanding ratings in case the fair lending review accompanying CRA exams identifies discrimination or another violation of consumer protection law that results in the rating being lowered. A bank with an initial rating of Outstanding would likely have its rating lowered to Satisfactory rather than one of the failure ratings. Finally, another motivation for exceptional CRA performance is the merger review process. As stated above, agency reviews of merger, branching and other applications includes scrutiny of CRA performance. Banks intent on merging do not want delays of applications or denials based on suspect CRA and fair lending performance.

Review of merger decisions

At first glance, the record of merger application reviews suggests that agency scrutiny ranges from streamlined to lackadaisical. CRA enforcement during the merger application process likewise appears to be insignificant. For example, the Federal Reserve Board probably considers most merger applications of the three bank agencies and their record would appear to strongly favor application approval. In a letter to Senator Elizabeth Warren, Federal Reserve Chairman Jerome Powell indicates that the Board processed 3,819 merger applications from 2007 through 2016 yet the Board did not deny a single application on CRA or other considerations. However, lending institutions withdrew 503 applications. Withdrawals can occur for a variety of reasons including deficiencies in CRA or some other aspect of banking. Chairman Powell's letter did not break down the reasons for the withdrawn applications.[144]

A more recent Federal Reserve semiannual report to Congress spanning the time period of 2018 through the first half of 2022 sheds additional light on the Federal Reserve's review process. During that time, the Federal Reserve considered 494 applications of all types including mergers, approved 455 of them and denied one application. The applicants withdrew 24 applications or almost 5% of the total. Of these, six involved substantive managerial or policy

Ending Redlining through a Community-Centered Reform of the Community Reinvestment Act

issues, but the report did not indicate if CRA was the cause for any of these six withdrawals.[145]

The Federal Reserve did not deny any merger applications from 2018 through 2022. However, average processing time increased from 57 days in 2018 to 81 days in the first half of 2022. Median processing times had a narrower range of 42 days in 2018 to 48 days in the first half of 2022.[146] This suggests that perhaps a few larger mergers or those with more ramifications regarding CRA or competitiveness took longer to process in the first half of 2022. In general, regulatory enforcement tends to wax and wane depending on the head of the agency and the overall atmosphere in Washington D.C (the agencies deny political considerations influence their decisions, but community organizations and other observers have noticed significant differences in agency oversight depending on the composition of the Congress and the inclinations of the President and who the President appoints to head the agencies).

Public hearings are another venue for increasing accountability to the public. The agencies have discretionary authority to hold hearings. Under some administrations, the federal agencies will not hold any public hearings on merger applications. Under others, hearings on large bank mergers occur occasionally. These hearings have been important in that they provide more information from a wider variety of stakeholders than the agencies would receive from the written comments alone regarding the merger. Yet, their full potential has not been effectively utilized because they often consist of several witnesses making short statements, including the banks' representatives. The agencies do not provide a format that allows for a discussion moderated by an agency official directly between the bank and at least a few community-based organizations most impacted. The discussion could allow for rebuttals and more detailed questioning by the agencies which would likely provide more insight into the validity of the arguments and positions on both sides.

In addition to approvals, denials and withdrawn applications, an agency will periodically approve an application subject to conditions, including mandated improvements in CRA performance. For example, in August of 2013, the FDIC approved the application of Renasant, a bank based in Tupelo, Mississippi to acquire Merchants and Farmers Bank. NCRC and its member organizations based in the South protested the application citing poor CRA and fair lending performance. In response, the FDIC imposed conditions on the approval requiring more marketing and outreach by Renasant to underserved communities.[147] Moreover, the approval required Renasant to establish goals for its home mortgage lending so that its level of lending to people of color and lower income borrowers at least equals its peers at the end of three years (NCRC had found that the bank offered considerably lower percentages of loans to LMI borrowers and people of color in its major markets). While this order increased accountability, the public was not granted the opportunity to review Renasant's plan nor to comment upon it.

The merger application process also presents opportunities for community groups to negotiate directly with banks in the development of plans for specific increases in loans, investments, and services to modest income communities and communities of color. These plans are similar to conditional merger approvals but often provide more publicly available details. Advocates previously called them CRA agreements, but they are now more commonly referred to as community benefit agreements (CBAs). They are named CBAs to reinforce the legal requirement that banks are required to demonstrate a public benefit of their merger in terms of serving community needs discussed above. Some banks respond to this requirement by negotiating an agreement that can be verified by publicly available data.

Overall, the CRA and fair lending enforcement during the merger application process would appear to be insufficient to motivate banks to be vigilant regarding their CRA compliance. However, while the possibilities of denial of applications are a remote possibility, more common actions can include delays, which cost the banks time and money. Moreover, uneven CRA and fair lending performance entail other costs for banks including more public scrutiny and exposure with possible repercussions to their reputations, oversight via a conditional merger approval or protracted negotiations over CBAs. Several large banks therefore take CRA seriously and attempt to have their CRA performance at a level that can withstand scrutiny before they embark upon mergers. The posture of the agencies seems to be that they will not generally overtly enforce CRA during the application process in most cases but that banks with problematic performance will face delays and other barriers.

While this is better than benign neglect, a more transparent process is needed. More denials and/or withdrawals on CRA grounds than the small amount that occurs currently would send a signal that the agencies are stepping up their CRA enforcement. It is implausible that thousands of mergers over the years involve banks without inconsistencies and weaknesses in their CRA performance. In addition to more denials, the agencies could employ conditional approvals more frequently to rectify weaknesses in performance. They could also require banks to submit community benefit plans describing how they would improve upon weaknesses in their CRA performance while maintaining commendable aspects of their CRA performance. Community benefit plans could be different from CBAs in that they are not negotiated directly with community groups. On occasion and particularly for the larger mergers with more widespread impacts including possible anti-competitiveness results, the agencies could encourage banks to engage in discussions with community organizations, which may lead to CBAs.

A more transparent process would reveal more about the inconsistencies in CRA and fair lending performance and would engage all stakeholders in a more frank and productive dialogue about how to create goals and plans to overcome these inconsistencies to better serve formerly redlined communities and those still experiencing discrimination. In addition, public hearings should be an important venue for dialogue and debate about how to improve CRA and fair lending performance. After mergers, the agencies should review bank compliance with either conditional merger approvals, community benefit plans, or CBAs on subsequent CRA exams. Ratings could be influenced depending on the extent of a bank falling short on conditional approvals or CBA goals or exceeding them.

Review of literature: CRA's impact on lending, investing and services

An initial reaction from a member of the general public in response to the trends of CRA ratings and the inconsistent agency review of merger applications is that CRA would not be effective in increasing access to credit and capital for traditionally underserved communities. However, despite its appearance as law not strenuously enforced, CRA has leveraged significant bank reinvestment in formerly redlined communities. At the same time, its full potential has not been realized because enforcement and transparency need to increase. The rest of this chapter presents evidence regarding CRA's track record and offers observations as to why it has had some important success.

One major factor accounting for CRA's significant if modest

success is its ability to correct for market failure. Market failure is a term in economics that refers to imperfections in the marketplace that impede economic transactions, resulting in frustrations experienced by both sellers and buyers and reduced economic output. An asymmetry of knowledge between buyers and sellers is one cause of market failure. Due to redlining or the refusal to serve communities of color and LMI neighborhoods, banks (as sellers) lacked knowledge about the quality of neighborhood housing and the creditworthiness of neighborhood residents. They thus passed up on opportunities to make profitable loans.[148] Neighborhood residents as buyers or borrowers also lacked knowledge about banking and lending because they were served infrequently by traditional banks. They were therefore often unprepared to qualify for loans or when they were offered loans, they did not know how to shop for the best loan terms and conditions. Lending institutions as sellers were able to exploit the unaware borrowers. Asymmetry of knowledge therefore results in fewer loans in neighborhoods or loans with onerous terms and conditions.

CRA corrects for market failure and asymmetry of knowledge by requiring banks to serve all communities continually and affirmatively. Under CRA, banks are required to acquire knowledge of community needs and how to best serve creditworthy neighborhood residents. Because they are also required to make safe and sound loans, the incidence of exploitation of borrowers is reduced under CRA. Finally, CRA requires all banks to serve neglected neighborhoods, which reduces the perceived risk of just one or only a few banks being pioneers in a formerly redlined neighborhood. The overall knowledge of the characteristics of neighborhoods and borrowers increases for all banks since the entire industry is required to create a robust amount of data and information (which is essentially shared via credit bureaus and other industry mechanisms).

Lending and service increases to neighborhoods as CRA helps to reduce market failure and information barriers as confirmed by academic and federal agency research. The Joint Housing Studies at Harvard University conducted one of the early studies about the impacts of CRA assessment areas on lending during 2002 in commemoration of the twenty-fifth anniversary of CRA. The study found banks made a higher percentage of their home purchase loans to LMI borrowers and census tracts in their assessment areas than outside of their assessment areas from 1993 through 2000.[149] In addition, rejection rates for LMI applications were eight percentage points lower in assessment areas than outside assessment areas.[150]

When a census tract gained eligibility as a LMI tract due to a metropolitan area boundary change, Federal Reserve economist Daniel Ringo found that lending by a single bank increased by two to four percent from 2003 to 2004. Moreover, Ringo found that the impact was greatest for low-income borrowers, those with less than 50 percent of area median income, than for moderate-income borrowers, those with between 50 to 80 percent of area median income. He hypothesized that banks face less competition in extending loans to low-income borrowers than to moderate-income borrowers, so efforts to increase lending to these customers—prompted by the new CRA eligibility of the tracts—were more effective at filling unmet demand.[151]

Similarly, Lei Ding and colleagues at the Philadelphia Federal Reserve Bank updated Ringo's analysis and applied it to the greater Philadelphia metropolitan area when the Office of Management and Budget (OMB) changed metropolitan area boundaries in 2013. The study utilized a set of difference-in-differences model and examined lending two years before and two years after the changes in census tract eligibility. They concluded that when census tracts lose CRA eligibility because they are no longer considered LMI, the number of home purchase loans decreased between 10 to 20 percent.[152]

Ding, Bostic, and Lee found a similar impact in small business lending. They also used the changes in metropolitan boundaries implemented by OMB but considered lending across the country instead of just one metropolitan area. After the changes, 549 census tracts that were eligible for CRA consideration became ineligible while the reverse occurred in 432 tracts.[153] The researchers compared small business lending trends in the newly ineligible and eligible tracts against lending trends in a control group of tracts that had similar incomes. They found that in the two years after the changes, the number of small business loans increased by 13.8 percent in the newly ineligible tracts while the increase was 19.5 percent in the control group of tracts. In addition, in the newly eligible tracts, the increase was about 2 percentage points higher than in the control group.[154] Regression analysis confirmed that becoming newly inel- igible caused about a 6 percent decrease in small business loans.[155]

Silver and Richardson's study using a Federal Reserve data- base of CRA exams corroborated the Ding and Bostic studies on CRA spurring greater lending efforts. In 2020, the Federal Reserve released a database on CRA exams from 2005 through 2017.[156] The database contained CRA data on retail lending, community development financing, and subtest ratings for a large sample of 6,300 CRA exams. In general, we found that a higher percentage of home loans made to LMI borrowers or tracts corresponded to higher ratings. For example, the median percentage of home loans to LMI borrowers was 12.8 percent for banks with High Satisfactory ratings on the lending test as opposed to 10.4 percent for banks with

Low Satisfactory ratings. Banks with Needs-to-Improve ratings had a median percentage of loans to LMI borrowers of just 2.1 percent.

We found some inconsistencies in the ratings. For instance, banks with Outstanding ratings made just 11.8 percent of their loans to LMI borrowers, which is almost one percentage point lower than banks with High Satisfactory ratings. These inconsistencies could be due to the prevalence of a variety of performance measures on the lending test so that a lower percentage of loans to LMI borrowers could be compensated by better performance on the other quantitative and qualitative performance measures for home and small business lending. Overall, however, if the ratings are sorting banks in descending order based on their performance, they would be effectively serving as motivations for enough banks to do better and thus would achieve the results observed by Ding and Bostic of more lending in eligible CRA tracts.

While the findings regarding ratings support the findings about increases in LMI tracts and to borrowers due to CRA, CRA's impact could be stronger if the subtests were improved to measure performance more accurately. Ratings would then be more reflective of performance and thus would be a more effective motivator, particularly if the overall rating categories were more like the five ratings on the subtests. The major inconsistency decreasing the effectiveness of ratings revealed by the Silver and Richardson study was the poorer performance of large banks over $50 billion in assets on the performance measure considering lending to LMI borrowers. The large banks rated Outstanding on the lending test had a median percentage of loans to LMI borrowers of just 9.4 percent, which was considerably lower than the median percentage of 14.3 percent and 12.8 percent, respectively, for the Outstanding rated regional banks (assets between $10 billion and $50 billion) and community banks (assets under $10 billon). In fact, the median percentage of 9.4 percent for large banks was lower than the median percentages for regional and community banks rated Low Satisfactory on the Lending Test.[157]

The Silver and Richardson study's finding that large banks trailed their peers was consistent with that of Calem, Lambie-Hanson, and Wachter (the Silver and Richardson study used the same bank classifications to see if the findings were similar). Calem, Lambie-Hanson, and Wachter used a multi-year period from 2000 to 2017 to assess how banks of various asset sizes performed compared to non-banks such as independent mortgage companies.[158] In general, over this multi-year time period and especially since 2010, large banks trailed community banks and non-banks in the percentage of loans offered in LMI tracts and to LMI borrowers.[159]

In contrast to banks' performance in lending, not much research has considered their CRA investment record. CRA-related investments support affordable housing and economic development. Silver and Richardson also used the Federal Reserve database to find that higher ratings on the Investment Test usually corresponded to higher levels of investment compared to bank deposits. Regional and large banks exhibited wide differences among the ratings categories. Large banks with Outstanding ratings had a median ratio at the assessment area level of 2.45 percent while those with High Satisfactory had a significantly smaller ratio of 1.2 percent. A similar difference was present for regional banks. The ratios for banks in those two categories with Low Satisfactory and Needs-to-Improve ratings were quite small.[160]

It appeared that the tendency for large banks to perform worse than their counterparts was not an issue on the Investment Test nor the community development lending portion of the lending test according to the Silver and Richardson report. It is possible that the community development aspects of the CRA exams are more effective in stimulating community development loans and investments for underserved communities than the Lending Test is for retail lending, particularly for large banks. However, a significant caveat is that the community development parts of the tests do not measure the impact of community development financing well in terms of jobs created, housing units built, or other outcomes. Ratios by themselves could award higher ratings to larger dollar amounts of financing that do not have the biggest bang for the buck in terms of outcomes (more on this in later chapters).

In one of the first studies of its kind, Federal Reserve economist Daniel Ringo used the Federal Reserve database on CRA exams to estimate the impact of community development financing on job growth. His econometric equations revealed that when banks with a greater propensity to engage in community development financing increased their deposit share in a metropolitan area, employment and total wages would increase in a statistically significant manner. About $80,000 in community development lending resulted in one more job. He also found that when community development increased by one-dollar, small business and farm lending increased by 21 cents.[161] Intuitively, if a community development loan supports the creation of a supermarket or an affordable multi-unit rental housing, small businesses or farms may have opportunities to expand their services and/or receive contracts to contribute to the community development projects. They may need loans to expand their plants, equipment and capacities. It is thus important that CRA exams not only encourage more community development financing, but that CRA exams promote holistic thinking on the part of banks to consider how home loans, small business/farm loans and community development financing can be best combined to revitalize neighborhoods.

Ringo did not find the job or wage growth impacts with community development investments.[162] This might be due to the different nature of investments which tend to be in funds that finance projects over a larger area while community development lending is usually more focused to the metropolitan area in which the bank branches and deposits are located.

A third major area of CRA is preserving and increasing access to bank branches and services. Ding and Reid conducted one of the few studies on whether CRA exams encouraged banks to retain branches in LMI census tracts by either opening new branches or not closing existing ones. They used a FDIC database and looked at a long period from 2009-2018.[163] Their econometric model estimated the probability of branch closure dependent on a bank's total number of deposits and branches in a census tract along with a variety of demographic and economic variables including population, number of housing units, poverty rates, number of college educated adults and businesses per capita.[164] These variables attempted to cancel out all other possible factors for closure as much as possible and to focus on CRA eligibility of tracts. They examined tracts with median incomes ranging from 70 to 80 percent of area median income (CRA eligible tracts) compared to tracts with incomes between 80 to 90 percent of area median income (tracts that are not CRA eligible).[165] The narrow range of median incomes between tracts that were CRA eligible and non-eligible was intended to control for the effects of income as much as possible.

They found that if a branch was in a CRA eligible tract, it had a lower probability of being closed, holding other factors constant.

Also, CRA eligible tracts were less likely to become branch deserts, meaning that it was less likely that the last branch in a tract would close.[166] In addition, the positive impacts were larger in the post-2013 period, which was a period of more rapid branch closures overall and a rise in internet banking. Thus, CRA exams should retain a subtest that measures branch availability, services, and deposit products in LMI census tracts as this subtest has had positive impacts. Branches are particularly important for small businesses to establish relationships with banks and to receive loans as documented by Mitchell and Richardson.[167]

Effectiveness of CRA agreements and CBAs typically negotiated during bank mergers

In addition to CRA exams, merger reviews can result in increases in bank loans and investments via CRA agreements or Community Benefit Agreements (CBAs). As discussed above, CBAs involve discussions and/or negotiations among banks and community organizations during merger reviews that commit banks to increases in loans, investments, and services in LMI neighborhoods and communities of color in the years after the merger. CBAs are one way that banks can meet the statutory public benefit requirement that they demonstrate that mergers will positively impact on their ability to meeting community needs. Without these commitments, mergers can result in decreases in loans, investments, and services as banks close branches, and cut staff after mergers in order to reduce their costs and increase their profits. CBAs arose soon after the passage of CRA and have occurred ever since.[168] From 1977 through the first part of 2007, lenders had committed over $4.56 trillion in reinvestment dollars. The lion's share, $4.5 trillion in CRA dollars was committed from 1992 through 2006. In contrast, $8.8 billion was negotiated from 1977 through 1991.

Structural changes in the banking industry and the rise of national level behemoth banks accounted for much of the acceleration of CRA commitment dollars in more recent decades. For example, 1998 was a year of mega-mergers that included the Bank of America and Nations Bank merger as well as Citigroup's acquisition of Travelers; CRA pledges totaled $812 billion dollars as a result. The following years saw fewer mega-mergers and considerably less reinvestment dollars. CRA pledges shot up again in 2003 and particularly in 2004. The year 2004 experienced watershed mega-mergers as Bank of America acquired FleetBoston Financial, JP Morgan Chase acquired Bank One, and Citizens gobbled up Charter One. Community organizations intuitively grasp that larger mergers pose anti-competitive outcomes, so they try to compensate by negotiating robust CBAs. This dovetails with the statutory emphasis that the positive impact on banks' serving convenience and needs must outweigh anti-competitive impacts. However, CRA pledges slowed significantly in 2005 and 2006, which saw less mega merger activity.[169] The financial crisis was also not a favorable environment for negotiating CBAs.

More recently, NCRC itself became more involved directly in negotiating CBAs (more on this in the next chapter). Since 2016, NCRC has facilitated the creation of CBAs with 21 banks worth a combined $580 billion for mortgage, small business and community development lending, investments, and philanthropy in LMI and other underserved communities.[170]

The other important issue to consider when assessing CBAs is the distinction between agreements and voluntary pledges. Agreements often involved a document negotiated and signed by banks and community groups. In contrast, voluntary pledges are unilateral pledges banks usually announce during merger reviews in an attempt to facilitate regulatory approval of their applications. Some voluntary pledges were genuine in that they can be verified with publicly available data, but others could not readily be verified since they used definitions of low- and moderate-income or other terms that were vague or that differed from the official CRA definition of these terms. These pledges could amount to smoothing public relations. For example, in 2011, Capital One issued a $180 billion pledge when acquiring two lenders, HSBC bank and internet-based lender ING. NCRC criticized this pledge as short on details of whether responsible lending would increase and how the bank would add safeguards in its higher cost lending operations.[171]

Overall, NCRC calculated that about $3.7 trillion of the dollars were in the form of voluntary pledges and that approximately $784 billion was in the form of agreements up through 2007. While pledges are better than a total absence of any commitments, it would be preferable for communities if these figures had been reversed over the years.

Using a database of about 200 agreements obtained from NCRC, economists Raphael Bostic and Breck Robinson calculated that CBAs meaningfully increased home lending during the 1993 through 2001 period. The average increase in CRA-eligible lending was 65 percent measured by the number of loans and 94 percent measure by the dollar volume of loans. The averages, however, masked wide variation in performance. More than 25 percent of banks increased their lending by 100 percent but 35 to 45 percent of banks had lending declines.[172] In addition, the average bank reduced their lending after the time period in the agreement expired (typical periods are three to five years).[173] However, enough banks increased their lending after the expiration of agreements as revealed by regression analysis to suggest that CRA and the merger application process has helped correct for market failures and led banks to discover new profitable lending opportunities.[174] Moreover, agreements that included mortgage counseling also boosted mortgage lending, as verified by the regression analysis (mortgage counseling often involves effective collaboration among banks and community groups). Some agreements contained provisions for a review committee of bank and community group representatives. Review committees that met more frequently resulted in increases in loans.[175]

Bostic and Robinson engaged in further analysis in a second paper on agreements to assess in more detail whether CRA agreements increased lending overall and corrected for market failure. If markets are "perfectly competitive" and do not experience any information asymmetries, lending institutions would not miss any opportunities to lend to borrowers that are creditworthy. If this scenario was correct, CRA agreements would not increase total lending but rather shift lending to the lending institutions with agreements that presumably are working harder to woe borrowers.[176]

The regression model calculated the percentage change in home lending over three years, controlling for a variety of economic and demographic factors on a county level. It found that the introduction of a CRA agreement increased total conventional home lending, conventional lending to LMI neighborhoods and borrowers, and conventional lending to people of color and communities of color. Unfortunately, lending stagnated or declined after three or more years.[177]

Overall, the results suggested that CRA corrects for market failure, redlining, and discrimination by requiring banks to work harder to find profitable lending opportunities to creditworthy people in overlooked communities. At the same time, however, the new lending opportunities might not be enticing enough (perhaps lending in more affluent communities is more attractive due to higher loan officer commissions for larger loan amounts) to interest some banks for the long term. Either continued community advocacy resulting in renewed agreements or regulatory enforcement is needed to maintain the positive impacts for longer periods of time. CRA serves as the proverbial "thumb on the scale" that pushes banks to serve formerly redlined and neglected communities. Yet, the thumb needs to be continually applied and should not be released.

Another interesting finding in the Bostic and Robinson study is that the increases in lending were not observed for government-backed FHA lending.[178] Bostic and Robinson suggested that CRA agreements tended to focus on conventional lending. As described in Chapter 1, advocates have long been concerned with the increased cost for borrowers of FHA lending. Focusing on a less expensive form of lending in CRA agreements is a sensible choice.

The positive impact of agreements appears to have held up over time. Casey *et al.* examined the likelihood of loan approvals before and after CBAs from 2007 through 2014 in St. Louis Missouri, using agreements obtained from the St. Louis Metropolitan CRA Association.[179] Regression results indicated that loan approvals increased after the implementation of CBAs.[180] In addition, African Americans were less likely to apply to independent mortgage companies and more likely to apply to banks when CBAs were in effect.[181] This is a positive alternative in that independent mortgage companies were more likely to offer more expensive FHA loans than banks.

Like the Bostic and Robinson papers, the Casey study reinforces the corrective nature of CRA and the merger application process to lending markets and increases lending to people of color. A caveat must be observed here. If CRA exams were the only enforcement mechanism and since exams only assess lending to LMI populations, it is conceivable that banks would only focus on LMI borrowers and communities when negotiating CBAs with community advocates. However, the merger review process also considers the fair lending record of banks, which likely encourages lending increases for people and communities of color.

Critics of CRA – it caused the financial meltdown

Despite evidence of success, CRA has its critics. Conservative law-makers and pundits tend to regard CRA as another misguided government attempt to regulate well-functioning private sector markets. This book does not have room for an exhaustive review of opponents' views, but recent papers and articles by Diego Zuluaga provide a comprehensive summary of them. He creates a list of complaints ranging from CRA's contribution to the financial crisis to its cost and ineffectiveness. Regarding the crisis, he stated "Pre-crisis evidence of the CRA's impact, even when it suggested significant growth in LMI lending by depository institutions, failed to show that such credit was sound. The crisis and its aftermath, on the other hand, showed that mortgage lending on lenient terms could harm financial institutions and borrowers alike."[182]

One of the best rebuttals to this is the work of Reid and Laderman. These researchers compared the performance of CRA-covered banks to non-CRA covered mortgage companies, using the Home Mortgage Disclosure Act (HMDA) data and proprietary data to control for a wide range of lender, borrower, and loan characteristics. They found that loans issued by banks in their assessment areas were about half as likely to result in foreclosure as loans issued by non-CRA covered mortgage companies during 2004-2006, which was the height of subprime and high-cost lending. In addition, while bank lending outside of their assessment areas was still considerably less likely to result in foreclosure than mortgage company lending, it was more likely to result in foreclosure than bank lending inside of their assessment areas. Laderman and Reid suggest that the retail branch bank channel contributed to safer and sounder loans than wholesale channels commonly employed by mortgage companies.[183]

Like Laderman and Reid, Federal Reserve economists Bhutta and Canner analyzed the 2005 and 2006 HMDA data and found that just six percent of all higher priced loans were issued by banks in their assessment areas to LMI borrowers or census tracts. In other words, 94 percent of all higher priced lending (a proxy for subprime lending according to Bhutta and Canner) were made by mortgage companies or banks outside of their assessment areas and thus had nothing to do with trying to serve LMI borrowers for CRA compliance purposes. In his speech quoted at the beginning of this chapter, former Federal Reserve Governor Kroszner cited the Canner and Bhutta study.[184] Established to investigate the causes of the crisis, the Financial Crisis Inquiry Commission (FCIC) also stated, "The Commission concludes the CRA was not a significant factor in subprime lending or the crisis."[185]

The Schweizer quote at the beginning of the chapter is misguided in this context.. He suggests that housing activists were egging banks onto making risky loans to vulnerable populations. The reality is that community advocates work and reside in underserved neighborhoods and they do not want lenders to give their neighbors abusive loans. They have internalized any harm caused by lending and insist that banks provide safe and sound loans as CRA requires. CRA agreements and CBAs succeed in providing safe and sound loans in part because of the role of community organizations in insisting upon carefully underwritten loans.

In contrast, the financial crisis was caused by lending institutions and financial intermediaries that did not internalize the harm of abusive lending. As research demonstrated, non-CRA regulated lenders made most of the high cost and abusive loans. They made commissions and fees from these loans and then were able to quickly sell these loans and unload risk to Wall Street investors that did not have complete information on the full extent of the onerous loan terms and conditions as documented by the Financial Crisis Inquiry Commission and other research. An argument can be made that if CRA's legal requirement of safety and soundness had been extended throughout the financial industry including mortgage companies, then the amount of risky lending would have been significantly reduced. Financial institutions would have employed more home mortgage counseling for borrowers and careful underwriting to ensure that borrowers could afford loans.

With this said, banks did not have clean hands in the financial crisis. They also had parts of their institutions that were not covered by CRA and thus did not have the same standards of safety and soundness. A handful of large banks had mortgage company affiliates that engaged in risky lending that were not included on CRA exams. An example of optional exclusion enabling abusive practices is Suntrust Mortgage Company, which Suntrust excluded from its CRA exam of 2013. Federal agencies reached a $1 billion settlement with the mortgage company over widespread abuses associated with underwriting FHA mortgages and mortgage servicing that occurred in the time period covered by the CRA exam.[186] According to former Attorney General Eric Holder, the mortgage company's lending from 2006 through 2012 "is a prime example of the widespread underwriting failures that helped bring about the financial crisis."[187] Yet, because of CRA's optional treatment of affiliates, Suntrust's CRA exam did not consider the mortgage company's lending practices and whether these practices should result in a ratings downgrade. The optional treatment is inconsistent with the interconnectedness of affiliates and their parents. Suntrust's CRA exam states, "SunTrust Mortgage Company is the primary originator of home purchase and refinance loans for the organization."[188]

Investment banks that are exempt from CRA but also part of bank holding companies played a large role in the financial crisis. They pooled and assembled subprime mortgage-backed securities (MBS) and sold these MBS to investors. They underwrote $2.1 trillion of MBS from 2000 through 2007. Citigroup is one large bank that had an investment company affiliate not covered by CRA that handled subprime MBS.[189] If the agencies had cracked down on the MBS activities earlier in the high cost lending years and Congress had imposed a CRA requirement for investment banks, perhaps their talents could have been more focused on equity investments for affordable housing and economic development in LMI communities rather than financing abusive lending that extracted wealth from these communities and helped cause the worst global recession since the Great Depression.

It would have been more accurate for critics of CRA to have asserted that the incomplete coverage of CRA created regulatory loopholes that contributed to the crisis.

Critics of CRA – it is not profitable and is costly

Zuluaga expanded upon his argument of the inefficiency and cost of CRA by saying, "Yet another problem with citing increases in LMI lending as evidence for the economic gains associated with the CRA is that the opportunity costs of CRA-induced lending may exceed the benefits."[190] Yet, a 2000 Federal Reserve survey mandated by Congress found that eighty two percent of all bank respondents said CRA-related home purchase and refinance lending was profitable or marginally profitable in absolute terms.[191] The median difference in return on equity in CRA and other home purchase and refinance lending was zero percent.[192] The median difference in charge-off rate (default minus recoveries) for CRA and non-CRA loans was zero.[193] Zuluaga cited the same Federal Reserve survey's finding that CRA lending was less profitable and costlier. It was less profitable or somewhat less profitable for 44 percent of the respondents, which was not an overwhelmingly negative finding.[194] Similarly, about 53 percent of banks reported that origination costs were higher for CRA loans; this was a slight majority and not an overwhelming one.[195]

LMI lending typically has lower dollar mortgage amounts, which usually means originators earn lower fees that are based on dollar amounts. In a sense, costs might be higher because fees are lower, but overall profitability is not impaired to such an extent to make the lending unsustainable for the lending institution as shown by the Federal survey. If it were not for CRA, fewer LMI loans would be made, and neighborhoods would continue to experience the impacts of redlining and economic distress. Likewise, banks cannot survive if they only make loans to affluent borrowers; eventually that market will become saturated. Just like any business that has different levels of profitability for different products and customer groups, banks have various levels of profitability for borrowers of various income groups. Were it not for CRA, the level of LMI lending would be lower than is optimal for neighborhoods and banks in the long run.

Overall, the Federal Reserve Survey points to the corrective function that CRA serves in the lending marketplace. Sixty three percent of survey respondents stated that CRA home purchase and refinance led to new and profitable opportunities. Even higher majorities indicated that this was the case for small business (81 percent) and home improvement lending (71 percent).[196]

Conservative pundits also like to assert that cost-benefit analysis would conclude that the costs are much greater than the benefits for CRA. NCRC decided to try this during the last round of comments on proposed changes to the CRA regulation. Using data from the federal agencies, NCRC calculated that the annual compliance cost associated with the proposed rule would be about $52 million.[197] We then assumed that about 10 percent of mortgage loans in LMI tracts were due to CRA per the Ding study mentioned above. As a result, the CRA-induced increase in loans in this tract category was about 66,000 loans.[198] According the Mortgage Bankers Association, per loan income recently was about $1,099 per loan.[199] Multiplying the per loan income by the CRA-induced increase in home mortgage loans yields $72,562,683 which exceeds the added data collection cost by more than $20 million.

This is just one loan type that produced a benefit exceeding costs. If this type of calculation is replicated for other closed-end home loans, small business, small farm, multifamily lending and automobile lending (the loan categories to be included by the proposed rule), it appears that the benefits for banks considerably outweigh costs. Moreover, this analysis does not even consider wealth gains from borrowers receiving CRA-eligible loans. The proposition that benefits do not exceed costs appears to fail under detailed analysis.

Critics of CRA: it causes gentrification

Zuluaga continued his line of attack against CRA by asserting in an op-ed in the Washington Post that CRA accelerated gentrification and displacement of people of color in Washington DC by inducing banks to make the vast majority of their loans to higher income borrowers in lower income areas.[200] He ignored findings in the Ding and Bostic studies showing that CRA increased loans to people of color.[201]

Unlike Zuluaga who uses supposedly negative findings to argue for a repeal of CRA, a more constructive approach is to take the issue of displacement seriously and to build in additional safeguards in CRA against displacement. Chapters 3 and 8 will discuss how to add anti-displacement protections in the financing of affordable housing. In addition, the CRA lending test can refrain from providing favorable consideration to loans to middle-income and/or upper-income borrowers in census tracts experiencing rapid home price increases and displacement associated with gentrification. The point of considering serious issues like displacement is not to discard CRA but to reform it.

Critics of CRA: it is not effective

A refrain in the list of complaints against CRA is that it is not effective. Regardless of the number of studies documenting increases in safe and sound loans, investments and branches, there will be others showing ambiguous results or no CRA impact. Even studies that do not seek to discredit CRA can nevertheless end up being used for that purpose by the law's opponents. A recent Federal Reserve Bank of New York paper, for example, concluded that under most of its econometric models, CRA did not increase consumers' access to credit.[202] In this case, however, the major unit of measurement in the study may have been flawed. The authors' assessed CRA's impacts on a borrower's total debt levels in moderate-income tracts eligible for CRA compared to those with slightly more income levels that were not eligible.[203] However, the result is almost pre-ordained since the Ding study discussed above revealed a 10 percent to 20 percent boost in lending in CRA eligible tracts, meaning that most borrowers in those tracts will not receive CRA eligible loans, exactly what the New York Fed study found. However, the 10 percent to 20 percent boost in home lending likely made the difference between economically viable and distressed neighborhoods in many instances.

There are other models in the New York Federal Reserve study that showed minimal CRA impact, but the methodology was designed differently from the Ding study. Ultimately, the readers of studies have to make judgements about their methods. The Ding study appears to be more persuasive because changes in metropolitan boundaries made by the Office of Management of Budget resulted in some formerly eligible tracts becoming ineligible. Bank CRA staff would likely respond by diverting CRA lending from the ineligible to eligible tracts. The Ding study's methods capture real world CRA practice better.

Nonetheless, the New York Fed study exposed some CRA weaknesses that need to be addressed in CRA regulatory reform. One of these was banks' purchasing loans made by other lenders in CRA tracts instead of focusing on making their own loans.[204] They would also sell loans they purchased to other banks seeking CRA credit for the same loans. This is exam manipulation, which must be prohibited by the agencies. Again, instead of using studies to assess how to make the law and regulation better, the opponents of CRA employ them as evidence arguing for CRA's repeal.

Conclusion

This chapter has provided an overview of CRA and the merger application process. CRA has succeeded in increasing lending, investment, and services to traditionally underserved communities. At the same time, the full potential of CRA to leverage reinvestment has not been realized due to loopholes and weaknesses in the law and regulation. CRA ratings inflation and deficiencies in revealing meaningful distinctions in bank performance reduce the amount of reinvestment activity by dulling bank motivations to work hard in reinvestment. Ratings reform, either adding a fifth rating or a point scale, is needed to reinvigorate CRA. The merger applications process likewise is not consistent in achieving public benefits for communities after bank mergers. The agencies need to increase the level of scrutiny of bank applications, issuing more denials and conditional approvals. Moreover, the process needs to become more transparent via a requirement that banks submit community benefit plans or enter in CBAs. Empirical studies have reaffirmed CRA's benefits but also point to these and other needed reforms.

3

Reinvestment: Leveraging the CRA at the Community Level

CRA requires banks to serve community needs. Accordingly, residents of underserved neighborhoods and community-based organizations should be at the center of the CRA process. Banks should design their programs and products in response to needs as articulated by the community. As practiced over the decades, CRA implementation has had a mixed record in this regard. The most success with community input occurs when banks submit merger applications. Large bank mergers are most often the ones involving Community Benefit Agreements (CBAs).

In contrast, community input has been less successful during CRA exams in part because CRA examiners tend to ask pro forma questions that scratch the surface of community needs. Also, CRA exams can involve several geographical areas, making it daunting for many community organizations to analyze data and comment on bank CRA performance. Lastly, CRA implementation can occur daily when community-based organizations engage bank CRA staff in partnerships and conversations on needs and opportunities. Partnership and product development can arise when banks are seeking to implement their public benefit plans after mergers. This chapter will review observations from stakeholders and case studies of CRA implementation with the aim of improving the robustness of community involvement and making the community the center of CRA.

Community Benefit Agreements as a method to meet convenience and needs

Community Benefit Agreements (CBA) and their predecessors known as CRA agreements have been negotiated between banks and community organizations for decades. Marchiel documented early CRA agreements shortly after the passage of CRA negotiated between banks and NPA affiliates.[205] While this chapter reviews CBAs negotiated between NCRC members and banks, it must be emphasized that CBAs or something like them have been around for decades, have preceded NCRC, and are likely to succeed NCRC. In my estimation, they are an important complement to CRA exams and agency enforcement activities.

Kevin Hill, NCRC's Senior Policy Advisor, stated in an interview, "Community Benefit Agreements (CBAs) are the ideal model for how the merger application process should go. Community groups are in conversations with banks about what the most pressing needs are in their communities. There needs to be tractable, measurable goals. This is the ideal way for banks to meet the convenience and needs requirement of the merger application process. Without specific goals, it is hard to measure success and whether banks are responding to needs in a reasonable way."[206]

NCRC tracks merger applications on the federal agency websites. When it finds a merger that it believes has significant impacts on communities, NCRC will conduct extensive data analysis and compare the merging banks' performance to their peers in home, small business lending, and community development financing. It will also assess whether anti-competitiveness concerns are prevalent, using measures of the degree of market competition employed by the federal agencies. NCRC will then notify member organizations in states and localities that will be heavily impacted by the merger.

As stated in the last chapter, NCRC started involving itself directly in CBA negotiations in 2016 and have negotiated $580 billion in lending and investments since then.[207] In earlier years, NCRC helped its member organizations with data analysis and reviewing the major issues in merger applications. However, as it became apparent that community organization capacity would remain uneven across the country, NCRC decided to become more directly engaged in CBA negotiations in order to ensure that areas of the country without extensive community group networks such as the South would also benefit from CBAs. At first, NCRC had to approach banks and engage them with various degrees of success. Now, however, the banking industry is accustomed to NCRC as major force in the merger application process and many banks proactively approach NCRC to enter into CBA negotiations.[208]

Before engaging with banks, NCRC organizing staff discuss in one-on-one and in group settings community needs and opportunities with its member organizations. NCRC staff ask what the biggest issues in communities exist that must be addressed by CBAs.

Then, NCRC and its members will engage bank CEOs and senior departmental staff in meetings, either in-person or virtual, discussing a list of needs and opportunities. Each meeting can involve 25 to 30 community organizations and overall, it is common for NCRC to enlist 100 to 200 community organizations in the meetings. Hill remarks that these meetings impress upon the bank "the level of sophistication of groups that can hold banks accountable to meet the CBA goals."[209]

Catherine Petrusz, Senior CRA analyst, maintained that "the CBA process should be a model for improving public participation in CRA. The role of community organizing should be lifted up as an integral part of the process. The CBA process starts as listening sessions. Getting the bank to understand that they should listen to the community first before making decisions about the products and services that will be meet community needs."[210]

After the meetings with the bank, NCRC will develop a first draft of a CBA and submit it to the bank. The bank responds by editing the CBA, deleting some provisions, and amending others. NCRC and its members review the merging banks' responses and make counterproposals. At a certain point, NCRC and its members decide whether to move forward with finalizing the CBA, depending on whether a significant number of community group goals have been met. A level of trust needs to be developed. Hill maintained that a majority of community group concerns need to be addressed in a draft CBA. Also, the merging banks need to strive to improve performance in a reasonable manner, not just maintaining the current level of performance and certainly not decreasing lending or other activities. If the negotiations break down, NCRC will comment on the banks' merger application and will oppose the merger in a letter to the federal bank agencies. In other cases, NCRC will indicate that the merger should be conditional on finalization of the CBA.[211]

The merger application process is a leverage point for injecting community needs that otherwise could be neglected. The prospect of a letter critical of the merger is a motivation for some banks to keep negotiating over programs, products, and community engagement mechanisms. Without the merger application process, community needs would receive less attention. As Chapter 6 describes in more detail, some CRA opponents criticize the process as a "shakedown" that extracts concessions from banks that lead to unsafe and unsound lending and other ill-conceived activities. Community advocates counter that this process ensures that formerly redlined communities have a seat at the proverbial table and that mergers are not just opportunities for banks to become larger, monopolistic, and neglectful of the community (Chapter 2 provides data on the performance of CBAs and Chapter 6 describes how this debate shaped legislation passed in 1999). Hill maintained that a key to securing a robust CBA that improves public welfare, does not unfairly promote a single interest, and that broadly responds to needs articulated by several groups serving multiple communities is to be transparent in all steps in the process including publicly sharing CBA details on NCRC's website after the CBAs are finalized.[212]

CBA quantitative goal setting involves home and small business lending and community development financing. Goals are often developed at a state level but also for cities or other local areas in which the merging banks are performing poorly. A challenge for CBAs is how to address local needs, especially in underserved cities and rural communities. As early as the 1970s as Marchiel documented, advocates were concerned about how to maintain CRA's focus on meeting local needs while banks were consolidating. Five decades later, consolidation has accelerated to the point where half a dozen banks are truly national institutions with assets in trillions of dollars and branches spanning across the country. Regional banks can also serve five to ten states. CBAs, in response, have not created goals for all local areas in the banks' geographic footprint, which would be a herculean task in the compressed time period of a merger application. Hill indicated that robust advisory boards at banks that have community groups representing geographical diversity as well as gender and racial diversity is critical. Groups from underserved geographies can articulate needs unique or pressing for their areas. Also, community-wide concerns across the entire bank footprint about issues such as high downpayment requirements or minimum loan sizes can also benefit underserved areas. Organizing a network of community groups in local areas, including smaller cities and rural areas, also helps impress upon banks the importance of credit needs in underserved areas. Finally, documenting needs or conditions in underserved areas such as high unemployment will help banks target solutions such as workforce training to those areas.[213]

A merger reorganization at the banks affects decision-making regarding CRA activities including community development financing. Community organizations in areas far from the new headquarters become concerned that CRA officers will no longer have as much decision-making over community development financing or other CRA products. Banks can address these concerns by committing to the retention or creation of regional directors with decision-making over CRA activities as PNC did in its acquisition of BBVA Compass.[214] Whether this structure reaches far enough throughout the bank's geographic footprint remains to be seen. CBAs may need to continue to innovate to elevate the banks' attention to local needs throughout their footprint. CRA exams, on their part, need to ensure that enough geographical areas and a diversity of areas including smaller cities and rural areas are considered assessment areas where activities are evaluated.

In terms of retail home lending, NCRC will analyze data from the previous three years and create a three-year average in terms of the numbers of loans made to separate racial and ethnic groups and to LMI borrowers and communities. NCRC will then identify peer banks in the geographical areas who exhibit a healthy percentage increase in the number of loans over the time period. NCRC will then ask the merging banks to meet or exceed this rate of increase. Multi-year goals in numbers of loans are then often converted to dollar goals by calculating average dollar loan amounts made to the target borrower groups.

NCRC does not set goals as a percent of total bank loans to LMI borrowers or for separate racial or ethnic groups. Bank lawyers have been concerned that this type of goal setting could be criticized as quota setting.[215] While CBAs are critically important to help realize public benefits as a result of bank mergers, the caution in goal setting points to how and why CRA exams should supplement and complement CBAs. CRA exams measure the percentage of loans to LMI borrowers and compare a bank's performance to its peers. This has been accepted practice for decades and does not amount to quota setting because the comparisons are conducted for past years, not future years like a CBA. Moreover, CRA exams do not require a certain percentage of loans to LMI borrowers or communities but will develop ratings from assessments of performance in several categories of lending based on how a bank compares to its peers and demographic benchmarks. Ideally then, CBAs and CRA exams work in tandem to commit banks to safe and sound increases in lending and equitable shares of lending to traditionally underserved populations.

Process goals accompany quantitative goals. Banks cannot merely decide on robust percentage increases in loans to underserved populations and then expect to meet them in a passive manner. Hewing to the CRA mandate that banks must affirmatively and continually meet needs, banks commit to marketing and outreach to underserved populations and product flexibility in CBAs. Outreach efforts involve employing loan officers that are people of color and come from the communities being served. Branches remain a vital method for serving populations traditionally underserved and wary of banks. An extensive literature has researched and documented that branches can serve as a means for banks and the community to gain knowledge and trust in each other, resulting in increases in loans and services for underserved communities.[216] Accordingly, some banks will commit to increasing branches in LMI and communities of color in CBAs.

Product innovations include the creation of Special Purpose Credit Programs (SPCPs). Federal regulatory agencies have allowed SPCPs to target communities of color or specific racial or ethnic groups of customers provided the bank documents that the target populations have been historically underserved.[217] In a CBA with NCRC, U.S. Bank agreed to a pathbreaking SPCP that targeted organizations controlled by people of color. These include nonprofit developers that would receive construction loans and other financing for affordable housing. Hill stated that "CRA has hurt itself by being as colorblind as it is. This is a metric (measuring dollars to community-based organizations led by people of color) that CRA exams cannot do because of their colorblind nature. Organizations led by people of color are very rooted in their communities and often most effective in reaching underserved populations."[218]

Historically, the amount of dollars for organizations controlled and directed by people of color has been quite small as a result. If CBAs are to direct more reinvestment financing to underserved communities of color, CBAs should directly target communities of color and the organizations that serve them. NCRC has succeeded in committing some banks to count the philanthropic dollars issued to organizations controlled by people of color. On their part, the agencies incorporated consideration of SPCP programs in CRA exams.[219] These developments are encouraging as a starting point. In order for communities of color to benefit from significant levels of reinvestment dollars, SPCPs reviewed in CRA exams and contained in CBAs must be numerous and widespread instead of episodic and periodic.

Other types of product innovations involve subsidies and underwriting flexibilities. Reducing downpayment requirements addresses a major barrier often frustrating homeownership for LMI and people of color who do not have the wealth or savings to afford the typical downpayment required for a mortgage loan. In addition to lower downpayments, banks have also agreed to underwriting flexibilities that address the lack of traditional credit history that pose barriers for people of color and populations without established relationships with banks.[220] Some banks have agreed in CBAs to use the record of rental payments or other non-traditional credit histories for populations with low or no credit scores. In CRA guidance, the federal agencies have also encouraged this approach to help underserved populations qualify for loans.[221]

Example of a robust CBA with First Merchants

Hill considered the CBA with First Merchants Bank headquartered in Indiana to be a robust CBA. First Merchants initially entered into a CBA in 2020 and renewed it in 2022.[222] Scott McKee, Senior Vice President, Director of Corporate Social Responsibility, affirmed that the CBA is a way for the bank to formalize a strategic approach to community reinvestment. He stated that the bank's CEO is fully committed to community reinvestment and provided the resources needed for a comprehensive CRA and fair banking program. The bank has a culture that promotes reinvestment and racial equity, holding internal webinars featuring people of color employees discussing their experiences with the bank. Racial equity is not just an issue of social justice, it is good business. McKee commented that his research showed that "the purchasing power of Black and Brown people in the United States equals the fourth largest GDP in the world. In the next twenty years, racial and ethnic minorities will be more than 50% of the people in this country. If any element of our community is suffering, everybody suffers. So, there is an opportunity to grow the community by being smart, and fair, and equitable, and intentional."[223]

It is this mixture of good business sense and social justice that motivates the bank and McKee. McKee stated that the bank must listen first. "In the past, society has made the big mistake of going into communities of color and saying we have the answer. We knew that is not the approach. It has been done and failed. It disenfranchised people. We don't have any preconceived notions of what the solutions are or even what the problems are. Instead, help us find solutions together." The bank designs products after listening to the community explain what is needed.

Implementing this philosophy involves rigorous monitoring and collaboration with community-based organizations. The CBA created an advisory board that includes community groups, which offers input and is actively involved in reviewing First Merchants reports of CBA goal progress. In addition to the board, bank staff will meet with community groups throughout its branch footprint and ask them what products they need. As it entered Detroit, the bank committed to locating a new branch in an underserved community. McKee reported that the bank engaged a dozen community-based organizations and funded a needs assessment and survey through them that identified five zip codes where a branch is needed.[224] NCRC also contributed research identifying communities with low levels of branching but nevertheless have high population density that can support bank branches.[225] The bank is closing in on a location; McKee predicted by the time this book is published, the new branch will be up and running.

The bank also committed in the CBA to increase philanthropic spending to people of color nonprofit organizations by 155 percent. McKee reported that in 2021, the bank offered $287,000 to 34 organizations, and almost doubled this to $590,000 to 89 organizations in 2022. Like Hill, McKee regarded nonprofit organizations controlled by people of color as key to the revitalization of their communities. The bank has committed to significant increases in grants to these organizations to help combat the barriers faced by organizations controlled by people of color.[226]

In its 2022 CBA renewal, First Merchants committed to a variety of products and initiatives designed to provide customers with a full banking experience. The bank promised to increase home purchase and home improvement lending by 800 loans to African

American borrowers over a five-year period.[227] The bank also committed to tracking progress with its Next Horizon Mortgage that features up to 100 percent financing, no required private mortgage insurance, history of rental and utility payments as alternatives to credit scores, and downpayment assistance grants up to $7,500 for borrowers completing home buyer courses.[228] According to McKee, community stakeholders tell him that Next Horizon is one of the best products on the market because of its flexibilities. The data bears this out. The most recent CRA exam for the bank reported that the bank made 169 Next Horizon loans in 2020 and more than 270 in 2021. By 2022, the number had surged to 594 according to McKee.[229]

The bank committed to financial wellness and education programs that included one-on-one counseling. The bank promised to provide safe and affordable bank accounts certified as such by the Cities for Financial Empowerment Fund.[230] First Merchants' Simple Access deposit account experienced growth of 18 percent during 2022.[231] The bank recognized the need for different products to respond to various needs including a home improvement loan product critical for weatherization and energy efficiency in the banks' Midwest markets. The bank also committed to increasing grants for community-based organizations serving immigrants and exploring possible mortgage and small business deposit and loan products sensitive to the beliefs and culture of the Muslim population, which has significant concentrations in Midwest cities such as Detroit.[232]

The breadth and depth of the partnership building and product offerings reflect the inclusive business philosophy of this bank. As the bank continues to grow, it will continue to expand its reinvestment activity according to McKee.

Inspiring CBA provisions in need of replication

The number of innovative CBA provisions and accomplishments would be too numerous to list, but here are some:

Huntington increased its home purchase lending by 37 percent to African Americans and outperformed its peers as a result of its CBA. It also used non-traditional underwriting such as considering rental payments.

First Tennessee increased its financing for Community Development Financial Institutions (CDFIs) that are dedicated to serving underserved communities to $9.4 million during the CBA, an exponential hike from its previous $100,000 in CDFI financing.

BMO Harris pledged to form a Native Land Advisory Group to help the bank better understand and serve the needs of Native Americans which will comprise a greater share of the bank's footprint in future years. BMO Harris also created a fund to finance mortgages to support homeownership on tribal trust land.

BMO Harris pledged to double its CRA mortgage loan specialists. This promising provision is likely to significantly increase lending to underserved borrowers.[233]

U.S. Bancorp committed to opening five new branches in LMI or middle-income Majority Minority (MMT) communities in California over five years. It will also open or preserve five additional branches in LMI or MMT communities in California over five years decided with input from the California Reinvestment Coalition.[234]

These CBA experiences illustrate that banks cannot develop product innovations or marketing approaches in isolation, with staff cloistered in the headquarters' offices. They must engage representatives of the community who have first-hand experience of barriers to banking. Just as banks must work to serve affluent customers effectively, they need to work even harder to serve communities that have been underserved. Yet, the work of CBAs is never complete. Banks will change their focus and exit product markets. Community groups must therefore always be engaged and identify opportunities for renewing CBAs with their existing bank partners and identifying new bank partners.

Not all CBAs work – The Experience with KeyBank

Announced and celebrated at NCRC's annual conference, NCRC and KeyBank entered into a CBA in 2016 to the tune of $16.5 billion that would be executed over five years starting in 2017.[235] However, starting in 2018, the banks' lending to people of color and LMI borrowers shrank every year. As shown below in Cleveland, NCRC mapping highlighted patterns of lending in which clusters of dots representing loans were concentrated in predominantly White neighborhoods while communities of color had few dots.

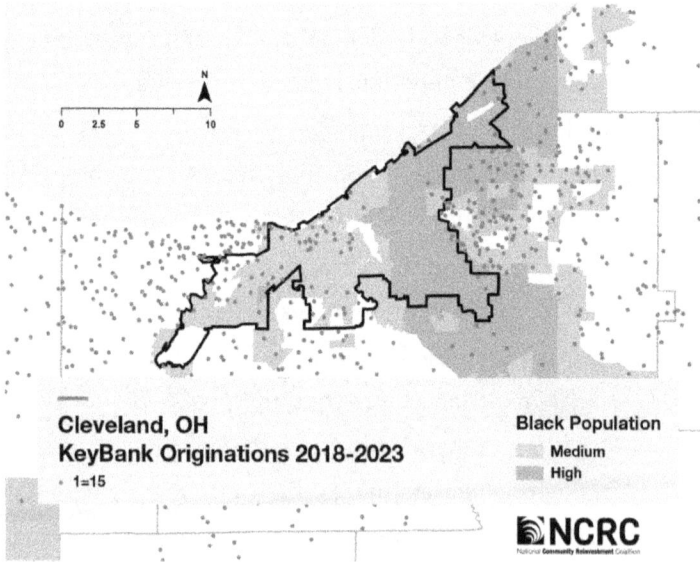

Cleveland, OH
KeyBank Originations 2018-2023
· 1=15

Black Population
Medium
High

NCRC
National Community Reinvestment Coalition

KeyBank's record of loans to communities of color

In a blog, NCRC's CEO Jesse Van Tol declared:

> "Of the nation's 50 largest mortgage lenders, KeyBank had the lowest percentage of home purchase loans to Black borrowers from 2018-2021. Across the bank's 10 largest markets, just 2.7% of its home purchase loans last year went to Black people, down from nearly 6% in 2018. Similarly, LMI borrowers accounted for just 17% of such KeyBank loans, down from 35% four years ago."[236]

Van Tol announced his resignation from the bank's national advisory council. Comparing KeyBank's unfulfilled CBA promises to those of a borrower who does not pay his loan and is foreclosed upon, Van Tol affirmed that banks must also face consequences for broken covenants with the community.[237] He hoped that this public break with KeyBank goads the bank into performing better and puts other banks on notice that they will also be held accountable.

Hill listed multiple reasons for the failure of the KeyBank CBA. The bank appeared to be in turmoil; it exhibited considerable turnover in executive and senior staff as well as loan officers on the ground. The bank did not make promised changes and was not forthcoming in reporting and abiding by CBA accountability mechanisms. For example, it had promised to change its compensation structure away from loan officer fees calculated as a percentage of loan dollars; this type of compensation favors larger loans made to more affluent customers since the dollar amounts are larger. Instead, compensation was to be tied to the number of loans made annually. Yet, KeyBank did not make this change until the last year of the agreement and was not keeping NCRC and the community organizations that were parties to the CBA informed of this development. KeyBank also did not make serious commitments to the innovative products in the CBA. For example, it had committed to a check cashing product but then did not inform its branch personnel to the existence of the product or its innovative features.[238]

A positive development during the spring of 2024 is that NCRC and KeyBank announced that they will work together in providing downpayment assistance, grants, and other subsidies to facilitate responsible lending.[239] Hopefully, this development will lead to a renewed partnership that will increase responsible lending to traditionally underserved communities.

Not all CBAs will work. All the parties need to be committed to the CBA. Chapter 2 included reviews of econometric studies that revealed that while CBAs were successful overall in increasing access to lending, there was a minority of agreements that failed in their goals. Since they work overall, the challenge is to keep making CBAs, identify more banks with philosophies similar to First Merchants, and to lock in more accountability mechanisms to guard against waning commitments.

Convenience and needs commitments of banks being acquired by others must be honored

The topsy-turvy world of bank mergers can involve consecutive mergers that occur at a rapid timetable. When the dust settles after the mergers, federal bank agencies must ensure that previous commitments regarding meeting needs are honored or else the merger will fall short of the legal requirement that it benefits the public. In a recent case, Citizens Bank, a large New England bank, acquired Investors Bank in April of 2022. Previously, Investors Bank had acquired the eight branches of Berkshire Bank. The FDIC approved Investors' branch acquisition in the summer of 2021, but the approval was conditional.[240] Investors had significant weaknesses in home lending to people of color. The FDIC required Investors to develop an Action Plan that included the following element: "The Bank will regularly monitor application and origination activity of home mortgage loans in majority-minority census tracts and from Blacks throughout the Bank's assessment areas."[241]

Less than a year later, however, Citizens acquired Investors and made no commitment to honor the FDIC's conditional merger approval despite its own weaknesses in home lending to people of color. NCRC and its member organizations had attempted unsuccessfully to negotiate a CBA with Citizens. Lacking any other recourse, NCRC and several of its member organizations commented on Citizens' CRA exam in the fall of 2022. As of this writing, NCRC has not heard from the OCC regarding its CRA comment or how the OCC will consider the previous conditional approval of Investors' branch purchases. Agency communications regarding CRA exams comments are lacking as shown in more detail immediately below, even in instances when clear and compelling compliance issues such as conditional approvals have been raised by community-based organizations.

Commenting on CRA exams not an easy or inviting task

The relatively few times that NCRC and its members have affected a CRA rating involved a systemic issue, meaning that it was significant enough to capture agency attention. In the case of Woodforest National Bank, for example, NCRC commented on a low loan-to-deposit ratio; that is, the bank was taking deposits but not making loans. The bank also made a low percentage of loans to LMI borrowers and neighborhoods. The bank failed its exam in 2012.[242] After this exam, the bank took significant steps to improve its performance including senior officials meeting with NCRC. In a 2015 exam, the bank's supervisory agency, the OCC, noted that lending performance was adequate.[243] By the 2019 exam, the OCC judged lending performance was excellent, including higher percentages of loans to LMI borrowers and communities. In its major operating area of Texas, for example, the percentage of small business and consumer loans to LMI areas and borrowers often exceeded those of its peers and equaled or exceeded the percentage of LMI households and census tracts.[244] In addition, the OCC stated that the bank's level of investments was excellent. In Austin TX, for example, the dollar amount of investments was 167 percent of Tier 1 capital, a very high ratio. The bank made a $125,000 equity equivalent investment into a Small Business Investment Corporation which was one of the few in the country led by Hispanics.[245] In this example, the bank stepped up its efforts and markedly improved its lending and investment performance across successive CRA exams over a long time period, including a 2023 exam, after a community group commented and met with them.[246]

Likewise, several NCRC members commented on a restrictive policy involving credit scores and FHA lending in the case of BBVA Compass Bank, which contributed to low levels of lending to LMI and people of color borrowers and contributed to a failed CRA rating.[247] In a 2018 exam, the Federal Reserve Bank of Atlanta had judged Compass to be Outstanding overall and Outstanding on its Lending, Investment, and Service Tests. This bank had transformed from a failing CRA performer to an Outstanding one on all of its tests.[248]

In February of 2023, the FDIC failed Transportation Alliance Bank (TAB), lowering its rating from Satisfactory to Needs to Improve due to an illegal credit practice that violated the unfair or deceptive acts and practices standard in Section 5 of the Federal Trade Commission (FTC) Act.[249] Led by NCRC and the National Consumer Law Center, 40 community-based organizations commented that TAB had an arrangement with a non-bank lender, operating under the name EasyPay Finance, that made usurious consumer loans financing a variety of purchases ranging from buying pets to auto repair.[250] Unscrupulous non-bank lenders have sought to partner with banks in order to evade interest rate caps of several states. While the non-banks must comply with the state law, banks can "export" the interest rates allowed in their headquarter states. TAB is headquartered in Utah which has a permissive law regarding interest rates. Therefore, when EasyPay partnered with TAB, consumers experienced rates as high as 189%. Moreover, unless a consumer read the contract carefully, the consumer would not know that if he or she did not repay the loan within 90 days, the interest rates charges would apply. Many consumers misunderstood this to mean that the loan was interest free. Often, consumers were signing the loan contract at the retail store and were not carefully reviewing the dense detail of loan terms and conditions. Several consumers complained to the Consumer Financial Protection Bureau about the practices of TAB and its partner, Easy Pay.[251] This case resonated with the public and generated many allies such as the American Society for the Prevention of Cruelty to Animals supporting the comment letter because in some cases, puppy mills used Easy Pay and TAB. The borrowers had sick dogs that died before the loan was repaid.

Adam Rust, a former NCRC Senior Policy Advisor, affirms that the strategy of commenting on CRA exams regarding abusive lending will be a continuing effort. He stated that "it is the rent-a-bank arrangement that is driving this engagement. Even if TAB bank changes their lending, the problem will still exist. We will use CRA as a lever. Other banks doing this will have CRA exams coming up."[252] Rust concluded that the subprime mortgage crisis taught us that the quality of loans is just as important as access to loans for underserved communities so agencies must address loan quality in CRA exams.

In most other cases in which NCRC and member community organizations commented, the impacts of those comments were harder to discern. NCRC commented a few years ago regarding the CRA exam of Texas Capital Bank. The comments concerned the low levels of lending to businesses with revenues of less than $1 million. The OCC did not contact NCRC for any follow-up regarding its concerns, leading NCRC to wonder whether its comments had any effect. Interestingly, the bank contacted NCRC, acknowledged the lending deficiency, and stated that it was in the process of hiring loan officers specializing in CRA activities.[253] The NCRC comment at least resulted in a conversation with the bank and the bank pledging orally to make improvements.

Identifying systemic issues is a high bar that will not be met in many cases, particularly when identifying systemic issues would involve analysis of lending and other activity across several geographical areas. Engaging in this intensive effort also is not encouraged when the agencies appear unresponsive to comments. Hill stated that "community groups do not report about good experiences and (agency) follow-up on CRA exams. It seems like comment letters go into a black hole." Hill maintained that with limited resources, community organizations will prioritize commenting on merger applications because those types of comments usually have more impact than commenting on CRA exams.[254]

Despite the high bar that community groups must meet in

commenting on CRA exams, public input of this nature can bolster bank reinvestment over a long period of time and also curb abusive practices. To my knowledge, no systematic study has been conducted regarding the impact of commenting on CRA exams and bank performance. Part of the difficulty is that the agencies have not established an easily accessible repository of comments on their websites. If the agencies did this and improved communication with community groups commenting on exams, perhaps public comments on CRA exams would increase and positive outcomes for both banks and communities would multiply. Also, researchers could probe more precisely whether there are positive qualitative and quantitative outcomes on bank performance associated with public comments on CRA exams.

Commenting on fair lending issues impeded by lack of exam transparency

CRA does not consider lending to people of color or communities of color. Instead, a fair-lending review section affirms that either the bank regulatory agency or the Consumer Financial Protection Bureau has conducted a fair-lending review. In a few brief sentences, the section often will state that the review did not detect discrimination or other illegal activity. The section does not include what methods were used to test for discrimination, which products were tested, or which demographic groups the examiners ensured did not experience discrimination.[255] Sometimes, the section will state whether occurrences of discrimination or other violations were widespread, thus resulting in a rating downgrade. Occasionally, the exam will describe the nature and type of violation, and which protected classes were victimized. Recently, some very large banks, including Wells Fargo failed their CRA exams due to serious violations of fair lending and consumer compliance, which were described in the fair-lending review section.[256] However, in many instances, the exam will not describe the violation.

When violations are not described or when the description lacks detail about methodology, community group input is stunted. Fair-housing groups are unable to engage in data analysis or mystery shopping the bank to determine if they agree or disagree with the examiner's analysis or conclusions. They are thus unable to finely tune their investigations to maximize the effectiveness of their input. Also, when CRA examiners do not describe community group comments on bank performance concerning communities of color, the community group does not know if the agencies took these comments into account when conducting the fair-lending review. Even if the agencies find that no discrimination occurred, the exam narrative should describe that community organizations raised concerns but that the agencies did not find violations. This would provide reassurance that the serious concerns of the public were at least addressed. Overall, the CRA examiner narrative on the fair-lending section needs improvement to be more transparent.

Using CRA daily and in partnerships with banks to meet small business and city needs

Bob Dickerson is Executive Director of the Birmingham Business Resource Center (BBRC) and a veteran CRA practitioner, having worked in management at banks and at community-based organizations. When he was 25 years old, he was a branch manager at a local bank when Congress passed CRA in 1977. Around this time, he and fellow African American bank employees protested a bank redlining policy that scored loan applicants higher if they resided in predominantly White zip codes than if they lived in African American zip codes. In response, the bank dropped the discriminatory policy.[257]

The BBRC grew out of conversations among banks and Birmingham city officials about the need for technical assistance for small businesses and African American businesses. Over its 25 years, BBRC has facilitated over $1.5 billion in small business finance. Dickerson says that BBRC makes lending possible for applicants that would not otherwise be approved for conventional bank loans. This is true for the hundreds of millions of dollars of Small Business Administration (SBA) loans that BBRC facilitated and for its micro-loan program that focusses on loans of between $10,000 to $15,000. Dickerson provides a good amount of one-on-one counseling and BBRC also has group seminars and workshops for training small businesses (capacity building and loan readiness). BBRC advocates for its clients and helps them find and utilize contracting opportunities with public and private entities.[258]

Over the years, Dickerson has developed strong relationships with senior CRA officers of major banks serving Birmingham and the South. He stated that on an annual basis he refers about a dozen BBRC clients to banks, judging them ready for traditional bank loans. Dickerson indicated that he succeeds not because he has changed bank underwriting approaches but that the bank has established a level of trust that he will refer clients that will pay back their loans. It is not so much changing underwriting guidelines as it is making banks understand that they need to be able to "color outside the lines;" that if a borrower does not meet all the underwriting criteria that there might be compensating factors making the borrower creditworthy. "Guidelines should not be used as a crutch to say no," Dickerson maintained. Instead, he sees CRA as a way to push banks to make loans that are safe and sound but that take a little more work since instead of checking all the underwriting boxes, they check most of the boxes and a couple of circles (compensating factors) as well.

Interestingly, the CRA field has discussions about how underwriting criteria for home lending has changed in response to CRA advocacy. Creditworthiness, for example, is judged by rental or utility payment history instead of sole reliance on credit scores. In small business lending in contrast, underwriting is stricter because it is riskier according to Dickerson.[259] It is the constant dialogue and level of trust among Dickerson and his partner banks facilitated by CRA that has opened small business and wealth building opportunities for his clients. Over the years, Dickerson observed that banks have become more aggressive in lending to small businesses with revenues under $1 million and those owned by people of color.

Dickerson has succeeded not only because of his partnerships with banks but also engaging in sustained dialogue with a series of Birmingham Mayors and city departments. In 1993, the City established the Birmingham Community Investment Partnership that involved conversations among city officials and about eight banks. Regular discussions among the stakeholders helped to strengthen bank partnerships with neighborhood-based nonprofit organizations including the local Neighborhood Housing Services affiliate. The partnership also facilitated banks applying for financing from the Affordable Housing Program (AHP) of the Federal Home Loan Banks. This and other bank financing contributed to the construction of affordable multifamily housing in Birmingham. Lastly, the Birmingham Community Investment Partnership led to the creation of BBRC, which has served the city for 25 years with Dickerson at the helm.[260]

CRA should be employed to utilize all local resources including city and county governments that receive program dollars from the Department of Housing and Urban Development (HUD) and other federal agencies for affordable housing and community development. Moreover, if banks, local public agencies, and community-based organizations are engaged in a constant and deep dialogue, chances increase that city revitalization efforts benefit long-term residents, people of color, and LMI residents. In contrast, if urban redevelopment efforts mainly feature discussions among local economic elites, the real estate industry, and city officials, economic development projects are more likely to benefit the affluent and displace long-term residents. Immergluck documents this result - gentrification and displacement – arising from a transit project in Atlanta called the Beltine. The City did not plan for sufficient amounts of affordable housing or strategies to maintain local small businesses in neighborhoods served by the Beltline.[261] In other words, the CRA process was not engaged since the underserved community was not at the proverbial table.

CRA has created opportunities to finance immigrant and asylee businesses

Namoch Sokhom is a Cambodian refugee who has devoted his professional life to assisting microbusiness to grow and prosper. Over three decades, Sokhom has worked as a loan officer and underwriter. He is currently the Director of Loan Services for the Vermont-Slauson Economic Development Corporation (VSEDC) located in South Los Angeles. Previously, he worked for the PACE Finance Corporation which had a focus on serving microbusinesses. Over the years, as he became educated from colleagues about CRA, he gained expertise about how to involve banks in financing microbusinesses, expanding upon the financing from the Small Business Administration.[262]

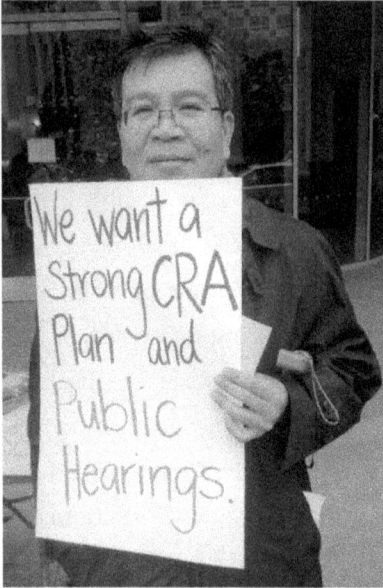

Community organizations demand that the merging banks OneWest and CIT Group develop a written CRA plan. California Reinvestment Coalition (CRC) Board Member Namoch Sokhom advocates, in front of CIT Bank's headquarters in Pasadena, for a strong CBA and CRA plan, in hope that banks reinvest more funding into his underserved clients, the micro- and small businesses owned by refugees, asylees, immigrants, and minorities.

Source: Sean Coffey

At PACE, several clients were asylees that were often at economic disadvantages compared to refugees. Refugees undergo a formal application process in their home countries and when they arrive in the United States, they have a sponsor who mentors them regarding how to pursue education and careers. In contrast, asylees often come to the United States on student and tourist VISAs. They will then apply for asylum, claiming that they will face persecution for their religious or political beliefs. When granted asylum, they do not have sponsors and thus lack the networks that help them prepare for successful careers. PACE would provide technical assistance and loans to asylees to situate them in small businesses for which they are well suited. Sokhom provided an example of a nurse from China who knew about Chinese funeral customs and procedures but lacked the capital needed for starting a funeral preparation business. PACE provided her with a $5,000 microloan and then subsequent loans in the $10,000 range. She received her first loan in 2003 and now, 20 years later, her business thrives in a suburb of Los Angeles.[263]

Another client was a Latina who worked cleaning hotels but wanted to start a side business as a seamstress. Again, PACE provided a $5,000 loan that helped her buy a couple of sewing machines. She ended up employing 17 to 20 seamstresses and works as a subcontractor to larger garment companies that receive contracts from retail chains for clothing orders. A more recent client of Sokhom's was a Korean convenience store that expanded into offering fresh produce and diary in a predominantly African American neighborhood that has a scarcity of grocery stores and a population without easy access to public transit. The VSEDC provided a couple of loans ranging from $20,000 to $35,000.

Sokhom stated that CBAs negotiated by the California Reinvestment Coalition (CRC) of which his organizations were members helped pave the way for banks to become involved in PACE and VSEDC. In PACE's case, for example, banks adhering to the CBAs provided funding for PACE to be able to meet Small Business Administration (SBA) match requirements for loan loss reserves used in microlending. Banks also served on PACE loan committees that approved microloans. The participation of bank staff on the loan committees earned banks points towards their CRA service test. But for CRA, Sokhom affirmed, there would be less participation of banks on these types of committees.

Service on small business loan committees are familiarizing banks with the microloan underwriting process that is rigorous yet flexible. In Sokhom's words, the underwriting seeks to find reasons to approve the loans, not reject them. While home lending features the three Cs of underwriting as described in Chapter 1, microbusiness lending has 5 Cs. These include credit, cash flow, cash injection or initial capital to start the business, collateral, and character. On each "C," the applicant is awarded a score from 1 to 5. If the total points over the five criteria exceed a threshold such as 18 points, the borrower receives the loan. Thus, an applicant can score poorly on one or more criteria but compensate by higher scores on the other criteria. For example, a start-up will have no cash flow and score a "0" on cash flow, but if a spouse of the applicant has a sufficient income of around $30,000 or more, the score on cash injection or collateral will be high. Given these flexibilities, banks also refer rejected applicants to PACE. Over time, banks may not only support more microlending programs but may bring these types of approaches to their small business lending programs.

When asked about CRA, Sokhom affirmed that "It gets us and the banks together. If they (the banks) don't have a CRA officer, we say, get a CRA officer. The CRA community is of the foremost importance."[264]

Indeed, dialogue is key for mutual learning opportunities. Sokhom reiterated that there "should be more awareness and consciousness about supporting the start-up" such as the funeral service provider. The start-up will then prosper.

At VESDC, since 2018, Sokhom and colleagues have used CRA to raise over $3 million in capital for the revolving loan fund of its Community Development Financial Institution (CDFI) and another $1.5 million in CRA-related investments and grants. The CDFI has made 58 loans worth $2.88 million.[265] CDFIs enable practitioners like Sokhom who have keen insights into refugee and asylee communities to employ flexible lending that enables budding entrepreneurs to provide unique services for their communities. It is critical that CRA continues to provide incentives to banks to support CDFIs. At the same time, banks need to take lessons learned from their interactions from CDFIs and apply it to their lending programs since CDFIs by themselves do not have the scale necessary to meet all the needs for small business finance (the issue of supporting CDFIs will be further discussed in Chapter 8 which reviews the most recent regulatory reforms to CRA).

An inherent tension in banking is to seek out the large deal over small dollar financing because large deals are more remunerative. This phenomenon has crept up into Sokhom's field. He left PACE in part because the organization eventually placed a priority on larger scale commercial real estate financing supported by newer SBA programs like Community Advantage. In contrast to the profits that can be made on large commercial financing, microlending is higher risk. Yet it satisfies a great need and can be done successfully.[266] CRA exams have quantitative measures that assess the dollar amount of community development financing, but these measures need to be balanced against qualitative measures that give more points to small dollar financing like microlending. It is hoped that the most recent CRA reform efforts discussed in chapter 8 provide sufficient consideration to the tireless and critical efforts of Sokhom and his colleagues.

CRA has some unfinished business financing rental housing and community services in rural farmworker communities

Maria Elena Guerra (Meg) is the executive director of the Farmworker Housing Development Corporation (FHDC) in Woodburn, Oregon, a rural community with large concentrations of immigrant farmworkers. Guerra came to the United States from Ecuador and pursed a master's degree in nonprofit management. She says she was inspired to go into nonprofit work after observing housing insecurity in her own family and after the collapse of the banks in her home country devastated people's savings. Her nonprofit career started in nonprofit property management; she held a property management position at FHDC before becoming the executive director. Like her, most of the farmworkers that FHDC serves are immigrants; about 75 percent are from rural Mexico and 25 percent from Central America. The agriculture in the upper Northwest consists of worm farming related to the fishing industry as well as dairy and fruit production.[267]

Guerra stated that FHDC's emphasis has been on developing and managing rental housing because FHDC can serve more people in rental housing than in homeownership. She cited the high cost of homeownership limiting opportunities. Farmworkers, like other immigrants not eligible for Social Security numbers, often have Individual Taxpayer Identification Numbers (ITIN) issued by the Internal Revenue Service. Guerra said that borrowers showing up at lenders with ITINs would have to pay 11 percent on their mortgages whereas the going rate at the time of my interview with her was around 7 percent. Thus, while FHDC does arrange for homeownership counseling for those interested, it has chosen to specialize in rental housing.[268]

Currently, FHDC manages 475 units in eleven properties in three counties. Of these eleven properties, FHDC owns most of them, including Low Income Housing Tax Credit properties whose investors have sold them to FHDC after 15 years. While Guerra is proud of the work of FHDC, she maintained that if "the system was fair" FHDC would be managing about 2,000 units, not 475, over the last 32 years. The impediments she cited is stiff competition for financing from larger for profit and nonprofit developers, rigidity on bank loan terms and conditions, and challenges and constraints faced by rural nonprofits serving immigrant populations. On the positive side, she says that "CRA is watching" and that more banks have more people of color in "positions of authority" including in community development initiatives. The newer bank staff in some cases came from nonprofit organizations or foundations, so they know how difficult it is for "communities of color to get loans and technical assistance."[269] These factors have opened doors and made banks more proactive.

An important aspect of FHDC's work is delivering community services at the rental properties. The farmworkers log long hours and are not home when their children return from school. FHDC arranges for after school programs to productively occupy the kids when they get home. In addition, the immigrant population can be afraid of venturing far from their workplace or residences. In response, FHDC arranges for mobile health and nutritional services to be delivered to their properties. Since farm working is seasonal, budgeting can be a challenge. Accordingly, FHDC offers financial counseling with an emphasis on savings for the lean winter months. Guerra observes that as banks are closing branches in rural communities, they should use organizations like FHDC as proxies in terms of generating a clientele for banks. Guerra maintains that banks should better utilize FHDC "because we have the trust of the people." She argues that banks should offer grants in the hundreds of thousands of dollars instead of grants in chunks of $20,000 so that FHDC can offer holistic community supportive services for a population that is not mobile and has limited incomes.[270]

She says that a limitation of the current CRA regime is that banks seem to be more focused on geography than people. This is a recurring issue of banks seeking to satisfy requirements to offer activities in their assessment areas where they are graded. They often want to ratchet up the number of activities in their assessment areas rather than focusing on the impacts of their activities. Chapter 8 will assess the extent to which CRA reform will address these imperfections since banks should in future years receive more credit for activities that are not in their assessment areas and the qualitative aspects of the exams will increase attention to impacts.

Guerra has a multigenerational view of wealth building and upward mobility. The tenants of her properties have limited socioeconomic mobility due to the lower wages of farm work. However, she believes that their children, if they find quality educational opportunities, will be able to ascend the ladder of mobility. She cited the example of one of the adult children as becoming an architect.[271]

Guerra has arranged for Casa of Oregon and the Oregon IDA Initiative to expand its Individual Development Account (IDA) program to be offered to tenants in her property.[272] IDAs are matched savings accounts; for every dollar that a consumer places in the account, the dollar is matched by a multiple by banks, foundations, or other funders. IDAs can be used for various wealth building activities such as pursuing post-secondary education or starting a small business. Banks can receive CRA consideration for participating in IDAs. Peter Hainley, Executive Director of Casa of Oregon, states that the two banks most involved in the IDA program are BMO Harris and Umpqua, two institutions recently undergoing mergers and needing to demonstrate a public benefit, in part, by participating in the statewide IDA program.[273]

CRA needs to continue motivating banks to provide holistic housing and community development funding for organizations like FHDC to improve the life chances of communities they serve. As much as possible, CRA exams must consider whether bank activities promote holistic development that emphasizes building skills and wealth for people and providing them with quality housing.

Can CRA steer private sector capital to Native American reservations

Dave Castillo is the CEO of Native Community Capital, a CDFI that serves Native American people and land areas in New Mexico, Arizona, and Utah and Colorado by the time this book is published. He exudes enthusiasm for fighting for justice mixed with passion and grace. He also does not hesitate to get to the nub of injustice. He stated:

"An investment in Indian Country could represent a shift in intention to use free market tools to rectify historic and grievous economic injustices leveled against Native nations in what is now the United States. Injustices that resulted in the taking of massive land holdings and raw materials used to build what the world knows today as the U.S. and that is nothing short of a global economic superpower. Those same actions resulted in a sad legacy of severe economic and social distress in tribal communities that remains to this very day. The challenge of rebuilding tribal econ-omies will be costly as well as time and labor intensive and it will not succeed by relying on public sector poverty programs in place now. A reformed CRA must put Native communities at the center of significant, sustained, and serious private investment. Investors have rallied around riskier propositions – including cryptocurrency. It's time to invest in the people and communities that have been here since time immemorial."[274]

Castillo is co-author with NCRC researchers of a hard-hitting study called *Redlining the Reservation: The Brutal Cost Of Financial Services Inaccessibility In Native Communities.* The study revealed the dearth of bank lending in Native American reservations in Arizona and New Mexico. Despite a federal guaranteed mortgage lending program called Section 184, traditional lenders have never fully committed to lending on reservations such that close to 90 percent of Section 184 mortgages have been issued to Native Americans living outside of Indian reservations.[275] Currently, three very large banks no longer participate in the program. As a result, residents of reservations rely on higher interest rate manufactured home lending to such an extent that almost half of all lending in tribal areas in New Mexico and Arizona is manufactured home lending, more than four times the rate elsewhere in the states. The story is similar for small business lending and access to bank branches. An average of only 5 small business loans were made for each LMI tract in tribal areas over four years, contrasted with 82 loans per LMI tract in non-tribal areas.[276] The federal bank agencies reported that counties where the majority of the population is Native American have an average of two bank branches compared with an average of nine in rural counties and 27 in all counties across the United States.[277]

The complexities of land ownership on reservations are often cited as an impediment to mortgage lending on reservations. About 75 percent of tribal land is trust land, meaning that the homeowner does not own it but leases it.[278] Castillo, however, believes that this issue is overblown, considering that the Section 184 program provides a 100 percent guarantee to the lender in the event of a default on the loan. Moreover, he maintains that federal legislation and regulation have enabled reservations to promulgate their own leases so that home lending on reservations now consists of mortgaging the home and any improvements to the land, and it is not more difficult than lending for homes on a "land trust in Vermont."[279]

"The real problem," Castillo asserts, "is that there is not enough volume or deal flow. It is just too nascent a business to justify the banks' expenditure," in the view of the big banks.[280] CRA is supposed to act like a thumb on the scale, pushing banks to pursue profitable but less lucrative loans in LMI communities because exiting underserved markets could imperil their ratings. However, the rub for Indian country is that serving LMI communities in urban areas often enables banks to reach higher loan volumes than on reservations. Banks, regardless of whether they are national, regional, or local, are inclined to pursue the urban deal, according to Castillo.

Despite the odds, Castillo adamantly refuses to accept minimal service from traditional banks. He declared, "Our mission statement from the very beginning is that private sector capital shall be as readily accessible and in use in tribal trust lands for housing as in any non-Indian community. We are saying we want parity."[281]

One way that Castillo is trying to lure banks back to the reservation is through the example of his Native CDFI. His Native CDFI finances about $2 million or 20 loans annually, about one third of which is new construction. The majority is for rehabilitation of existing housing stock, which addresses the higher incidence of physically inadequate housing on reservations.[282] Rehabilitation loans are also less expensive for the lender and hence more economical. Historically, most of Native Community Capital's loans are for Native Americans residing on reservations, but a revised business model will result in loans to Native Americans living off of reservations to subsidize the more expensive lending on reservations.[283]

Castillo hopes that the innovations of Native Community Capital show the traditional lenders that they can scale up and make more loans on or near reservations. Scaling up is difficult because there are over 500 tribal communities each with their own legal systems. And most banks do not have relationships with tribal leaders. As a result, most tribal leaders do not know what CRA is. There is a need for an intermediary role such as that taken by Native Community Capital to familiarize tribal communities and banks with each other. Castillo envisions that the report he co-authored helps to "light the fires and let people know that there is an opportunity here, and let's get after it." He adds that stakeholders need to further develop a legal infrastructure and a business-friendly environment that invites investment in Indian country.[284]

A reinvigorated CRA needs to motivate stakeholders to work together to facilitate lending in Indian county. Without reducing bank reinvestment in urban communities, a strengthened CRA must increase the total resources for reinvestment so that banks invest more on or near reservations. Since market failure as discussed in Chapters 1 and 2 continues to impede bank lending and investment in underserved communities, a new CRA can be a plus sum proposition identifying more profitable reinvestment opportunities in rural and urban areas. As will be discussed in more detail in Chapter 8, the CRA regulatory reform in 2023 added reinvesting in Native Land Areas and financing CDFIs as explicit categories of community development. For large banks, community development is assessed in a separate test. Moreover, banks will now receive favorable consideration for community development regardless of whether it is in areas with bank branches or beyond bank branches, which should help Native American areas which experience a dearth of bank branches. Perhaps more bank branches will return in conjunction with successful community and business development activities.

But as helpful as a new CRA could be for Native American

communities, Castillo concluded that more resources are likely needed to rectify centuries of injustice on the scale of the Marshall Plan that America directed to a devasted Europe after World War II. Castillo referenced the Truth and Reconciliation Commission in Canada that prompted some large banks like Bank of Montreal to commit to a $8 billion reinvestment program for indigenous communities. CRA directed to one industry, by itself, will not address all the brokenness in all victimized communities as this book maintains. Yet, a stronger CRA can succeed in increasing reinvestment and should be part of a national commitment like the Canadian Truth and Reconciliation Commission. In the meantime, Castillo believes that CRA can be paired with the federal infrastructure funding in the Inflation Reduction Act to further enhance reinvestment and counter redlining in Native American communities.[285]

Referral housing services need CRA's support

Imagine being a first-time and first-generation homeowner and running into an unexpected and significant repair expense. Imagine losing your job and facing foreclosure – is there any alternative to the streets? Created as part of Washington State's Foreclosure Fairness Act, a telephone hotline operated by the Washington Homeownership Resource Center (WHRC) helps about 1,650 distressed homeowners and renters monthly seek assistance. The hotline provides referral to legal aid agencies, housing counselors, or reputable repair assistance programs.[286] The high volume of calls reflects a pressing community need. This type of service is called community supportive services in CRA jargon.

Denise Rodriguez, the Executive Director of WHRC, has a background in public policy and started her career focused on banking services and establishing the Bank On Washington initiative in

Washington state. Bank On features partnerships between banks and community-based organizations to help underbanked and unbanked populations establish affordable deposit accounts and other bank services. Her experience in community outreach and teaching financial education classes motivated a career interest in housing. She stated that she saw how important "housing stability was to financial stability. I was asked by a local women's shelter to come and teach a class about rebuilding your credit. One of the women in attendance raised her hand and said, 'How am I supposed to care for my credit when I don't even know where I am going to sleep.'"[287]

In Rodriguez's estimation, homeownership represented the most stable form of housing and intergenerational opportunities for wealth building. At the same time, stability is not guaranteed, hence the need for referral services.[288]

To reduce the racial wealth gap, WHRC has embarked on an initiative called the Black Home Initiative with allied financial institutions, nonprofit organizations, and public sector agencies in the Greater Seattle Tacoma area to create 1,500 new African American homeowners over a five-year period.[289] WHRC has teamed with a foundation to provide training to nonprofit organizations, real estate agents, and banks about how to prevent racism in the lending process. Rodriguez affirms that when she refers clients to partners that she wants to them to have a "good experience and not be micro-aggressed."

In addition, WHRC provides referral services to consumers with limited English proficiency. It has Spanish speaking staff, and it also works with a telephonic interpretation service that provides live interpreters who can translate about 220 languages over the phone. In WHRC's experience, the most common non-English languages are Spanish, Korean, and Vietnamese. Several other

Asian languages and Russian are also spoken by numerous clients. Latino clients often have ITIN numbers which, as described above, are for residents without Social Security numbers. Lending options are fewer for these clients since most lenders will not offer loans to ITIN holders and those who do have requirements like 15 to 20 percent downpayments that make these loans unattainable for most households.[290] WHRC sees its role as connecting these borrowers to responsible lenders. Another group in need of specialized lending are practicing Muslims whose loans need to be structured to avoid interest payments.[291] Muslims consider interest as income that is unearned and therefore unfair.[292]

"CRA brings institutions to the table. We have been involved in some of the Community Benefit Agreements for banks based in Washington, and what I have typically seen is that the folks who are representing the financial institutions are really there to listen. They have an open mind to meeting the needs. There is usually some follow-up. We have been seeing that there is more investment in housing," states Rodriguez.[293]

While CRA has spearheaded the conversations that led to more affordable housing financing and support, Rodriguez also emphasizes the need for patient capital or patient grants. "All funders need to have realistic expectations of how much work can happen with a certain size team and with a certain amount of money, and oftentimes funders expect unrealistic results. You just cannot give somebody a grant for one year, and then after one year say 'bye.' We would be scaling up a program and hiring a person, but the program is just going to stop at the end of the grant."[294] Thus, the multi-year commitment for grants is critical to scaling up a program and giving it a chance to last.

Rodriguez continued, "Because this (nonprofit services) isn't a good that could be commodified for the people who need it. It's always going to be supported by people who have so that we can provide a service to people that may not be able to pay for that service, or who otherwise wouldn't receive it at all. We (nonprofits) are sort of the moral catch all for things that neither of those sectors (private and public) can do. If there's an expectation to figure out how to sustain the program without the grants, it's not a very realistic expectation."[295] Thus, the CRA reform covered in more detail in Chapter 8 must not only encourage funding for community supportive services but must encourage responsive and multi-year funding.

Using CRA to protect tenant rights and preserve multifamily rental housing

Kevin Stein is Chief of Legal and Strategy at the California Reinvestment Coalition (CRC) and has been there more than 20 years. CRC, now called Rise Economy, is a diverse coalition of 300 member organizations dedicated to fair lending and increasing access to credit in underserved communities. In the midst of CRC's work, Stein was approached by a tenants' rights organization around 2012 complaining about a slumlord that was trying to evict modest income renters. It turns out that that property owner had received a loan from a lender called Circle Bank. The tenants' right organization wanted to know if CRA could be used to pressure the bank to stop financing abusive property owners. By a quirk in California law, it is legal for a property owner to acquire a building with rent control units and then convert the building into a luxury condominium if the previous property owner was seeking to sell and exit the real estate business. Unscrupulous property owners sped up the process of tenant departure by evicting them. Circle Bank was aware of the new property owners' intentions and underwrote the loan to the higher revenue streams associated with the new use of the property.

Stein asked Circle Bank's regulator, the FDIC, if CRA could be used in a way to prevent this behavior since CRA's purpose is to ensure that community needs are met. The FDIC did not provide much guidance to Stein, and instead hinted that the bank may receive favorable consideration on the exam for this financing since the property was in a low- and moderate-income area. It was in the Mission District that was working class and Latino. Stein felt that this was "CRA turned on its head" since it was being used in a manner to harm communities, not help them.[296]

Subsequent to Circle Bank, advocates documented this type of displacement financing by First Republic Bank. CRC and several partners protested outside the bank's headquarters. The protests featured speeches, including testimony by two sisters that had lived in one of the properties being converted for 40 years but now faced displacement. First Republic promised reforms, but follow-up research identified the bank as one of the foremost financers of questionable property owners in the Oakland area. Stein and CRC commented on First Republic's CRA exam. The bank's rating appeared unaffected since the exam did not contain any narrative documenting the concerns of CRC and its allies. Stein remarked, "It was like a tree fell and nobody heard it."[297]

CRC did not give up. CRC and its allies commenced CBA negotiations in separate mergers involving BMO and Banc of California. The CBAs sought to address displacement and the preservation of affordable rental housing. The Banc of California CBA includes the following language, "The Bank agrees to review its policies, procedures, and practices to see how they align with

CRC's Anti Displacement Code of Conduct and agrees to discuss ways to support the reduction of involuntary displacement of LMI individuals and people of color. In addition, the Bank will support nonprofit legal services and fair housing organizations in its service areas to help prevent and address evictions and discrimination."[298]

A recent CBA with BMO Harris stated, "BMO Harris commits to being unreceptive to clients whose activities include wrongful evictions, single family property flipping, poorly managed properties, and other problematic behavior."[299]

A central provision in CRC's Anti-Displacement Code of Conduct is that a bank should underwrite a loan using existing rents and complying with local rent control laws. In addition, a lender should meet with tenants and tenant advocacy organizations and ensure that the property owner is not harassing or unduly evicting tenants. Critically, banks agree not to seek CRA credit for loans that lead to the displacement of tenants.[300] CRC credits the development of its code of conduct to a partner organization, the Association for Neighborhood and Housing Development (ANHD) in New York City, that confronted widespread evictions in a high-cost market like San Francisco and other large California cities. ANHD's code of conduct influenced the development of New York State regulations mandating responsible bank multifamily lending.[301] Like CRC, ANHD tracks bank financing of multifamily property and informs community-based organizations of banks financing abusive landlords. ANHD's research contributes to their CRA and merger comment letters.[302]

Stein is not satisfied with the progress to date and wants to keep pressing. He observes that banks are acknowledging CRC's code of conduct but have not yet implemented specific practices committed to in CBAs. CRA exams appear to be still in their infancy in terms of dealing with this important issue, but examiners are becoming sensitized to this issue thanks to the advocacy of Stein and his colleagues. Stein and CRC have opened the door to more CRA scrutiny by insisting that CRA enforcement include penalties for financing abusive practices that result in displacement. As he puts it, exploitative financing is the "opposite of CRA." He stated:

"If CRA is about community credit needs, harm should be taken into account. Instead of meeting needs, displacement financing is harming tenants. After eviction, they may have a hard time finding a place to live. Their credit is affected by the bank facilitated eviction. Units that were affordable are now going to be completely unaffordable to low- and moderate-income people. In contrast, if they were able to keep living there and paying modest rents, even with modest incomes, maybe someday they could get home and small business loans. Now that is much less likely to happen because of the loan that Circle Bank financed. CRA should be better for accounting for harm. If you are helping a little but harming a lot, you should not be getting better CRA grades."[303]

Indeed, CRA ratings should account for the whole picture of bank activity. In the final 2023 CRA rule, the agencies did not adopt specific best practices regarding anti-displacement features for rental housing but stated that "examiners will retain the discretion to consider whether an activity reduces the number of housing units affordable to low- or moderate-income individuals."[304] Hopefully, this will change the situation in which Stein and allies commented on CRA exams, but the examiners did not seem to consider the comments regarding displacement. If CRA examiners, taking agency cues in the final rule, change their approach, Stein and advocates scored a major advance for preserving affordable housing.

Agencies should create speed dating opportunities for banks and community organizations

As the experiences of housing and small business practitioners reveal, CRA works best when it fosters regular dialogue between banks and community organizations regarding credit needs. The federal bank agencies should be a natural facilitator for this dialogue. Hill recalled that the Federal Reserve Bank of San Francisco would promote sessions involving community groups and banks that amounted to "speed dating" opportunities. The community organizations would describe needs, their programs and projects for addressing needs, and the geographical areas they served. Banks listening to these quick presentations could then engage the community organizations that served the areas on the bank CRA exams.[305]

Hill reported that these sessions were productive, but they occurred infrequently, an observation with which I agree. I have attended federal agency sessions in which banks and community groups are in separate rooms discussing CRA, which is not useful in matching needs and resources. The agencies, at least some Federal Reserve Banks, have a model that works to promote thoughtful dialogue among all CRA stakeholders which they should employ frequently.

A multifaceted approach is needed to generate CRA dialogue. Commenting on merger applications and CRA exams is a difficult exercise that several under-resourced community organizations do not have the time to undertake. They are busy with the work of affordable housing development, small business development, or counseling. However, the agencies can engage them meaningfully with banks regarding needs and opportunities in underserved communities.

At NCRC conferences and workshops, Hill and I have asked community-based organizations if they have commented on CRA exams, merger applications, or talked to CRA officers of banks. Relatively few hands raise up. We attempt to explain that CRA is only effective if community organizations engage in regular CRA dialogue. On their part, the agencies via workshop sessions and other types of communications should encourage discussions directly between banks and community organizations. The objective would be to create more confidence and skill among community organizations in engaging in the sustained dialogue that practitioners featured in this chapter have undertaken for several years.

Do the federal bank agencies facilitate or impede public input into CRA exams and merger applications?

It would be unfair to say that the agencies discourage public comment on CRA exams and merger applications. That would be a dereliction of their duty to adhere to their legal requirements to facilitate public participation in laws designed to protect against discrimination and ensure community needs are met. There is no better way to meet needs than to provide forums for community residents to articulate their needs and banks' record in meeting them. I have encountered several professionals at the agencies that take this mandate seriously and are responsive to public inquiries. At the same time, the agencies' institutional commitment to the public waxes and wanes depending on their leadership. The agencies also have outdated technology and procedures that can act more like an impediment to public partici-pation rather than facilitating it.

Commenting on CRA exams and merger applications is not easy

The ease of commenting on CRA exams and merger applications is uneven across and within agencies. In the case of merger applications, the Federal Reserve System has the clearest information about which part of the agency (that is, the regional banks) is receiving comments on mergers and to whom to ask questions and send written comments.[306] In contrast, the OCC's website is harder to navigate. A user searches for bank applications to merge or engage in other activities in one part of the website and then must use another part to download applications.[307] The OCC and FDIC list regional offices that receive comments on applications but in contrast to the Federal Reserve website, no specific individuals are designated for receiving questions or comments.[308] I have experienced difficulties receiving responses from OCC and FDIC regional offices to inquiries, which suggests that the general public that is much less familiar with this process can be easily discouraged. The OCC gets one thing right: a user can download applications easily and immediately while one must ask the Federal Reserve System and the FDIC to email applications. The process of emailing applications can sometimes entail delays which consume valuable days in a short comment period of 30 days.

The agencies have parts of their website that announce the calendar quarter in which CRA exams will occur.[309] The Federal Reserve System and the FDIC have online boxes in which a user can click and then send comments on CRA exams.[310] In contrast, the OCC system is opaque. A hotlink on the OCC CRA webpage instructs a user to file a comment on an upcoming CRA exam to the "subject bank or appropriate supervisory office." Not many community groups, particularly ones new to this process, will have the gumption to send comments to the bank being examined. Thus, this OCC instruction can deter comments.. The hotlink leading a user to a supervisory office lists the major divisions of the OCC such as Bank Supervision Policy or Office of Public Affairs.[311] Most users would be defeated at this point or spend considerable time trying to contact one of the divisions. I would contact OCC staff that I have known for many years, but this inside knowledge of who to contact should not be necessary. As of this writing, the OCC website does not facilitate comments on CRA exams.

The OCC is not the only agency with deficiencies in terms of facilitating participation in the CRA process. In general, it is not easy for the public to navigate the websites and figure out how the public can comment on CRA exams and merger applications. Each of the agencies should have a prominent box towards the top of their websites that says something like "Members of the Public Click Here to Offer Your Views of Bank Service to Communities: Comment on Banks' CRA exams, merger applications and compliance with consumer protection and fair lending laws." The link would then take the user to one section of the website for all the information for commenting on CRA exams, bank applications, and compliance with fair lending and consumer protection laws. The section of the website should also have contact information for specific individuals or departments that would be clear about deadlines for submitting comments and would interact with the public as they are figuring out how to submit comments. When an individual or department receives an inquiry, the website should send an immediate confirmation acknowledging receipt. Agency staff should then respond within the next business day. Any further delays should result in the comment period being extended for each day of delayed response. The current lack of clarity and responsiveness impedes public input into bank compliance with CRA.

Seriousness with which the agencies consider comments varies

Receiving public comments is just one step. Responding to them in a reasonable manner is the next step the agencies must take. The agencies tend to elevate the visibility of comments to a greater extent on merger applications than on CRA exams. When agencies issue decisions on merger applications, they discuss past CRA performance and the mergers' impact on future reinvestment and fair-lending performance in a section called "Convenience and Needs." The Federal Reserve tends to respond in the most detail to public comments received. In this section of the merger decision, it is common to see numerous footnotes summarizing community group comments on specific aspects of CRA and fair-lending performance.[312] The footnotes and the body of the narrative include the agencies' responses to the community group comments. Through this discussion and the final decision, it is possible to determine whether community group comments affected the agencies' analyses, conclusions, and final orders.

In contrast, community group influence on CRA exams is more difficult to discern. CRA exams have a section called "Community Contacts." This section often offers generic and cursory observations of community groups regarding the credit needs and economic conditions of a locality. From these general observations, it is usually not possible to determine if the public input influenced the CRA examiner's analyses, conclusions, or ratings. As discussed above in the case studies, community organizations have made specific comments about some banks' lending records and abusive practices contrary to CRA, but the exams are silent regarding these comments.

While it is not practical for examiners to respond to every point in every comment letter submitted, the agencies should at least keep a public record of all comments received on the CRA exam. The comments would be available on agency websites and upon request. In this manner, stakeholders can assess the extent to which examiners responded to comments in general and to pressing issues in particular. This would be an important mechanism for holding examiners and agencies accountable for rigorous exams.

The agencies should add an "Expectations for Improvement" section on CRA exams that could encourage more comments by indicating that the agencies incorporate them in their CRA review. This section could identify unmet needs that the examiner agreed that the bank has the capacity to address, even when community groups' concerns do not lead to a lower rating overall or in a specific geographical area. Examiner narrative indicating expectations for improvement would increase the chances that non-systemic issues, which will probably not impact a rating, would nevertheless be addressed. Also, if a need remains unaddressed and community organizations issue comments to the bank's CRA public file during subsequent years, these comments should influence a bank's rating in one or more assessment areas or the overall rating on the next exam.

The seriousness with which community input is solicited and reflected on CRA exams and merger applications motivates or discourages public involvement. If members of the public regard either CRA exams or merger applications as rubber stamp processes—in which public input is formally solicited, acknowledged in a brief manner, but then not discussed in detail —then public participation will be infrequent. On the other hand, if substantive comments are elevated in importance, and influence analyses or conclusions, then public input will be more frequent.

Developing a meaningful discussion of community needs on CRA exams is needed

CRA exams have a section called performance context that describes community needs, economic conditions, and demographic characteristics of localities. It also considers bank capacity and expertise when assessing the banks' ability to meet various needs. The performance context analysis could be one of the most important parts of the exam in order to determine whether banks are identifying the most pressing needs and designing products and programs for addressing these needs. Unfortunately, most CRA exams do not have illuminating performance context analysis.

Most performance context analyses will present tables of census statistics regarding demographics by income level and major industries in the geographical areas served by the banks. They will then present the results of "community contacts" or discussions that the examiner had with community-based organizations. This section usually presents bland conclusions such as more affordable housing or more jobs are needed in the geographical area, observations that could apply to most areas. For example, a recent Federal Reserve exam of Sandy Spring Bank, a large bank serving multiple counties in the District of Columbia, Maryland, and Virginia reported:

> Local affordable housing officials were contacted recently to discuss local housing conditions and community credit needs. The contacts indicated that area unemployment rates have significantly improved since the declaration of the worldwide pandemic. They also noted that the supply of affordable housing remains stagnant, while demand continues to remain high. The contacts suggested that affordable housing developers would benefit from flexible financing options from financial institutions: however, they acknowledged that area financial institutions are reasonably meeting local credit needs.[313]

This performance context analysis failed to distinguish among employment and affordable housing conditions in the three jurisdictions, which could have vastly different experiences concerning affordability in the rental and homeownership stock in addition to employment trends. The analysis did not provide helpful hints for either the bank or community organizations as to how to target affordable housing and economic development activities across this large area. It alluded to the need for flexible financing for affordable housing developers, but lacked information providing insights into what types of financing is in short supply.

A few years ago, I wrote a white paper in which I urged the agencies to develop and present a concise set of economic and demographic indicators that would facilitate needs comparisons across the geographical areas served by the banks.[314] For example, housing needs could be summarized by presentation of vacancy rates and the number and percent of LMI renters and homeowners with cost burdens (households are generally not supposed to pay more than 30 percent of their income for rent or mortgage payments). Summary statistics should also be developed for people of color and people of color with modest incomes in the CRA income range with a focus on subgroups that have population concentrations in geographical areas such as the Hmong in areas in the Midwest and California.

The geographical areas that the bank serves with the highest percentage of cost burdened households and lowest vacancy rates would receive priority attention for affordable housing finance. In addition, the agencies should develop a few clear statistics about economic conditions such as unemployment and poverty rates. The geographical areas with the highest percentage of unemployed and impoverished residents would be priority candidates for economic development financing. Other geographical areas that may not be priority areas for either affordable housing or economic development would still receive financing addressing these needs. However, if an examiner discovered a considerable mismatch in terms of an area with the most pressing needs for affordable housing or economic development and low levels of financing for these needs and the bank had the capacity for financing addressing these needs, then the rating should likely be affected.

The examiners should also present the summary economic and demographic statistics to the community-based organizations they engage with while conducting the exam. The statistics should generate more meaningful discussions. For example, if a geographical area has an affordable housing crunch, the examiner can ask follow-up questions about whether the crunch is more pressing for certain subgroups in the population such as people of color, senior citizens, or families with children. The examiner can then ask the banks about whether the banks considered programs for these subgroups or worked with the community organizations to address the needs of these subgroups.

A further series of inquiries concerns whether banks are engaging in financing that is needed by community-based organizations. For example, in the case of nonprofit housing developers, there is a range of financing needed that includes pre-development financing before house building commences, construction finance for rental and homeownership developments, lines of credit for ongoing operating costs, and grants for services like homeownership counseling. In my experience at Manna, the housing nonprofit developer in Washington D.C., banks were inconsistent in providing these different types of financing. An examiner should determine if there is a particular type of financing that is most difficult to obtain in a geographical area as well as information about which banks tend to be more forthcoming in general with various types of financing. The examiners should develop checklists for financing needed by various types of community-based organizations ranging from housing non-profit organizations, small business technical assistance providers, and community facilities such as childcare and health clinics.

If desired by community organizations, the examiner can collect these observations in a confidential manner since community based organizations depend on bank financing and may not want comments about specific banks relayed to the banks (the statute describes procedures regarding confidentiality in CRA exams when warranted).[315] In the course of assessing bank performance, the examiners could report observations about the banks' responsiveness to various needs without identifying the organizations they spoke with and then see how the banks respond.

Overall, the performance context analysis can be considerably more informative and lead to more accurate assessments of banks' responsiveness to needs if the federal bank agencies develop more systematic and compelling ways to collect data on needs for various types of activities such as affordable housing and economic development as well as financing needed and received by community-based organizations addressing these needs. Unfortunately, the change in CRA regulations in the fall of 2023 (discussed in Chapter 8) did not adopt these recommendations for improving performance context analysis or community input mechanisms.[316] Stakeholders should work with the agencies on incorporating some of these recommendations as the agencies implement the new rule.

The agencies should provide lending data in easily accessible formats for the community to use

CRA and fair lending enforcement depends on data analysis of lending trends to determine if banks are lending to all segments in the community. Accordingly, the agencies should provide the Home

Mortgage Disclosure Act (HMDA) data and the CRA small business and farm lending data to the public in a manner in which the public and stakeholders can meaningfully analyze and use the data to comment on CRA exams and to educate the community about access to credit. John Taylor, former President and CEO of NCRC, lists the improvements in data accessibility as one of NCRC's biggest achievements. He stated,

> Banks are motivated by CRA and fair lending and the data that we (community organizations) could look at. You remember the way it all changed. Initially, you would have to have a mainframe computer with data that was not organized in any particular fashion. Then the Fed provided two CD Roms to the general public, which they changed to being free of charge. Information was power so our effort was to change the flow of information… to get it into the hands of organizations all around the country.[317]

Taylor was alluding to the meetings that NCRC had with former Federal Reserve Chairman Alan Greenspan regarding public dissemination of HMDA data. The Chairman's subsequent actions suggested he agreed with NCRC about increasing the accessibility of public data disclosure

In addition to providing CDs, the Federal Reserve, as the former disseminator of HMDA data, made it available over the internet in raw form for sophisticated data users and in summary excel tables for the community organizations that were not as familiar with data analysis.[318] The data tables nevertheless had important information like the number and percentage of conventional home purchase loans and government guaranteed loans for people of color and LMI borrowers.

More recently, the Consumer Financial Protection Bureau (CFPB) took over the processing and dissemination of HMDA data. They improved the means for sophisticated data users to download data from their website but made the summary tables less useful and unable to provide breakouts of different types of loan approvals such as conventional as opposed to government-guaranteed home purchase loans.[319] That is one important aspect of analysis since as discussed above, government-guaranteed lending can be more accessible for traditionally underserved populations but is more expensive. In lieu of summary tables, NCRC has suggested the creation of a CFPB query engine that can supply these types of summaries. Conversations are ongoing as of this writing; accessibility improvements are still needed in order to maximize community group input into CRA and fair lending exams. Meanwhile, NCRC operates a data query engine over its website but feels that the CFPB should do the same in order to make the data as widely accessible as possible.[320]

The power of the data is illustrated by a previous NCRC publication called Best and Worst Lenders that compared banks based on how many home loans they made to traditionally underserved populations. Taylor said the publication "Blew the roof off of the world of CRA investment because we named names. That's one of the things you got to do."[321] In other words, the report identified banks that did well in making loans to traditionally underserved populations and increased overall lending to underserved populations by motivating the banks with lagging performance to bolster their lending. For CRA and the fair lending laws to work, easy public access to data is critical so that the public can offer informed opinions and issue their own reports about bank CRA performance to hold them accountable.

Public hearings on mergers and CRA exams are needed

Advocates are not the only stakeholders that believe that more frequent public hearings on merger applications are desirable. These hearings enable the public to present their views and data analysis on the performance of the merging banks and whether the mergers should proceed. Acting Comptroller of the Currency Michael J. Hsu asserted:

> "CRA performance and ratings are only a starting point, however. Community feedback on the impact of a proposed merger also is important. I recall meeting with a bank CEO who was touting the extraordinary success of a branch the bank had recently opened in a low-income neighborhood. I asked what prompted them to open that branch. He acknowledged it was requested by community organizations in a meeting related to the bank's most recent merger. Without that community feedback, that branch would not have been opened."

> "In recognition of the value that public input can provide on mergers, the OCC is considering options to facilitate such input. For example, for mergers involving larger banks, the OCC is considering adopting a presumption in favor of holding public meetings. We partnered with the Federal Reserve to hold a public meeting in March for the proposed U.S. Bank and MUFG/ Union bank merger. Over 120 community members attended and shared their views on the needs of the community and how they may be impacted by the merger."[322]

In the wake of this speech, the OCC proposed and then finalized a rule and guidelines implementing the views Hsu expressed about the value of public hearings. One feature of the guidelines is that the OCC indicated that public hearings are more likely in the case of large mergers involving banks with combined assets of $50 billion or more that have outsized impacts on access to banking services and the level of competition in local geographical areas.[323] The FDIC likewise indicated the likelihood of hearings in mergers involving banks with combined assets of at least $50 billion.[324]

Hsu's comments reinforce the positive role of public hearings. Hearings generate more information on bank performance, particularly if there is opportunity for debate and discussion moderated by agency officials in which banks answer challenging questions about their CRA and fair lending records rather than the agencies only receiving two-minute oral testimonies from several witnesses. As of this writing, the agencies have not altered their hearings format to also include moderated discussions. Nevertheless, when hearings occur, agency decisions including conditional approvals are likely to be more thoughtful, since hearings enable agencies to gather more information during the application process. Bank responses to pressing issues are also likely to improve the more robust the conversation is during the merger application process.

The number of public hearings varies depending on agency leadership. Under some leadership, there might not be a single hearing in three or four years, but in more recent years there have been more hearings. The frequency of hearings seems to depend on the outlook of Presidents and the officials they appoint to lead the federal bank agencies. Under administrations that consider themselves pro-business, the frequency and rigor of oversight over business including banking decreases. Under administrations that are concerned about consumer welfare, oversight tends to increase, including the number of public hearings on bank mergers.

Acting Comptroller Hsu is correct in my estimation that a presumption in favor of hearings should be the case in larger mergers. The largest mergers, however, are not the only situation in which convenience and needs could be impacted significantly. Regional and even smaller mergers can involve adverse impacts if, for example, one of the banks has a poor CRA and fair lending record or if the combination dramatically reduces the level of competition in local geographical areas. Agencies should be guided by the number and substance of public comments when deciding whether to hold hearings. In addition, if one of the banks has a poor CRA record, even if a passing record, a hearing is warranted, particularly in assessment areas where a bank has scored Low Satisfactory or less.

Marchiel's research revealed that National People's Action also wanted public hearings to inform CRA exams, not just merger applications.[325] This is an intriguing suggestion, particularly since the agencies need help with more robust performance context analysis and more detail about whether credit needs in a variety of areas are being met. Without more facilitation and easier formats for commenting like public hearings, it is unlikely that agencies will receive many comments on CRA exams, especially for the largest banks that span several states. A community organization contemplating a written comment may be deterred thinking that it would have to conduct sophisticated data analysis or opine about performance in all states. In contrast, a hearing format could reinforce the importance of whether the bank being examined or banks in general are meeting credit needs across a variety of areas. This may empower underserved, remote, and disenfranchised areas such as Native American reservations if hearings are virtual as well as in person.

A combination of in-person and virtual hearings can accommodate a robust number of annual hearings. The agencies should not just hold one or two hearings a year. It should be a considerably higher number considering the number of mergers and CRA exams that have profound implications on access to affordable credit and other banking services. Some virtual hearings occurred during the pandemic. Reports from NCRC member organizations suggest that agencies still need to work through unnecessary impediments such as awkward and limited platforms that make it difficult for community groups to access virtual hearings.[326]

The agencies should stop stating that CBAs are not a CRA requirement

In one of the most recent merger approvals in January of 2023 as this book was being written, the Federal Reserve Board approved the application of BMO Harris to approve Bank of the West. A footnote in the approval order stated, "The Board consistently has found that neither the CRA nor the federal banking agencies' CRA regulations require depository institutions to make pledges or enter into commitments or agreements with any private party."[327] This footnote, with slightly different phrasing, has popped up over the years in Federal Reserve approval orders. This time, the footnote even acknowledges that BMO Harris negotiated a $50 billion CBA with community-based organizations. Like the Federal Reserve, the OCC sends mixed messages. An OCC application form asks whether the merged banks would continue honoring any previous "commitments" with community organizations.[328] However, in a recent merger approval order, the agency cites a multi-billion community benefit plan but then also states that these types of agreements are not required or enforced by the OCC.[329] The agencies' schizophrenia of acknowledging CBAs and then stating they are not required should stop. Footnotes and language of this nature implicitly deter CBAs by sending a message to banks that they are not required.

However, banks are required to demonstrate public benefits as a result of their merger. CBAs are a clear and verifiable method for doing so. The agencies should encourage them or at least dispense with stating they are not mandatory. Even though they are not required, they are currently a voluntary mechanism used by some banks to demonstrate public benefits as a result of their mergers. In perhaps the first instance of a change in approach, the FDIC recently issued a policy statement saying that commitments banks make during the merger application process will be considered by the agency in further enforcement and supervision activities. The FDIC stated that its approval of a merger application could include an order stipulating that the agency will subsequently examine "adherence with any such claims and commitments" regarding public benefits of the merger.[330] The agency shied away from using the term community benefits agreements in its policy statement but the preamble to the policy statement referenced community benefit agreements when discussing the section of the policy statement regarding bank commitments.[331]

For the longer term, a requirement added to either CRA or the bank merger regulations that either CBAs be negotiated, or a bank submits a community benefits plan with measurable goals after consultation with affected communities, would not only be consistent with the convenience and needs standard but would help facilitate the realization of public benefits.

CBAs are quite similar to the CRA strategic plan option that allows banks to establish measurable goals in lieu of traditional CRA exams. A CBA can form the basis for a newly merged bank strategic plan should it opt for one instead of the regular CRA exam.

Alternatively, a community benefits plan would be less formal than a CBA and would not be a negotiated contract signed by banks and community groups. It would be a plan with measurable goals developed by a bank after it consults with community-based organizations. A community benefits plan should be part of bank applications and can replace vague descriptions of public benefits that do not have measurable goals and can be just a few short paragraphs that have occurred on previous merger applications.[332] A community benefits plan could also form the basis for a strategic plan.

Conclusion

CRA is a dialogue among parties – banks, community groups and residents, and regulatory agencies. When the dialogue is stilted and formulaic, opportunities for improving reinvestment is missed. When outcomes are only binary – pass or fail CRA exam – or merger approval or denial - the communities will often miss opportunities to improve bank reinvestment activity. The great majority of banks likely will continue passing their CRA exams and receiving merger approvals. On the other hand, when outcomes are more nuanced and multi-faceted, communities have a better chance of their needs being served. If a bank passes its CRA exam, but the examiner cites specific needs for improvements in either certain geographical areas or product lines, chances increase that the bank will then make improvements. Low ratings in poorly served geographical areas would also serve as a motivation to improve for the next CRA exam. Likewise, when mergers are approved, community needs are more likely to be met when CBAs are negotiated or if the merger application process required the development of community benefit plans.

4
Breakthrough! CRA Squeaks through Congress

Senator William Proxmire, the legislative parent of CRA

Source: The U.S. Senate Historical Office

Congress enacted the CRA in 1977 as a community development initiative that sought to leverage the financial resources of private sector institutions. Senator William Proxmire of Wisconsin was the primary architect of the CRA. In the wake of the large public sector Great Society programs of the Johnson years in the 1960s, the public was wary of massive new government programs to revitalize communities. The genius of the CRA is that it was designed from its inception to tap into the financial might of the banking industry. Moreover, the Senator emphasized that the banking industry had a public duty to serve all communities because of the charters banks received from state or federal governments and to atone for the redlining that the financial industry had practiced for decades.[333]

The chapter reviews the passage of CRA in 1977, early implementation of CRA in the 1980s, limitations of CRA, and subsequent Congressional amendments to CRA in the 1980s and 1990s.

Premise and purpose of CRA

As Chairman of the Senate Banking, Housing, and Urban Affairs Committee, Proxmire convened three days of hearings on the CRA starting on March 23, 1977. In his opening statement, the Senator outlined his four premises necessitating the CRA. The four premises are:

- The government cannot and should not revitalize cities with its own resources;

- Financial institutions are the main source of capital for economic development in cities and rural areas;

- Financial institutions do not need to engage in risky lending to serve communities, and can often do so with relatively little risk because of their first-hand knowledge of communities; and

- A public charter bestows economic benefits and "in return it is legitimate for public policy and regulatory practice to require some public purpose, without the need for costly subsidies, or mandatory quotas, or a bureaucratic credit allocation scheme."[334]

In his hearing statements, Proxmire elaborated on each of the four premises. He defined redlining and indicated that the devastation wrought by redlining is large scale and cannot be remedied solely by government funding. Proxmire stated:

> By redlining let me make it clear what I am talking about. I am talking about the fact that banks and savings and loans will take their deposits from a community and instead of reinvesting them in that community, they will actually or figuratively draw a red line on a map around the areas of their city, sometimes in the inner city, sometimes in the older neighborhoods, sometimes ethnic and sometimes black, but often encompassing a great area of their neighborhood.[335]

Systemic discrimination and disinvestment require both private and public resources be directed to revitalize redlined areas. Proxmire stated:

> We have the appalling facts of our cities. President Carter was right when he said . . . in Milwaukee that the number one economic problem in this country, is our cities. I think you would agree with me. We don't want to solve the problem with Government money. We couldn't do it with a Marshall plan for the cities. We have to do it with the people who are there, people

who understand the city, live in the city, who know the economy, loan officials who understand the value of the property, who understand what it is to require effective discipline.[336]

As described in Chapter 1, advocates such as Gale Cincotta and the group she led, National People's Action, did not want the government to abandon financing community revitalization and were uneasy with Proxmire's fixation on this rationale for CRA, particularly since the first NPA HMDA studies revealed paltry amounts of bank lending in urban neighborhoods.[337] At the same time, economically disadvantaged neighborhoods could not be revitalized if banks continued to redline them. While banks know their localities, they often do not exercise their talents to meet credit needs of underserved communities. Proxmire did not directly say why this is the case, whether it is because of a lack of effort or discrimination. He implies, however, that banks were not trying hard enough:

> When the committee did a survey of banking services here in Washington, we found one bank with a policy of making no home mortgage loans. This same bank was making a great volume of loans to the outside real estate interests of its own board. We found a savings and loan chartered in Washington with [ninety-nine] percent of its mortgage loans in the suburbs, and this story is repeated throughout the country. Banks that claim there is no demand for local housing and small business and agricultural credit, or who argue that they need to protect depositors' money precludes such lending, are often the same banks that have squandered money on speculative real estate loans or credits to shaky foreign regimes.

Demand in our economy is not a passive, fixed thing. It is manipulated and promoted. If a banker is willing to get out of the office, he will find it. This bill would encourage him to do so.[338]

If a banker hustles, he or she can find safe and sound lending opportunities. Lending in his or her community does not entail risk. On the contrary, a community cannot prosper if banks are not lending to them. Lending in the community is often safer than the speculative loans banks were making to well-healed insiders. On this point, Proxmire stated:

> Moreover, there is no reason to assume that a higher degree of community reinvestment is incompatible with bank safety. Financial institutions cannot prosper in the long run unless we have balanced growth and development throughout America. Finally, there is no evidence that banks and thrift institutions have gotten into financial difficulty by overinvesting in their local communities. On the contrary, most of the recent financial difficulties suffered by banks arose from making insider loans to affiliated persons.[339]

The extra push for banks to lend in their communities needs to come from the federal bank agencies. The agencies should view conferring a bank charter to be a privilege, not a right. In the hearings on the CRA, Proxmire stated: "The Community Reinvestment Act, which I am introducing today, is intended to establish a system of regulatory incentives to encourage banks and savings institutions to more effectively meet the credit needs of the localities they are chartered to serve, consistent with sound lending practices."[340]

When considering bank mergers, the agencies must consider the convenience and needs of communities. The agencies, however, only consider the needs for deposit accounts, and not credit needs. Proxmire explained: "The federal bank regulatory agencies have considerable influence over financial institutions. One of the most significant powers is the authority to approve or deny applications for deposit facilities. Persons wishing to organize a bank or savings institution must apply for a charter."[341] The agencies, however, do not fully assert their influence over banks. Proxmire continued:

> The regulators have thus conferred substantial economic benefits on private institutions without extracting any meaningful quid pro quo for the public. Other regulatory agencies have not been as timid when awarding charters.[342] But the other side of the coin—the credit needs of the locality and the applicant's capacity to service these needs—have been almost ignored by the regulatory agencies.[343]

In addition to providing statutory authority for the agencies to enforce CRA, Proxmire's staff and community groups saw CRA and the Home Mortgage Disclosure Act (HMDA) as a means of allowing community groups to influence banks and challenge bank mergers if banks were not meeting community credit needs.[344] Robert Kuttner, former Senate Banking Committee staff, praised the savvy of National People's Action, the Woodstock Institute, and the interracial coalition it organized as promoting CRA as a community empowerment tool. He stated that:

> "The brilliance of HMDA and CRA is that it created leverage and provided something (evidence of lending disparities) for people

to organize around. It created a sense of empowerment when you come together with other people and achieve something (such as CRA agreements negotiated in the early years by NPA).[345] If you normalize credit flows to these marginal neighborhoods that are at risk for being block busted, you will create a situation where African Americans can have homeownership opportunities but not in a context where a neighborhood flips from being all White to all Black and middlemen benefit."

He added that this type of federal legislation promoting problem solving through community empowerment is like labor law providing unions with a formal role in bargaining contracts with corporations.[346] In her detailed account of the early years of CRA advocacy, Marchiel describes how Gale Cincotta and NPA advocated for strengthening Proxmire's draft of CRA. They urged the Senator to adopt clearer performance measures showing bank progress (or lack thereof) in lending to historically underserved neighborhoods identified as those with lower incomes, undergoing racial transition, and with older housing stock.[347] These prescient recommendations foreshadowed policy debates decades later when advocates urged regulatory agencies to adopt more specific performance measures in CRA exams. Since politics is the art of compromise, advocates understand that this is a long struggle since all recommendations are unlikely to be adopted at any legislative or regulatory moment but over time, hopefully, the law and regulation moves to more rigor and ability to increase reinvestment.

While Proxmire did not adopt the strengthening amendments offered by NPA, the cooperation among the Senator, his staff, and NPA advocates built a strong case with substantial evidence about the need to combat redlining and how a law empowering communities could help do so. Kuttner recalled, "Grassroots lobbying is terribly, terribly important. I mean, if a Senator is hearing from folks at home, and you've got the churches…civil rights groups, and the labor unions, who were a lot more powerful in those years…A Senator who is working with a coalition of groups to try to enlist the support of other Senators."[348]

Evidence convinced Proxmire that banks needed to be pushed to reinvest in neighborhoods

Several witnesses during the three days of hearings on the CRA explained that banks were not meeting the needs for credit in communities of color and working-class neighborhoods. Their descriptions of unmet credit needs made for a compelling case that the public sector needed to intervene to remedy market imperfections and impediments to access to credit.

Calvin Bradford, Senior Research Fellow at the Woodstock Institute and a Northwestern University researcher working with community groups at the time CRA was moving through Congress, emphasized the priority that Proxmire placed on testimony from community groups setting the framing for the hearing and questions for the regulators to answer. He affirmed that "When you have a hearing, the regulators testify and the media sits there, and they write all the stuff down, and then the media disappears. The community groups then testify. Proxmire did not like this system." Instead, after the community groups testified first at his hearing, the Senator "could ask the government people about the issues they (the community groups) raised. That was something NPA really respected him for. So, if you look at those hearings, one thing you get is a huge amount of information from the community, redevelopment banks, people who ran state reinvestment programs, more than you would normally get.

It is a very important part of what goes on, not only in the bill, but later on in the groundwork that got laid that people can refer to."[349]

In his testimony, renowned consumer protection advocate Ralph Nader provided statements from Advisory Neighborhood Commissioners (ANC) in Washington D.C. regarding the barriers neighborhood residents confronted in accessing credit. Neighborhood residents seeking home purchase loans from banks often had to make twenty-five percent down payments, which were prohibitive in many instances.[350] The neighborhood residents then had to rely on the inferior option of mortgage companies. Mortgage companies foreclosed faster than banks when borrowers fell behind.

Small business owners also confronted frustrations in securing loans. In a survey of seventy-four small businesses in ANC neighborhoods, only twelve percent had loans while forty-nine percent tried unsuccessfully to apply for loans.[351] In addition, branch personnel in two AS&T branches told neighborhood residents that they did not have the authority to make mortgage loans. AS&T had issued only five mortgage loans in the ANC neighborhoods in a four-year time period.[352] While shunning the ANC neighborhoods east of Rock Creek Park, the institution made millions of dollars of mortgage loans west of the park in affluent and Caucasian neighborhoods.[353]

Bank reluctance to offer low-cost loans in communities of color occurred across the country. Gale Cincotta of National People's Action discussed a 1975 study from Northwestern University documenting racial disparities in lending in Chicago neighborhoods. Hispanic residents of the Logan Square neighborhood had to rely on high down-payment FHA loans while mostly White residents of an adjacent neighborhood received low down payment conventional loans.[354]

Proxmire and witnesses at the hearing had access to new data required by the Home Mortgage Disclosure Act (HMDA) passed in 1975 that effectively documented stark racial disparities in lending compelling policy responses. Proxmire declared on the floor of the Senate that "The data provided by [the HMDA] remove any doubt that redlining indeed exists, that many credit-worthy areas are denied loans. This denial of credit, while it is certainly not the sole cause of our urban problems, undoubtedly aggravates urban decline."[355] For example, newspapers in New York presented a series of reports pointing out that only eleven percent of the deposits in Brooklyn remained in the borough while eighty-nine percent was loaned outside of the borough. This pattern was repeated in Chicago, Los Angeles, and St. Louis.[356]

The Senator maintained his position that disinvestment occurred in smaller towns as well as larger cities. He stated, "We also know that small town banks sometimes ship their funds to the major money markets in search of higher interest rates, to the detriment of local housing, to the detriment of small business, and farm credit needs."[357]

Notable neighborhood-based efforts dispelled the notion that lending in underserved neighborhoods was risky and that combating redlining was futile. The Philadelphia Mortgage Plan (PMP), for instance, involved a partnership between the Neighborhood Housing Service (NHS) nonprofit organization and thirteen banks. On a proactive basis, the PMP reviewed results every two months and adjusted lending criteria as necessary. According to the hearings testimony, delinquency rates were low despite millions of dollars being loaned out.[358] In eighteen months, the program extended 1,500 loans with a default rate of six tenths of one percent.[359]

Another instance of a well-intentioned bank highlighted by the hearings was the South Shore Bank based in Chicago whose

Chairman was Ronald Grzywinski. Grzywinski testified that his team purchased the bank after the Office of the Comptroller of the Currency (OCC) denied a request by former owners to relocate the bank out of a neighborhood experiencing racial transition from White to African American.[360] Instead of fleeing the neighborhood, Mr. Grzywinski adopted a neighborhood-based lending model that featured extensive dialogue between the community and senior officials of the bank. Grzywinski and his team had countless meetings with the community to regain their trust. He also established review committees composed of senior officials including himself that carefully reviewed loan applications while at the same time assuring that the loans were safe and sound.[361] At the end of the first year of operation, his bank had made fifty-two loans in the surrounding neighborhood and only two were delinquent. This was in stark contrast to other banks located in city neighborhoods that used local deposits to make most of their loans in the suburbs.[362]

Grzywinski realized that his model of banking would not organically replicate itself since it involved more costs than the typical bank at that time would incur. Most banks sought to maximize their earnings via deposit activity rather than concentrating on lending, particularly in underserved neighborhoods. In advocating for the CRA, Grzywinski stated:

> The unfortunate conclusion I have come to is that bank managers may be well-intentioned on that issue, but the simple fact of the matter is that the system rewards earnings, and development or reinvestment in neighborhood is an additional short-term cost. If any bank decides to do that by itself, it is, in effect, self-imposing a tax on its earnings. Therefore, what is needed is a universally applied system of incentives and/or sanctions to encourage development.[363]

Market failure caused by years of discrimination and disinvestment made it difficult for banks to assess creditworthiness in underserved neighborhoods. The banks encountered barriers to underwriting due to a lack of information on borrower creditworthiness and neighborhood characteristics. Many banks were unwilling to roll up their sleeves and do the background work necessary for lending like South Shore Bank. Hence, Proxmire and others felt a federal law was needed to compel an entire industry to reinvest time and energy to serving neglected neighborhoods and discover profitable lending opportunities. Costs would be diminished over time as they learned how to assess creditworthiness of neighborhood residents.

Early Precedents for CRA – Experiences of Massachusetts and Connecticut

Proxmire asked the Banking Commissioners from Massachusetts and Connecticut to testify about their experiences implementing reinvestment obligations on banks as a means of demonstrating that a federal law would be feasible and effective. The Massachusetts Commissioner of Banks, Carol Greenwald, testified that before allowing banks to branch into the suburbs, they were required to serve all the areas in which they did business. She observed that one bank responded by saying that mortgage loans would now be available in all of its branches.[364] Massachusetts also stipulated that banks applying for permission to open new branches or merge were required to analyze the credit needs of their service areas. According to Greenwald, banks would maintain that demand for mortgage loans were low but "we have found that there were a number of home sales; there just wasn't a substantial number of bank mortgages being made in the area."[365] Greenwald reported that mortgage companies were doing brisk business because neighborhood residents had concluded that banks would not loan to them.

The Bank Commissioner of Connecticut, Lawrence Connell, testified regarding differential service at bank branches in the city compared to the suburbs. The banking department's survey of branch hours revealed significant disparities. In the cities, only about thirty percent of the branches were open in the evenings and Saturdays whereas in the suburbs more than fifty percent were open for extended hours.[366] In response to the survey findings, the Connecticut Bank Commission placed a moratorium on branch applications. Eighteen savings banks and six commercial banks then indicated that they would change branch hours of operation.[367]

Precursors to CRA at the state level seemed to be having their desired impact of reducing inequities in bank lending and service. It would stand to reason that a federal CRA would create a more level playing field nationwide.

Rebuttal of criticism of CRA as bureaucratic credit allocation

Despite the comprehensive data analysis showing disparities in lending, and despite positive indications of banks responding to state law, federal bank regulatory agencies opposed Proxmire's proposed CRA legislation during the three-day hearings. Robert Bloom, the Acting Comptroller of the Currency, testified that CRA would be largely duplicative of existing bank merger law and regulations. The OCC already required banks to describe how they would respond to credit and deposit needs. He asserted that "[The OCC] [does] not agree with your assertion that the credit needs of a locality and the applicant's capacity to serve these needs have been almost ignored by the regulatory agencies."[368] In addition, a CRA law would be too restrictive and would not allow the regulatory agencies to exercise discretion in evaluating bank applications. Requiring banks to indicate how they will serve local needs was not appropriate in all cases. Mr. Bloom stated, "Geography plays a limited role in the operations of the largest commercial banks which are national and international in scope. Also, people make deposits on their way to work rather than in their home communities."[369]

The Chairman of the Federal Reserve Board, Arthur F. Burns, echoed Mr. Bloom's concerns. Mr. Burns stated:

> To restrict the activities of these institutions through Federal regulation could well prove counter-productive. It could block the flow of funds, for example, mortgage credit or new funds for capital investment from an established community with excess savings to a growing community unable to generate sufficient savings to meet its expanding financial needs.[370]

Burns continued, "Each time a particular credit use is mandated by law or regulation, some other credit use that otherwise would have been accommodated must go unsatisfied."[371] He tempered his concerns about government restriction of optimal use of capital for lending by saying, "We recognize, of course, that markets do not always work in ways that maximize social priorities and that thus there may be particular needs that public policy will need to encourage."[372]

A.A. Milligan, testifying on behalf of the American Bankers Association, seconded the concerns of the Federal Reserve Chairman about inadvertently restricting lending to where it was needed most. Mr. Milligan stated:

Banks in urban areas such as Milwaukee, Chicago, or Minneapolis, that are providing the necessary funds for rural community development in Wisconsin would not be considered to be meeting the needs of their own communities. They would be labeled derelict in their responsibilities to their own communities even if their communities had no current need.[373]

Growing frustrated during the hearing, Senator Jake Garn ratcheted up the criticism of the proposed CRA, declaring that it would be: "Building up a regulatory burden that is going to destroy the housing industry in this country."[374] He calmed down later during the hearings and confessed, "Redlining does exist. I may surprise you after hearing my initial outburst. What I disagree with is how do we solve the problem of redlining."[375] He then discussed how deteriorated neighborhood conditions made banks reluctant to lend and that comprehensive solutions must include code enforcement, eliminating neighborhood health hazards, as well as advocating for government grants for community development.

The essential debate between the proponents and opponents of the CRA was whether market failure existed that was a significant cause of neighborhood deterioration and whether government regulation was needed to rectify market failure. Opponents of the CRA subscribed to the views of the bank regulatory agencies that markets worked well to identify areas of credit excess and scarcity and that regulations would interrupt the optimal flow of capital from areas of excess to areas of need. They harped on the notion of credit allocation, which in their mind, referred to government agencies telling banks where to lend and how much to lend. Credit allocation is often referred to as regulation mandating specific quotas or percentages of loan to specific groups of borrowers or specific loan-to-deposit ratios that must be reached.

Proponents of the CRA, in contrast, maintained that market failure was pervasive in inner city areas and that credit was not flowing to where it was needed. Banks located in inner city areas were receiving deposits but refusing to meet pent up demand for loans. According to this view, it was not the case that these banks were judging that needs were greater in rural areas for loans and therefore directing their deposits there.

Reasonable observers and stakeholders can disagree about the problems and the needed solutions. However, as documented in Chapter 1, inner city areas as well as rural counties continue to be underserved and CRA still needs to address market barriers to lending. Contrary to Garn's assertion, it is also clear that forty years after Congress passed CRA, the law has not destroyed the housing industry. In fact, it may have saved the banking industry from itself by reducing the amount of risky financing including subprime lending as Proxmire had the prescience to predict.

The CRA statute passed in 1977 avoided credit allocation and simplistic performance measures, but had clear limitations

The debate over the CRA influenced Proxmire's design of the bill. After listening to the criticism, he changed the bill to make it less prescriptive and instead sought to emphasize that banks must serve the needs of the community. Proxmire noted that the revised bill was "drastically revised" and that "the substantive objections have been satisfied."[376]

As originally introduced, the CRA started by affirming that banks have a continuing and affirmative obligation to serve the

convenience and needs of the community in which they are chartered to do business. The convenience and needs of the community
included the needs for credit as well as deposit services. When
chartering, supervising, and examining banks, the federal regulatory
agencies must encourage banks to meet needs consistent with "safe
and sound" operation of banks. Kuttner affirmed that "safe and
sound" was added in order to overcome regulators' resistance and
defang the criticism of credit allocation. He stated "The bugaboo of
all of this is credit allocation and that you are increasing risk. And
so, we very carefully put in the language of safety and soundness."[377]
Calvin Bradford, Senior Research Fellow at the Woodstock Institute, added that Proxmire sought to garner the votes of Republican
Senators by addressing credit allocation since that is "anti-capitalist
and against the free market. It's all those things at a time when free
market capitalism was a big political issue as well."[378] Also, Bradford
asserted that the safety and soundness provision was also critical
for community group support. He stated, "Nobody wants a loan to
fail in their neighborhood because then the program dies and the
people in the neighborhood lose their neighborhood."[379] Chapter
2 further discusses the perspectives of supporters and opponents of
CRA regarding safety and soundness.

When banks applied for charters, deposit insurance, opening
branches, or merging with other banks, the bill required banks to
describe in their applications how they would serve convenience and
needs. In the first draft of the bill, banks were required to designate
a primary service area in which they anticipated they would receive
more than one half of their deposits. They were then supposed to
indicate the proportion of loans that they would reinvest into their
primary service area. Also, banks were to indicate how they were
meeting the needs of their primary service area.[380]

When considering applications from banks, the federal agencies were to assess the extent to which banks were meeting needs in their existing primary service areas as well as how they would meet needs in any new or enlarged primary service areas associated with their application. The agencies were to permit and encourage members of the public to testify regarding how well the banks or their subsidiaries were meeting needs in their primary service areas. Finally, the agencies were to obtain periodic data from banks regarding how many deposits they obtained from their primary service areas and how many loans they made in those areas.[381]

Congress passed the CRA on October 12, 1977. The final version of CRA became Title VIII of the Housing and Community Development Act of 1977.[382] CRA almost did not make it into the Housing and Community Act; a Senate Banking Committee vote to delete it from the Housing and Community Act resulted in a 7-7 tie. A tie vote allowed it to remain in the Act by the closest of margins. As chairman of the committee, a tie enabled Proxmire to keep CRA in the Housing and Community Act.[383] Proxmire realized that the might of the banking industry would not enable CRA to survive as a stand-alone bill, so he made it part of the Housing and Community Development Act. His staff person Ken McLean remarked, "he (Proxmire) realized that CRA cold never get through as a stand-alone measure because the banks had too much political power."[384] On the floor of the Senate, opponents tried to strip CRA out of the Housing and Community Act. The vote to strip out CRA was close. In an oral history recounting this vote, McLean recalled that about 20 Senators were absent that day and of these, 17 probably opposed CRA. The supporters of CRA prevailed by a margin of 3 or 4 Senators on that vote.[385]

The Senate passed the Housing and Community Development Act by a vote of 79-7 in June of 1977. The House agreed to a Senate and House conference report of the bill by a vote of 384-26 in early October of 1977.[386] While the votes on the housing and community bill appear overwhelmingly in favor, this vote reflects more the bicameral approval of federal funding of housing and community development programs in the larger bill than CRA itself, which narrowly passed the Senate Banking Committee.[387] This political context helps explain why Proxmire needed to compromise and water down some of the bill's provisions.

In its final form, the purpose of the CRA remained the same, that is, requiring banks to meet credit needs. However, the final version shifted its emphasis from details expected from the banks in applications to requiring agencies to examine banks. During regularly scheduled examinations, the agencies were to assess the record of banks of meeting the credit needs of their entire community, including low- and moderate-income communities. The agencies were then to take bank records of meeting needs into consideration when they were considering bank applications. The details required on bank applications regarding bank designation of primary service areas and the proportion of loans expected in service areas were deleted from the final version. Also, deleted were bank data reporting requirements regarding their deposit and lending activity in their primary service areas.[388]

Proxmire altered CRA in response to criticism that it would be difficult for banks to determine how many loans they would make in their primary service areas. He was also probably sensitive to the issues of not deterring banks from lending in rural areas or other underserved areas with lower incomes if they thought they were adequately serving the primary areas in which they were doing business. The examination regime established in the final version of the bill would help ensure that banks were meeting credit needs in all areas in which they were chartered to do business. On the first day of hearings in March of 1977, the Senator stated:

> [The proposed CRA bill] does not provide for credit allocation. To criticize reinvestment incentives as a form of credit allocation is disingenuous. It would not allocate credit, nor would it require any fixed ratio of deposits to loans. But it would provide that a bank charter is indeed a franchise to serve local convenience and needs, including credit needs.[389]

From the inception of the CRA bill, Proxmire was insistent that CRA was not establishing a system of credit allocation that would force banks to hit any specific ratio or other measure of loans to specific populations that could entail making risky loans in order to do so.

Even though the primary service area requirement did not require a fixed ratio of deposits to loans, it did require banks to estimate such a ratio for their primary service areas. Yet, the Senator most likely dropped this requirement so CRA would not be subjected to continued criticisms of credit allocation. Instead of the ratio requirement, perhaps he calculated that regular exams would catch any bank that was not meeting the needs for credit in the areas from which they took deposits and/or in which they were chartered to do business. In response to Senator Morgan's question, Proxmire stated on the Senate floor that the revised bill "also redefine[d] the primary service area to be served on a broader basis, so that there be no question that it is not simply the immediate community where the bank was located."[390]

It is not clear what Proxmire meant by a broader basis. The final version discussed the requirement for banks to meet credit needs in all communities in which they are chartered, including low- and moderate-income communities. As Dennis pointed out, meeting needs of the "entire community" replaced the phrase "primary service area."[391] It also provided room in the future for the federal bank agencies to take a more expansive view of the communities to be served by banks. Communities were not only those from which the banks received deposits though these remained important. Instead, the essential impetus of CRA was to focus on redlined and underserved communities, and these can be located in a broader area including rural areas discussed during the hearings. As Dennis corroborated based on the data presented during the hearings, "There is evidence in the record that when Congress speaks of "local credit needs" it is utilizing an interchangeable shorthand reference to the housing and community development needs of areas in which there has traditionally been a statistically low level of conventional financing of home sales or home rehabilitation areas which may be on the threshold of decline."[392]

Thus, CRA examination of activity beyond the branch footprint is justified because it focuses on underserved communities. As discussed in more detail in future chapters, the federal bank agencies proposed changes to the CRA regulation and examination that requires scrutiny of lending beyond the branch network to include geographical areas that the bank is serving via non-branch means whether by loan production offices, brokers, or the internet. As described below, Congress amended the CRA statute to specify examination in geographical areas containing bank branches, but these additions were in the context of the expansion of banking across state lines and thus not inconsistent with the passed version in 1977 that dropped primary service areas and allowed banks to serve additional underserved areas.

The deletion of the ratio of primary service area loans to deposits should also deter federal agencies in the future from designing CRA exams that rely primarily on a single ratio or performance measure to judge performance. As discussed in Chapter 7, in 2022, the Office of the Comptroller of the Currency rescinded its CRA rule promulgated during the Trump administration that had relied largely on a ratio of the dollar amount of CRA activities divided by bank deposits to assign ratings. During the 1977 hearings, one of the lenders, Todd Cooke, critiqued the original requirement for banks to indicate a ratio of loans to deposits in their primary service areas on the grounds that banks could not easily anticipate future economic conditions.[393] This type of critique five decades later similarly doomed the Trump era CRA rule. Instead of overreliance on one measure, CRA exams need to contain a variety of measures that more accurately assess bank performance and that allow banks to compensate by stronger performance in some aspects of lending or service for weaker performance that could be caused by economic conditions inhibiting other types of lending or investing.

The new law did not require an evaluation of lending by race

A conspicuous omission in the CRA statute was any mention of race or the needs of communities of color. This was likely due to the political environment in the late 19070s, which included a backlash against proposals that appeared to mandate affirmative action.

Immergluck mentioned that during the debate on CRA, supporters focused on the needs of neighborhoods and that race was only discussed once.[394] Moreover, author and former Committee staff person Robert Kuttner maintained that the absence of race, "was deliberate and strategic. Although African Americans were the disproportionate victims of redlining, the coalition (of community groups) was working class people and middle-class people of all races, and that the need was to require reinvestment and create a vehicle of pressure by community groups. We wanted to make it clear that CRA was not a racial affirmative action bill. We (political leaders and community advocates) felt this would be stronger if we did not put race in it explicitly. If you do this (however), you're disproportionately going to help Black people and put blockbusters out of business."[395]

Kuttner's astute observations reflected the dynamics of organizing in racially transitioning neighborhoods. The coalition of groups promoting CRA was careful not to discuss race often in efforts to keep everyone united and focused on the destruction of redlining. Calvin Bradford, Senior Research Fellow at Woodstock, recalled that Shel Trapp, one of the leaders of NPA, told him that they would focus on the destruction of older neighborhoods by unscrupulous actors instead of harping on the racial injustice of redlining since they were organizing White and African American residents of redlined neighborhoods.[396]

Yet, the decision to delete an explicit mention of race was not a quick one and involved a considerable amount of discussion among advocates and Proxmire's staff. NPA pushed for explicitly prohibiting discrimination in the statute, according to Bradford.[397] In addition, a draft of NPA's version of the CRA bill included requiring banks to develop affirmative marketing plans in conjunction with their merger applications that would indicate how banks would market to people of color, women, lower income people, and underserved communities.[398] The CRA evaluations would develop standards for determining what is acceptable and unacceptable lending in underserved communities.[399] NPA's draft CRA bill was not a mandate to examine lending by race but was a nuanced effort, perhaps to be more universally acceptable, that included a prohibition against discrimination and the development of marketing plans to reach out to overlooked populations including women, people of color, and lower income people. Moreover, the category of underserved census tracts was not an exact proxy for race since the concept was aimed at racially transitioning neighborhoods that would likely experience segregation if there was not intervention.

The Senator and his staff replied that stakeholders would understand that CRA was concerned about race even if race was not addressed in some fashion in the statute. They reasoned that CRA was one of a series of laws including the Fair Housing Act, the Equal Credit Opportunity Act, and the Home Mortgage Disclosure Act (HMDA) that sought to eliminate racial discrimination in lending. The Senator also cautioned that he could lose votes and that CRA was "hanging by a hair" according to Bradford. The deletion of race also helped lessen regulator opposition Bradford recalled.[400] Finally, a common understanding was that reducing racial disparities in lending would be incorporated into the regulations implementing CRA (Indeed, considering bank lending by race was one of the "assessment factors" in the first regulation but was deleted in the 1995 regulatory rewrite as described in Chapter 5).

Clearly, the lawmakers sought to direct the benefits of CRA to people of color, but did the absence of race in the statute curtail regulatory efforts to do so? This is a question to be grappled with in upcoming chapters. Kuttner added that the color-blind nature of CRA was reacting to the politics of a certain place and time, and the need to keep a multiracial coalition of advocates together. If the times are different now and regulators are willing to adopt approaches to further benefit communities of color, he would be supportive of that.[401]

CRA was focused in the early years on bank merger applications

The passed version of the law did not specify the performance measures the agencies should use on exams while assessing banks' records of meeting needs. The vagueness led to lax enforcement and ratings inflation in the early years of implementation. The architects of the law, however, hoped that the merger application process would be a lever that community-based organizations could use to offer their views during agency consideration of merger applications although lawmakers removed an explicit reference in the original draft that agencies were to hear testimony from community groups at hearings.[402] Robert Kuttner suggested that the language may have been altered because Proxmire had to negotiate intensely to bring Banking Committee swing votes to favor CRA's passage. He was very clear, however, that a key purpose of the law was to empower community groups and use "federal legislation to create countervailing power," in order to enable community groups to safeguard neighborhood interests in safe and sound lending.[403]

Kenneth A. McClean, Senate Bank Committee staff director, stated that neighborhood groups could challenge bank mergers "on the grounds that a particular bank didn't have a very good lending record. Our idea was essentially to empower the neighborhood movement."[404]

Defending CRA after 1977 required mobilization of community organizations around the country

After CRA passed in 1977, the bank industry and allies in Congress tried to repeal, or if that failed, to weaken the law. John Taylor, the founder of NCRC and former President and CEO, maintained that the key to preventing legislative weakening of CRA was to mobilize the community constituency. He explained that since all politics is local, it is not enough for a community association based in Washington DC to opine about CRA. "A Congressman would care less about what..." a DC-based organization would say "because it did not represent a single vote." "Community development corporations (CDCs) were at the front lines beyond the Federal government in creating affordable housing. We started hearing about people in the districts where they were voters contacting their members of Congress. It wasn't that difficult to derail the effort to weaken CRA because it was a good law. It made sense. Hearing this was an issue in the community woke up a lot of folks." Opponents of CRA "didn't want newspapers to be writing about how they were opposed to affordable housing in their Congressional districts."

Over the years, NCRC operated on the premise that community groups did not have the dollars to spend on lobbyists or campaign contributions like the bank trade associations, but that community groups had the votes if they mobilized. Taylor emphasized community voice and community members weighing in with their Congressional delegation. Several times, NCRC member organizations would give their members of Congress tours of neighborhoods with affordable housing and economic development projects financed in part by CRA. This solidified support from CRA proponents and converted some opponents like former Representative Jim Leach (R-Iowa) to supporters.

After these concerted efforts from the community constituency to preserve the law, how well did CRA empower community-based organizations to hold banks accountable and leverage reinvestment? The early regulatory implementation and experience of community-based organizations provides some insight.

Early regulatory implementation of CRA half-hearted and tentative

After passage of CRA, the federal bank agencies implemented the first regulations in 1978. The agencies adopted a conservative approach that focused exams on process rather than measuring outcomes. In other words, the first regulations emphasized scrutinizing activities such as a bank ascertaining community needs and marketing as opposed to measuring actual lending in LMI neighborhoods.[405] In addition, the agencies required banks to publicly issue CRA statements that described their CRA efforts to meet their community needs. However, these statements were often vague and lacked specifics about the level of lending in LMI communities or how they planned to maintain or increase this lending.[406]

The tentative approach to CRA reflected the agencies' wariness regarding credit allocation. Immergluck reported that the Federal Reserve System in its 1980 "Community Reinvestment Act Statement" maintained the CRA "was not intended to establish a regulatory influence on the allocation of credit. The Board believes that there are many reasons why a particular neighborhood may generate more deposits than loan requests."[407] This approach errs too far in excusing lackluster CRA performance and suggests that either regulatory or community group impact on the "allocation of credit" such as increasing lending in LMI neighborhoods amounts to undue interference in the marketplace.

Yet, redlining is a perverse form of credit allocation in that it is the systematic denial of credit in neighborhoods. In other words, under redlining, the allocation for credit in these neighborhoods is zero or close to zero. Moreover, correcting for market failure implies that credit will increase in LMI neighborhoods. An increase in credit, however, does not equal credit allocation because increasing credit is not the same as specifying a certain percentage of loans for formerly redlined neighborhoods. CRA examination and enforcement do not amount to government fiat if it involves reasonable performance measures that compare banks against each other in lending to underserved communities. A major part of this analysis is assessing performance by comparing private sector actors against each other in the marketplace. Bank performance should also be judged against demographic benchmarks that help examiners determine the potential level of market demand for loans.

The early CRA exams ratings for individual banks were confidential, further impairing public accountability. Interestingly, however, they consisted of five ratings from 1 to 5 instead of the current four ratings. Although, an early Federal Reserve Board analysis of ratings conducted in 1980 revealed laxity in the form low failure rates, a potentially positive outcome was that the ratings distribution revealed more distinctions in performance than current ratings. In its analysis, the Federal Reserve Board did not reveal individual bank ratings but looked at overall ratings distributions. Just 3.5 percent of the banks received the highest rating of "1" and 56.7 percent received a rating of "3", which is analogous to Low Satisfactory ratings on current CRA exam subtests.[408] Although the confidentiality of ratings was counter to CRA's public accountability purpose, the five ratings categories could be viewed as a favorable precedent for CRA reform efforts to introduce more nuance into the ratings system.

Despite federal bank agency torpor, advocates seize opportunities

John Taylor is the founder of NCRC and served as President and CEO for three decades. NCRC is an association of 700 community-based organizations that use CRA to increase access to credit for underserved communities.

Prior to that, he had a career in Massachusetts, eventually becoming director of the Sommerville Community Development Corporation (CDC). The CDC was in the business of building affordable housing and providing social services to low- and moderate-income residents. The Sommerville CDC sought to provide opportunities for public housing residents to become homeowners. Taylor lined up an impressive array of financing for a development of 32 homeowner units. The city would donate land and Fannie Mae had pledged to purchase the mortgages made to the new homeowners. The only financing piece that remained was to secure a construction loan from a bank. Taylor approached Somerset Savings Bank and its President Tom Kelly. Kelly gave Taylor the cold shoulder, even going to the lengths of leaving the bank building from a back door when Taylor and his staff had camped out in front of Kelly's office asking for a meeting. Taylor eventually went to a suburban branch of the bank to make a pitch for the project. A commercial loan officer at that branch liked the project but that endorsement was met with silence from Kelly.[409]

At around this time, the bank wanted to switch charters and had applied to the Federal Reserve System to be placed under its oversight. Taylor took advantage of the new CRA law and opposed the charter application in 1983. The protest letter caused quite a ruckus. It even drew condemnation from the Mayor of Sommerville who was upset at a protest of a well-connected bank. Nevertheless,

Taylor's letter eventually found its way to a sympathetic officer of the Federal Reserve Bank of Boston who convened a meeting with Taylor and Kelly. After listening to a rambling discussion from the Somerset Bank's lawyer, Kelly asked a question to the Federal Reserve officer, "what do you think of us signing an agreement with this group to commit funds for affordable housing." The Federal Reserve officer responded, "We would be very, very, very predisposed for you to sign an agreement with this organization." Taylor stated that "each very" suggested that the agreement would be larger. Taylor and Kelly signed a $20 million commitment to fund affordable housing.[410]

Previously, Taylor had worked in Cape Cod, Massachusetts attempting to obtain home improvement financing for modest income homeowners that needed to weatherize their homes against the cold Northeast winters. Taylor presented the math to various banks, showing that the energy conservation savings would eventually equal or even exceed the amount of the home improvement loans. Astonishingly, he had no takers from the banks. Taylor then decided to have a public townhall meeting with the Office of the Comptroller of the Currency and the Massachusetts Bank Commissioner about the credit need for home improvement loans. Media attended and reported. The next day, several banks contacted him.[411]

It seemed that in the early days, CRA enforcement was largely up to the initiative of community-based organizations aided by the periodic assistance of sympathetic regulatory officials. Thus, CRA victories were achieved on a per bank basis. A more widespread industry response would wait until changes in the CRA regulatory regime. According to Taylor, this occurred after the CRA ratings for individual banks became public and up to 10 percent failed in the first few years. Then the funding for affordable housing and community development became more readily available.

"Any law or regulation that protect people is only as good as the sheriff who is charge of enforcing it," concluded Taylor.[412] Clearly, that is true, and if it was not for the dogged determination of community organizations in the early days, the sheriffs would not have been as motivated to enforce the law and regulation vigorously. This pattern would repeat itself over the years: the sheriff would need a push by the community. That is one important reason why CRA must remain a law and regulation that empowers community-based organizations to be involved in the process and hold regulators as well as banks accountable.

Amendments to CRA bolster Proxmire's objectives of public and local accountability

After the passage of the CRA in 1977, Congress strengthened Proxmire's objectives of bank accountability to the public, community organizations, and to local areas. As discussed above, limitations in the original statute such as confidential exams curtailed the accountability and effectiveness of CRA. The first time Congress amended CRA was in 1989 when it passed the Financial Institutions Reform, Recovery, and Enforcement Act (FIRREA). FIRREA focused on the bailout and rescue of the savings and loans industry. Section 1212 of Title XII of the law included an amendment to CRA requiring the federal agencies to make publicly available CRA exams including the rating awarded to banks. The exams were required to reach conclusions about assessment factors described in the CRA regulations measuring the extent to which banks were meeting credit needs of communities, including LMI neighborhoods.[413] FIRREA also changed the ratings from a point system of 1 to 5 to four possible ratings ranging from Outstanding to Substantial Noncompliance.[414] While it was a well-intentioned reform to increase bank accountability, the four ratings categories eventually contributed to ratings inflation and was not as supple as five ratings categories in revealing gradations in performance.

An amendment to CRA in the Federal Deposit Insurance Corporation Improvement Act of 1991 was designed to further improve the rigor of CRA exams by directing the agencies to not only describe conclusions about bank performance but also to include data verifying conclusions. The intent was to enhance public scrutiny of exams by allowing the public to review data and determine if examiners properly and convincingly used data to support conclusions.[415]

As discussed by Taylor above, bank financing for community development projects increased significantly after CRA exams became public starting in 1990 and between 5 to 10 percent of banks failed exams for a few subsequent years (see Chapter 2 for a chart of CRA ratings by year). Visibility increases accountability which in turn improves bank performance.

The Riegle-Neal Interstate Banking and Branching Efficiency Act in 1994 expanded the geographical scope of CRA exams. Prior to Riegle-Neal, unless permitted by state law, bank holding companies generally were not allowed to buy out-of-state banks but served the state in which they were chartered.[416] Interestingly, in 1977 Proxmire predicted that the CRA would facilitate interstate banking by reassuring the public that banks would reinvest back into the communities making deposits instead of taking the deposits across state lines for investing and lending.[417] Section 110 of Riegle-Neal requires federal agencies to conduct CRA evaluations in each state in which a bank has a branch and to reach conclusions about performance for metropolitan and non-metropolitan areas of each state where banks have branches. Evaluations are also to be conducted for multistate metropolitan areas in which banks have branches. Since

Riegle-Neal anticipated that banks would serve multiple states, it insisted that CRA retain a local focus and conduct evaluations in metropolitan and rural parts of each state they served.[418]

As stated above, amendments to the original statute per Riegle-Neal increased the references of geographical areas around branches as areas evaluated by CRA exams. However, it is doubtful that the amendment authors intended to restrict CRA exams to areas with branches, which would be inconsistent with the original bill and the removal of primary service areas in the original bill. Criticism by bank representatives motivated Proxmire to remove primary service areas in response to the points raised that banks were becoming multi-state and national and should be able to serve underserved areas beyond their branch footprints. Instead, the Riegle Neal amendment allowed CRA exams to expand and continue to hold larger banks accountable for serving all communities in response to the interstate growth of banks enabled by Riegle Neal. The Clinton administration supported interstate banking but wanted to make sure that CRA could still ensure that a bank "with branches serving widely separated areas helps meet the needs of all the communities it serves," according to Comptroller of the Currency Eugene Ludwig.[419] Another House Banking Committee hearing on interstate banking and the House Conference Report on the bill references updating CRA for interstate banking and does not discuss intentions to limit CRA's coverage to areas with bank branches.[420]

Amendments to CRA made by the Resolution Trust Corporation Refinancing, Restructuring and Improvement Act of 1991 and the Housing and Community Development Act of 1992 included traditional bank support to minority-owned banks, women-owned banks, and low-income credit unions as favorable factors on CRA exams. Investments in and loans to these institutions could be considered on CRA exams as supporting the credit needs of local communities.[421] In addition, donating branches or selling branches at a discount to these institutions would likewise be considered.[422] These amendments were attempts to further focus CRA on underserved communities and communities of color by supporting institutions dedicated to serving these communities. They provide precedents justifying increased attention to communities of color continuing to experience disadvantages due to redlining and discrimination.

Conclusion

The passage of CRA required all the considerable legislative skill of a lawmaker such as Senator Proxmire and an interracial coalition of community groups pushing for passage. Proxmire had to make compromises that simultaneously improved and impaired the law and early regulatory implementation. A more expansive definition of community was an important precedent for recent regulatory efforts to incorporate bank lending beyond bank branches. At the same time, a lack of specific performance measures or instructions about how to evaluate banks led to the creation of CRA exams that focused on process rather than results in terms of measuring bank lending to LMI borrowers and communities. Importantly, however the language in the 1977 law did not preclude the future adoption of rigorous performance measures and did not constrain community input. In fact, senior staff from the Senate Banking Committee confirmed that community participation and input were central for the implementation of CRA.

Subsequent amendments attempted to fix the flaws of the original bill. Exams and ratings were made public. Riegle-Neal expanded CRA's reach to accommodate the interstate growth of banks unleashed by the bill, but exams were to remain focused on

Ending Redlining through a Community-Centered Reform of the Community Reinvestment Act

evaluating local areas in the states. Lastly, amendments were added to increase CRA's attention to serving communities of color by supporting minority-owned banks and other institutions dedicated to serving underserved communities. While important, these fixes were not enough to unleash CRA's full potential. A further regulatory overall was needed, which is discussed in the next chapter.

5

Revisions: Clinton-Era Regulatory Reforms an Incomplete Advance

In July of 1993, President Bill Clinton issued an executive order directing the federal bank agencies to revise the CRA regulations. In his remarks on the south lawn of the White House introducing his order, President Clinton declared:

> While the CRA has played an important role in making credit available to underserved urban and rural communities, I think we would all admit that it hasn't lived up to its potential. The current enforcement system relies too much on public relations documentation and not enough on real lending performance.
>
> This has been a pain for everybody involved –too much paperwork for the banks and not enough investment for the communities.

That's why I am sending a memorandum to the four federal banking regulators that requires them to implement a series of reforms
around CRA – designed to increase investment in communities
that need it, while simultaneously streamlining and clarifying the
regulatory process. The policy will be good for banks, good for
communities, good for borrowers, and it represents real change.

These actions today fulfill a commitment I made during the last
campaign when I promised that we would work hard to unlock
the energy and the entrepreneurship that lies latent in the hearts
and souls of men and women in this country in every community.
This proposal will enable them to take a small loan and start a
business; to turn their dreams into storefronts, and then expand
those storefronts into chains, creating jobs for their neighbors
and bringing opportunities to their neighborhoods. It will make
them a part of the movement for democratic capitalism and
growth that is reshaping the entire world but has left too many
Americans behind.[423]

The President correctly asserted that CRA's potential was yet to
be realized due to an examination methodology that emphasized process over measuring performance. Both major stakeholders – banks
and community-based organizations – had expressed frustration
with this. John Taylor explained that if banks "had something on the
wall that signified that you were an equal opportunity lender and
had a CRA file, you were like two thirds of the way through your
exam. This (executive order) was to change it from an administrative
review to a performance review. That's what we had argued for over
and over again."[424]

Community groups not only argued but organized to generate massive numbers of comment letters to the agencies. When issuing their final CRA rule in 1995, the agencies stated that community groups had issued 3,082 comments on the proposed rule as opposed to 2,544 for banks.[425] John Taylor asserted, "Banks were shocked that they were out commented by a four- or five-year-old coalition of working class and poor people organizations."[426] This mobilization by community organizations was critical. Had NCRC and its allies not organized as effectively, the voice of the community would not have been amplified and the final rule would not have emphasized performance reviews as much as community groups had desired. The agencies watered down the final rule compared to their proposals but the reduction in rigor likely would have been greater had community groups not weighed in as much as they did.

Clinton indicated that if exams became more consistent, performance-based and objective, banks would be motivated to make more loans and investments in underserved communities. His July 1993 Executive order asked the agencies to "replace paperwork and uncertainty with greater performance, clarity, and objectivity."[427]

The agencies took three years to propose and then finalize new CRA regulations with these goals guiding them. They initially proposed changes in December of 1993 and then in response to several thousand comments, proposed a second draft of changes in October of 1994. Finally, the agencies issued a final CRA regulation in May of 1995, which took two years to fully implement. This was a massive effort conducted with thoughtfulness and deliberation as reflected in three drafts of the CRA regulation over multiple years. The final rule established a solid foundation and components for CRA exams, which could promote objective assessments of bank performance and include robust community input. However, the agencies opted to leave too much to the discretion of examiners, which caused continuing frustrations by all parties over the inconsistencies of CRA exams. Several exams were objective but too many were subjective and contributed to CRA grade inflation. This chapter will review major parts of the agency rulemaking, focusing on key decisions that promoted President Clinton's objectives for reform as well as those that impeded the objectives. For each subject area, such as community group involvement or the creation of objective measures on CRA exams, the chapter will discuss proposals in the 1993 and 1994 draft rules and the final decisions made in the 1995 rule.

Agencies recognize importance of community group involvement but back away from most expansive proposals for facilitating community input

A CRA examination regime should include robust community involvement to ensure that exams are rigorous. Firstly, community-based organizations and residents have first-hand knowledge of credit needs and opportunities for banks to respond to those needs. Without their input, examiners will have incomplete context with which to evaluate banks. Secondly, if the examination process mostly entails interactions between banks and examiners, the chances for bank-friendly exams with inflated ratings increase. Some on-site examiners could have a natural tendency to become too acclimated and accepting of the bank's perspective. The best assurance of objective exams is creating a process that is not only open and solicitous of multiple points of view but also carefully documents the views and inputs of all parties.

The 1993 proposed rule included the most discussion about the role of community group participation in CRA exams. In particular, the agencies devoted attention to the role of community organizations in CRA agreements (known now as Community Benefit Agreements or CBAs) and how these agreements could influence the CRA exam process. According to the agencies:

"A number of respondents, both from the financial service industry and community-based organizations, expressed interest in the idea of financial institutions developing strategic plans for CRA performance in conjunction with the representatives of the communities within which they operate. Some wanted the regulatory agencies to make enforceable agreements between financial institutions and community groups a central focus of the CRA process."[428]

Notably, the agencies repeated the requests from both community groups and some in the banking industry that CRA agreements and plans jointly developed by community groups and banks be a central part of CRA examination. In addition, the agencies in the 1993 proposal contemplated awarding banks CRA points if they involved community organizations in their CRA programs.

The agencies proposed in 1993 that "an institution could also receive an upward adjustment to its lending rating based on the operation of a program under which the institution would reevaluate applications that, based on an initial evaluation, the institution planned to deny." These "second look" programs could involve community-based organizations.[429]

Both ideas – making CRA agreements a key part of the CRA process and formally recognizing community organization participation in bank programs on CRA exams – did not make the final 1995 rule. The notion of making CRA agreements part of bank plans that could be submitted in lieu of CRA exams did not even make the 1993 proposed rule. Instead, banks were allowed to pursue a strategic plan option in lieu of a traditional CRA exam. The strategic plan option featured the development of measurable goals. The 1993 proposal required that banks publicize the draft plans and solicit public comment on them.[430] The 1994 proposal expanded the public solicitation requirement modestly by requiring the banks to informally gather input from community stakeholders before publicly releasing its plan for comment. The agencies stated:

"These changes would increase the opportunity for productive community input in the plan process. By requiring an institution to seek informal suggestions in formulating a plan, and then to solicit formal comment before submitting a plan to the agency, this process will encourage consultation between an institution and its community, including local government, community leaders, and the public."[431]

The agencies clearly desired to encourage community input into the CRA process but likely backpedaled on including CRA agreements as an option for strategic plans in response to bank opposition to community group involvement in what they viewed as undue meddling in their operations. The agencies stated:

"Several industry comments were concerned that under the strategic plan option, community organizations would play an *inappropriate* (italics added) role in an institution's operations. However, the purpose of the consultation would be for the institution to develop information about the needs of its community and how they might be met so that it can make better judgments when formulating its plan objectives."[432]

Some industry stakeholders have repeated the theme of inappropriate or undue interference in bank operations over the years. The agencies appropriately responded that the purpose of community input is not to dictate a bank's product decisions or underwriting approaches but to provide insight into how it can respond to needs.

Ending Redlining through a Community-Centered Reform of the Community Reinvestment Act

While the agencies made the correct decision not to jettison the strategic plan option, they erred by not at least allowing banks to use agreements as the basis for the plans. While some banks would shun this approach, others like First Merchants welcome it. The agencies missed an opportunity in the 1995 rulemaking to promote and formally acknowledge a role for CRA agreements. Perhaps the agencies could have explicitly stated that CRA agreements could help a bank formulate a strategic plan.

Stephen Cross, Deputy Comptroller for Compliance at the OCC during the time of the rulemaking, remarked that:

"I believe that at the end of the day, the agencies concluded that they should not be in the business of enforcing private contracts (that is, CRA agreements). But I think community benefit agreements can serve as a framework for a strategic plan option. I look at introducing the strategic plan option as a significant step forward, a way of having an agreement with an agency but that allows for public input and get to an agreement that makes sense for the bank and the community, but that the agency could actually enforce because it was a strategic plan approved by the agency."[433]

Cross also mentioned that most banks have regarded strategic plans as burdensome and so have not executed them. He does not understand that because his more recent experience as a consultant suggests that strategic plans can end up with goals and measures that are less rigorous than traditional exams. He said that the state of the art must improve so that the strategic plan option is no longer regarded as daunting but at the same time reflects robust goal setting with substantial community input.[434] The agencies could help achieve that if they at least hold up CBAs as mechanisms to help banks develop robust strategic plans.

In addition, the agencies dropped the proposal that explicitly listed "second look" programs for denied applicants operated by community groups as earning banks favorable consideration on CRA exams, most likely due to some industry complaints about undue interferences. In future years, however, the agencies recognized community-bank partnerships that provided financial counseling and other community development activities eligible for consideration on CRA exams.[435] This revision basically achieves the same end of encouraging community participation but is couched in a more nuanced fashion in an interagency Question and Answer document rather than in a regulation so that perhaps it would be more palatable to some banks.

The agencies incorporated another means for incorporating community group input in the 1994 proposed rule when they adopted performance context as a part of the CRA exam. Performance context analysis as described in Chapter 2 is a part of the CRA exam that describes a local geographical area's economic and demographic conditions and how these conditions influence community needs and the ability of banks to respond to them.[436] The 1994 proposed rule introduced the collection by the examiner of information on needs and conditions from community-based organizations and local and state governments as part of data that would inform performance context analysis (called assessment context in the 1994 proposal).[437]

While this is an important opportunity for community participation in the exam, it should not be the only role for community participation. Community groups must be able to comment as well on a variety of bank performance issues ranging from the quality and affordability of their products to analysis of publicly available data on their record of lending to LMI and other underserved populations. The final 1995 regulations should have explicitly listed the range of community participation and input since it must be central to the CRA process. In later years, one of the agencies, the OCC, tried to limit community group input to just performance context issues, an inappropriate confinement considering the legislative intent of empowering communities and rectifying redlining.

Per the statute, the CRA record of the bank would influence the agencies' determination of whether to approve bank applications to merge. At the same time, the agencies recognized during the 1990's rulemaking that CRA ratings cannot be the only factor influencing merger decisions. Not only would this violate banking law's requirement that future public benefits be considered in the decisions, but public input would also be cut off during merger deliberations if CRA ratings were the sole factor.

In the 1993 proposal, the agencies stated:

> The CRA examination rating is not conclusive, however, and the proposal recognizes that other information related to CRA performance and the convenience and needs of communities, including information collected through public comment and through periodic and special reports, is also relevant and must be considered. As proposed, an "Outstanding" rating generally would result in a finding that the CRA aspect of the application is consistent with approval of the application and would receive extra weight in reviewing the application.[438]

In the 1994 proposal, the agencies changed their language regarding passing ratings because they admitted that it could be construed as truncating public comment opportunities. Specifically, the agencies stated that:

The agencies deleted language suggesting that ratings of Out-standing and Satisfactory would generally result in approval of applications since the agencies did not want to create an impression of a safe harbor. Agencies also wanted to make clear that they will consider comments on applications. The revised proposal explicitly states that interested parties would have the opportunity to comment on applications and that the agencies would take their views into account in considering the CRA performance of an institution in the applications process. The revised proposal also would specify that an institution's record of CRA performance would be considered in an institution's expansion proposals (as defined in the CRA) and may be the basis for approving, denying, or conditioning approval of an application.[439]

The industry pushed for a "safe harbor" in comments submitted in response to the 1994 proposal. They desired automatic approvals of merger applications if the banks involved had Outstanding ratings. The agencies declined to adopt this suggestion affirming that "The final rule implements without change the balance given in the 1994 proposal between CRA performance ratings and material information presented through public comment in the applications process."[440] The agency recognition of the importance of public comment has the added benefit of considering changes in CRA performance since the last rating and exam. Even a bank with an Outstanding rating can have performance that has declined in one or more local areas, particularly large banks with several assessment areas on their exams.

Restricting public comment would cut off opportunities for the agencies, banks, and community stakeholders to address bank weaknesses in performance, through an agency conditional merger approval order, a CBA, or informally with a bank stepping up its collaboration with local stakeholders in areas where performance needs to improve. In other words, a safe harbor is antithetical to CRA's mandate that banks have a *continual* and affirmative obligation to serve communities, not just a one-time obligation consisting of the years on the most recent CRA exam.

Objective measures created but agencies allow too much examiner discretion

In the 1993 proposed rule, the agencies sought to address the subjective and inconsistent nature of CRA exams by introducing relatively few performance measures that would involve clearer correlations between ratings and banks' performance on the subtests. On the lending test, for example, the agencies created a market share test that compared a bank's market share of home and small business loans in LMI tracts to its market share in middle- and upper-income (MUI) tracts. The proposed regulation provided examiners with clear guidance regarding ratings to be assigned based on the results of the market share test. An Outstanding rating would be earned if a bank's market share in LMI tracts "significantly" exceeded its market share in MUI tracts.[441] To illustrate this proposal, a bank could be eligible for an Outstanding rating if it made 4% of all loans in LMI tracts and 2% of all loans in MUI tracts.

Confronted with widespread industry opposition to this approach, the agencies modified their approach. In the 1994 proposal, the agencies stated,

"Many comments agreed that the mechanical application of numerical ratios would not foster fair and appropriate CRA assessments. The agencies continue to believe, given the wide diversity of institutions and communities, that it is inadvisable to provide such specific numerical ranges or ratios. The agencies expect the current (1994) proposal to increase the consistency and clarity of the examination process. By identifying a set of performance-based assessment criteria, and expanding the objective performance data available to examinations, institutions and the public will be better able to evaluate the basis on which examiner judgments are made. In addition, by providing more detailed profiles that involve several criteria, assessment under the current proposal will not turn on the evaluation of a single factor."[442]

The agencies were about half correct in their revisions. They correctly recognized that CRA performance includes several elements. In addition to examining lending in LMI tracts, the 1994 proposed rule expanded the lending test to include assessments of lending to LMI borrowers, community development lending and innovative and flexible practices.[443] If CRA exams include too few measures, bank attention could be inordinately focused on too few needs, which would be counterproductive. Cross confirmed that the agencies were concerned that an exclusive focus on LMI tracts could motivate banks to chase after MUI borrowers in those tracts, neglecting LMI borrowers and intensifying gentrification in some communities.[444] Meanwhile, LMI borrowers that sought to move to MUI communities could be neglected by banks.

While understanding the importance of several performance measures, the agencies erred by completely removing the correlation among results on performance measures with ratings. In order to achieve an Outstanding, the agencies replaced the guideline that the market share in LMI tracts needed to be higher than the market share in MUI tracts with a guideline in the 1995 rule stating that Outstanding in lending in LMI tracts could be earned when a bank achieved "An excellent geographic distribution of loans in its

Ending Redlining through a Community-Centered Reform of the Community Reinvestment Act

assessment area(s)."[445] This guidance is too vague and most likely resulted in findings reported in Chapter 2 in which large banks earning Outstanding ratings on the lending test had lower percentages of loans in LMI tracts and to LMI borrowers than smaller banks. Examiners likely made too many subjective judgements in the absence of any correlations between performance on ratios and ratings.

A more sensible compromise could have been achieved if the agencies had specified that generally certain ratios or results would correspond to certain ratings. If the examiner wanted to deviate from this in one or more assessment areas, the examiner would need to document reasons why on the CRA exams. In that manner, the guidance would allow for flexibility in the face of extenuating circumstances that is carefully documented in the exam while also providing a benchmark to be followed in most cases. It also would place the burden of proof on the examiner to document an exception rather than a vague guideline generating inconsistencies across exams and examiners. Stephen Cross agreed and stated, "you can always allow for exceptions, they just have to be explicitly identified and justified.[446]"

The bugaboo of credit allocation most likely moved the agencies away from a more prescriptive approach to the tests on the CRA exam. As Stephen Cross recalled, "That (the 1993 proposal) was lost for fear of being charged with credit allocation. The concept of credit allocation was front of mind among at least some of the agency principals."[447] Yet, several performance measures mitigate concerns of requiring banks to hit specific marks on a few measures since a bank could compensate for poor performance on some measures with better performance on other measures. Cross responded to the concept of several measures by stating, "If you have a range a metrics and allow a bank to fall short on some metrics and still pass. That seems to be another reasonable response (to concerns about credit allocation)."[448]

Moreover, the introduction of qualitative measures allows for the possibility of a bank boosting its rating on a test or overall if the bank made concerted efforts to offer innovative and flexible lending, investing, and service products. Qualitative measures can also cause ratings inflation in that some examiners do not carefully document why they judge performance to be outstanding on these measures and then award generous ratings. However, if qualitative measures are well constructed, they can help a bank compensate for some weaknesses in the quantitative measures and thus pass their exams. In other words, sensible and feasible methods existed for responding to bank criticism of formulaic approaches without erring too far towards examiner subjectivity.

The agencies reasoned that examiners would present data on exams that showed why an examiner may have judged performance to merit certain ratings.[449] However, exams tend to be so dense in many cases that a layperson reading them can skim over an examiner conclusion that seemed too cursory or lacking justification. I can pick up questionable calls because I have looked at exams for almost three decades. However, even for me, a lack of clarity on the weight of various performance measures or geographical areas in current exams can make it difficult to judge whether questionable calls can inappropriately influence ratings. For quantitative measures, clearer correlations between performance and ratings are needed to reduce inflation and to make exams more useful for the general public. The public can more readily see how ratings or points correspond to performance on specific metrics when rules are clearer than the 1995 final rule. That makes it easier for community organizations to participate in the CRA exam process. Chapter 8 will discuss agencies' efforts in the 2023 regulatory revisions to introduce more precision in the performance measures.

Like their decision on the lending test, the agencies opted against requiring a common metric on the investment test. The 1993 proposed rule had included a ratio of investments divided by capital.[450] The 1994 proposed rule eliminated this ratio, citing industry opposition, which claimed that such a ratio would penalize well-capitalized banks.[451] The bank opposition has some merit since the denominator would be larger for banks that have higher capital levels, making the ratio of investments to capital appear smaller for banks that are actually safer and sounder. However, this flaw should have been fixed by comparing investments to either assets or deposits. As it was, this ratio was replaced by a few other metrics including the dollar amount of investments and their innovativeness and complexity.

With a lackadaisical examiner, the dollar amount of investments can be used inappropriately since a simplistic analysis could equate a larger dollar amount with better CRA performance. However, a more revealing statistic would be the dollar amount of investments divided by bank capacity to make investments, which could be represented by either assets or deposits. This ratio would normalize the measure; in other words, it would basically reveal the dollar of investments per $1 million or $1 billion worth of capacity. It would therefore make comparisons among banks easier and facilitate scoring and rating.

Again, the upshot of too much examiner discretion was the creation of inconsistencies over a period of several years. OCC exams tend to compare investments against Tier 1 capital while FDIC exams compare investments against assets.[452] Moreover, the exams do not compare banks against their peers on these ratios, which renders the quantitative analysis less meaningful in terms of rating banks partly due how they compete against each other in their CRA programs. As a result, the measurement is less useful for community groups and other members of the public.

Agencies propose and then delete data on race and gender of small business borrowers and also remove explicit examination of lending by race

In the 1994 proposed rule, the agencies proposed that small business lending data not only include the census tract location of the business and the revenue size but also the race and gender of the small business owner. The agencies stated:

"The one significant new data reporting requirement would be that small business and small farm loan data reported to the agencies would include information on the race and gender of small business and farm borrowers to respond to concerns that the December (1993) proposal did not give enough weight to the fair lending aspect of an institution's CRA performance."[453]

In their comments on the 1994 proposed rule, community organizations reiterated fair lending concerns and urged the agencies to include an evaluation of lending by race and gender. However, even though the agencies had acknowledged these concerns, they backpedaled when issuing the 1995 final rule, saying that the CRA exam would not evaluate lending by race or gender but that fair lending reviews which accompanied CRA exams would test bank compliance with the Fair Housing Act and the Equal Credit Opportunity Act (ECOA). The final rating would be adjusted if discrimination was found.[454] Along the same lines, the agencies deleted their proposal to require banks to collect and report race and gender small business loan data. They stated:

"This provision, which was the most frequently addressed issue in the comments, was proposed to support the fair lending component of the CRA assessment. The agencies have removed this proposed requirement from the final rule. These (supportive) commenters believed that the information was critical to determine whether discrimination was occurring in small business and small farm lending. Nearly every industry comment opposed the collection as proposed. These commenters stated that the requirement was burdensome and the data, as proposed to be collected and reported, would be of limited utility."[455]

This was a regrettable agency decision in response to a stale industry argument. Data collection is not unduly burdensome as revealed by a multi-decade history of banks successfully reporting data, including Home Mortgage Disclosure Act (HMDA) data on home lending, without exiting lending or hiking interest rates charged to consumers. Data helps banks figure out how to compete better in markets as well as helping the public achieve fair lending purposes such as increasing responsible lending to traditionally underserved populations. For example, shortly after the HMDA data included demographics on borrowers in addition to census tract locations of loans, the more affordable conventional home purchase lending to African Americans and Hispanics increased at a considerably faster clip than such lending to Whites from 1993 through 1995.[456] Data increases accountability and enhanced data encourages banks to increase lending to populations that had been traditionally underserved. The data on race and gender for small business and small farm lending would have to wait upon an act of Congress, the Dodd Frank Wall Street Reform and Consumer Protection Act of 2010 (as discussed in chapter 6).

Accompanying the decision to remove data on race and gender of small business borrowers, the agencies also deleted parts of the CRA exams that had explicitly analyzed lending by race. Before the CRA regulatory reforms in 1995, federal CRA exams conducted data analysis regarding applications from people of color as part of Factor D, which considered special purpose credit programs and whether banks discriminated by discouraging applicants from using these programs.[457] The deletion of this analysis was a significant loss that reduced the accountability of banks to reach populations burdened with a legacy of redlining and continuing redlining in some cases. While the overall thrust of the 1995 final rule was positive in introducing more rigor in CRA exams, this deletion was a loss.

Stephen Cross concluded:

> Agency lawyers were uncomfortable with race and gender because the statute was about lending and low- and moderate-income areas, and some agency principals were particularly vociferous on that score as well.[458]

The challenge going forward would be whether stakeholders could revisit the issue of racial and gender disparities in a way that would be rigorous and also pass legal muster, an issue that will be revisited in Chapter 8.

The agencies introduced nuance in ratings but then removed penalties for subpar performance

As discussed above, the initial numerical ratings had five categories. The agencies recognized the importance of five ratings in terms of revealing gradations in performance. In the 1993 proposed rule, the agencies affirmed that they "have proposed five ratings rather than four ratings for each test to measure as accurately as possible variations in performance among institutions. The agencies propose to have only four composite ratings, however, because the four ratings are required by the statute."[459] The 1995 rule retained this important decision. The agencies stated that, "This will permit the agencies, banks and thrifts, and their customers to recognize the stronger performances on the lending, investment, and service tests of those institutions that are doing a very good, but not quite outstanding, job of helping to meet the credit needs of their communities."[460]

Nuance in ratings was not accompanied by either penalties for poor performance or incentives for good performance. In 1993, the agencies had proposed the possibility of terminating a bank's federal insurance of its deposits if it received a Substantial Noncompliance rating. The agencies reasoned that this was "a method of improving the effectiveness and fairness of CRA. If the consequences for inadequate performance are restricted to the application process, then institutions not contemplating applications may have little incentive to comply."[461] The 1995 final rule discarded this approach with sparse discussion and a mere sentence stating that "based on further analysis of their statutory authority, the agencies have removed these provisions."[462]

The agencies were attempting to address a flaw in CRA. Unless a bank submits an application, including a merger application, CRA does not factor significantly in agency enforcement actions. While termination of federal insurance for bank may seem like an appropriate penalty for the lowest CRA rating that represents a failure to reinvest in communities, it might be too blunt. It could result in political pressure on examiners to never mete out a Substantial Noncompliance. Another possibility is adjusting fees banks pay to the agencies for supervising them and ensuring that they are safe and sound and non-discriminatory. Higher fees could be paid by banks with lower ratings. This way, each rating has a consequence with better performance being rewarded with lower fees and worse performance being penalized by higher fees. In addition, as discussed in Chapters 6, proposed CRA legislation has included improvement plans subject to public comment when a bank scores Low Satisfactory and below in either a geographical area or on a subtest. This is a form of a penalty – albeit a corrective one – that provides an incentive to perform better and that can also benefit communities in terms of increasing CRA-related loans, investments and services.

Conclusion

Rulemaking involves a series of equitable and carefully thought-out compromises between the desires of various stakeholders. In CRA's case, the main stakeholders are banks and community organizations. In some cases, the desires of the constituencies coincided such as the desire for more objective and consistent exams. The agencies achieved a degree of success in their balancing act by introducing objective quantitative measures but erred when removing most guidelines tying scores on metrics to actual performance.

The agencies hewed to the spirit of CRA by upholding most forms of community input and participation in the CRA exam process. However, they missed an opportunity to more formally incorporate CBAs into the CRA process such as the strategic plan option. This had been requested by community groups and some industry stakeholders. They also missed an opportunity to comprehensively enhance data on CRA exams in the case of small business and farm lending to include race and gender in addition to the location and revenue size of the small business. The deletion of proposed data collection was accompanied by deletion of an exam component that assessed lending by race. This diminished accountability and community input. At the same time, the agencies recognized that nuance was important in CRA exams and introduced five ratings on the subtests though they felt constrained from altering the four overall ratings described in the CRA statute. On a series of choices and compromises, the 1995 rule got it about half right, which established a foundation of reasonably thought-out subtests. A poor rule would have gotten a lot more wrong in terms of not abiding by the intent of the statute and would have not formed a foundation upon which to build. Overall, the 1995 rule withstood the test of time and endured for several years. However, all rules become dated due to technological changes and business models. Chapter 8 discusses the process of updating the 1995 rule.

6

Rollback: Congress Weakens CRA

After the 1995 CRA regulatory reforms, Congress undertook an effort that some lawmakers considered modernizing or reforming the financial industry. Free market proponents desired to tear down the barriers between banking, insurance, and securities that the 1933 Glass-Stegall Act created in the wake of the Great Depression and the excessive risk taking by the nation's big banks leading up to the economic crash.[463] At the same time, opponents of CRA, most notably former Senator Phil Gramm saw this as an opportunity to discourage community group participation in the CRA process and to weaken CRA generally.

Community-based organizations were skeptical about the free market benefits of the Gramm-Leach-Bliley Act of 1999 that Senator Phil Gramm and two of his colleagues promoted. Firstly, community organizations were concerned that allowing banks, insurance companies, and securities firms to merge would increase concentration in the financial industry, leading to oligopolistic pricing and inferior service. Secondly, they were concerned that if CRA was not applied across all the companies (affiliates and subsidiaries) in the new financial holding companies created by this law, the conglomerates could shift assets from their banks to the non-CRA covered parts of the holding company and thereby decrease their CRA responsibilities. If Congress allowed financial holding companies to become substantially larger and more powerful, shouldn't there be a concomitant increase in reinvestment requirements? While some sympathetic lawmakers tried to amend the bill to apply CRA to the non-bank parts of the holding companies that lend and introduce data disclosure requirements for insurance companies, they were unsuccessful.[464] Moreover, even these friendly amendments would have fallen short of a systematic application of CRA across all affiliates and subsidiaries of the new holding companies.

This chapter begins with a discussion of the CRA sections of the Gramm-Leach-Bliley Act (GLBA).[465] The CRA sunshine section of GLBA diminished the original purposes of CRA to empower communities and elevate them as partners working with banks to rectify redlining and increase reinvestment. In addition to CRA sunshine, the other main provision that Senator Gramm succeeded in incorporating into the law was less frequent CRA exams for banks under $250 million in assets. Proponents of CRA countered the Gramm amendments by attaching a modest CRA requirement imposed upon banks seeking to become financial holding companies.

After GLBA, lawmakers sympathetic to CRA introduced CRA modernization acts during the 2000s that attempted to apply CRA broadly throughout the financial industry and mitigate the harm to

CRA inflicted by GLBA. While these bills did not pass, they created important blueprints for modernizing CRA. One key provision of these bills, improving small business and farm data by including race and gender (which the federal bank agencies flirted with in their CRA regulatory update as discussed in Chapter 5) became law upon passage of the Dodd Frank Wall Street Reform and Consumer Protection Act of 2010. Moving on from GLBA, the chapter discusses major provisions of these CRA modernization bills.

CRA sunshine seeks to lessen participation of community groups in the CRA process

Senator Gramm was the driving force behind efforts to weaken CRA as GLBA was working its way through Congress. Gramm's name is included in the law's title as one of three main authors of the bill along with former Representatives James Leach and Thomas Bliley. Despite considerable opposition from CRA supporters in Congress, Gramm saw the GLBA as a vehicle to diminish CRA since GLBA had powerful support in the financial industry and had bipartisan support in Congress. He cleverly couched his main proposal, CRA sunshine, as a means to increase transparency in the CRA process. After all, what was wrong with publicly disclosing CRA agreements made between banks and community groups? Isn't that how CRA is supposed to work – increasing accountability through disclosure?

While he protested that the attempt was to promote disclosure, his views suggest additional objectives behind CRA sunshine. Gramm declared in an interview:

> Nobody in 1977 ever envisioned that you would have banks making cash payments to community groups. Nobody ever envisioned that banks would enter into agreements with individuals

whereby they would give them hundreds of thousands of dollars cash in return for them signing contracts to not oppose CRA applications (merger applications).

We're trying to deal with these abuses…No one is talking about repealing CRA or undercutting CRA. The debate is about bringing integrity, sunshine, and relevance to CRA. If a merchant was paying a kickback racket, the fact that they (banks) were still making money would not make the Mafia action OK. The point is, should CRA produce cash payments? I don't think so. It was never anticipated in the law.[466]

One of the pundits in the Gramm camp wrote an article around this time calling CRA a "trillion dollar bank shakedown," using figures on agreements that NCRC had provided to him.[467] What is curious is that these CRA opponents perceived harmful activity by community organizations to be a preeminent problem in the banking sector, instead of documented discrimination and redlining that occurred over decades. Proxmire and his allies designed CRA to empower the victims of discrimination, community residents and their organizations, to have a role in rectifying redlining. As Congress was passing CRA, advocates were already striking agreements with banks to channel loans and investments in underserved neighborhoods. Far from undue interference in the marketplace, it would seem that contracts among banks and community stakeholders is a time honored mechanism in our capitalistic system to conduct business and tap underserved markets.

Nevertheless, Gramm designed CRA sunshine to deter community groups from participating in the CRA process and offering comments during exams or when agencies were considering merger applications. GLBA defined a CRA agreement as a contract between a bank and a non-governmental third party that involved grants in excess of $10,000 or loans in excess of $50,000 over a year. The dollar amounts were low in order to ensure broad coverage. Requirements to disclose these agreements were only triggered if the non-governmental entity "commented on, testified about, or discussed with the institution" CRA performance or issues associated with CRA.

If a community organization, as a non-governmental third party, declined to disclose its agreement by providing a copy to a federal agency, the CRA agreement would not be enforceable, meaning the bank would not have to comply with its promises to reinvest. If an agency determined that the non-governmental third-party misspent funds such as using funds for "personal financial gain," the penalties included surrender of any funding received from banks that were misspent and a prohibition against the community organization from entering into any future agreement for a period of ten years.

The disclosure requirements included submission of the original agreement and annual disclosures of grants, loans, and investments required by the agreement. In addition, a non-governmental entity would be required to annually disclose the use of any funds received by a bank including for "compensation, administrative expenses, travel, entertainment, consulting and professional fees paid."[468]

In totality, the sunshine requirement would be broadly applicable, would be triggered by speech protected by the First Amendment, would require detailed annual disclosures, and would involve stiff penalties if a federal bank agency deemed that the non-governmental entity was in violation. A ten-year prohibition on securing agreements is unsettling in that if a regulatory agency erroneously determined that a nonprofit misspent funds, a nonprofit housing developer or other entity could not secure construction loans or other contracts for a decade. In other words, it could put community-based organizations out of business since it would make it very difficult for them to carry out their normal business of revitalizing neighborhoods. In opposition to CRA sunshine, NCRC maintained that strenuous enforcement of it would violate a core purpose of CRA to encourage community group participation in reinvestment. It would also interfere with the exercise of free speech by burdening the use of speech with detailed disclosure requirements, the violation of which would result in significant punishment. Commenting to the federal agencies, NCRC referred to a Supreme Court decision:

> Justice William Brennan's majority opinion of NAACP v. Button, 371 U.S. 415 (1963) stated, "(T)here is no longer any doubt that the First and Fourteenth Amendments protect certain forms of orderly group activity..(A) vague and broad statute lends itself to selective enforcement against unpopular causes…In such circumstances, a statute broadly curtailing group activity leading to litigation may easily become a weapon of oppression, however, evenhanded its terms appear…"[469]

After passage of GLBA, the agencies promulgated CRA sunshine regulations as they were required to do. However, perhaps, the counterproductive nature of the CRA sunshine provision motivated the agencies to adopt a posture of benign neglect. Over the years, banks have disclosed the CBAs that they negotiated with NCRC to the agencies. To my knowledge, the agencies have not required NCRC to make annual disclosures. As discussed in Chapter 5 about the 1995 CRA rule, the agencies decided that they should not enforce private contracts in the form of CRA agreements. Their decision was an astute one in the context of enforcement of the CRA sunshine law as promoted by Gramm.

During the GLBA debates, NCRC willingly disclosed agreements to Senator Gramm's office to show that there was nothing to hide. After the agencies implemented CRA sunshine, NCRC submitted a Freedom of Information Act (FOIA) request to the agencies asking for copies of agreements. Covering the period of 1999 through 2001, NCRC obtained about 700 agreements. Of the $3.6 billion in loans and investments committed by CRA agreements, NCRC only found $11.8 million or .3 percent of the total funding devoted towards general operating support for community groups.[470] This large sample size showed that contrary to Senator Gramm's assertions, agreements did not mostly channel funds to community organizations negotiating the agreements. Instead, the great majority of the funds supported loans and investments in local affordable housing and economic development. In addition, the support received by community groups typically funded housing counseling and other activities that help banks make home purchase and other loans in underserved communities.

Periodically, skeptics recycle complaints about CBAs as justification for CRA sunshine.. In an opinion piece published by the American Banker, the fair lending consultant Ken Thomas alleged that CBAs were the "real basis for (agency) approval" (of mergers) even though the vast majority of mergers do not involve CBAs. What these skeptics do not acknowledge is that community-based organizations have maintained that CBAs should be an option for banks to demonstrate public benefits arising from mergers, not a requirement. Moreover, the skeptics keep insisting on CRA sunshine disclosure.

Thomas continued, "The Fed should not only require all financial details of CBAs be made public, but also monitor and enforce them, since they are a de facto condition of merger approval. Without a public accounting of a CBA, there is no way to know how much money is going to the communities and how much to the coalitions and local community groups. At least one member of Congress agreed on the need for total disclosure, arguing it would be consistent with the CRA sunshine requirements of the 1999 Gramm-Leach-Bliley Act."[471]

Community-based organizations and CRA advocates have never opposed disclosure and believe deeply in transparency as an accountability mechanism. What they are opposed to are attempts to discourage free speech and participation in the CRA process.

Congress and the agencies should consider methods for modifying CRA sunshine to maintain the benefits of disclosure and avoid unnecessary penalties. A possible way forward is for the agencies to acknowledge the role of CBAs and then monitor their implementation. If a bank includes a CBA in its merger application and represents it as a public benefit arising from the merger, then the agencies should follow up in subsequent CRA exams to verify that the public benefits occurred. To the extent that this is an enforcement activity, it is quite different than the penalties imposed by CRA sunshine for failure to follow difficult disclosure rules.

Another aspect of replacing CRA sunshine with a more effective accountability mechanism is the use of the community development financing data required as part of the 2023 regulatory reform of CRA described in Chapter 8. The data could serve well as an accountability mechanism for CBAs since it would include grants to community organizations. Under the CRA regulation, banks would report community development finance data including grants to the agencies. The data reporting would include whether the grant or other financing benefited low-income households or areas with high poverty levels or areas with low levels of community development financing.[472] Accompanying information on grants could be impact data such as how many clients were helped under a grant for housing counseling and how many of them purchased homes or improved their credit scores. Banks and community groups could collaborate in developing and submitting impact data, such as that described in Chapter 1 regarding equity accumulation for homeowners residing in nonprofit developments. Data of this nature would separate out grants made under CBAs that were used for the time-honored business of community revitalization targeting underserved communities versus those that were not effective because of any shortcoming by the bank or community organization recipient.

A rigorous CRA exam would encourage banks to fund community organizations and activities that were effective versus those that were not for whatever reason, including any instances of malfeasance. The CRA examiner would have a role in identifying and recommending to banks that they continue supporting effective partnerships and programs with community groups and cease supporting the ineffective ones. The CRA examiner could also monitor community development lending and investment levels motivated by CBAs using the new data. Using community development financing data in his manner would be a more appropriate and less punitive method than CRA sunshine of supporting successful reinvestment activities and discouraging ineffective ones.

If CBAs were submitted as part of merger applications and/or part of developing CRA strategic plans, the CBAs should be publicly available on the agencies' websites. The subsequent CRA exam can then assess bank compliance with the CBA. The bank's rating can be positively impacted it the bank met or exceeded its CBA goals or negatively impacted if it fell far short of its goals. Any member of the public can comment on whether the CBA and the partnerships it motivated served communities well and/or whether the bank needs to reach out to other geographical areas and nonprofit organizations not included in the CBA. In this manner, the public and the examiner can gage whether the CBA helped the bank serve all communities equitably or whether there were any deficiencies in the CBA's coverage that the bank should address by seeking out additional opportunities to serve communities that were not included in the CBA. Ratings and scores for assessment areas would help steer the bank to increase lending, investment, and services in communities not served well, whether because a CBA did not include the communities or the bank's performance lagged for another reason.

Besides CRA sunshine, the other significant weakening that former Senator Gramm secured in GLBA was less frequent exams for small banks with assets under $250 million. As mentioned in Chapter 2, GLBA specified that exams were to occur once every five years for small banks whose most recent rating was Outstanding and once every four years for those whose most recent rating was Satisfactory. For small banks with the two failed ratings of Needs to Improve and Substantial Noncompliance, the statute provides the agencies with discretion regarding exam frequency.[473] The agencies had already streamlined small bank exams so less frequent exams were not necessary from a point of view of reducing burden. However, from the point of view of accountability, mandating exams for a category of banks to occur once every four or five years could mean in practice that several small banks are examined only once during a decade, particularly if the exam occurred in the middle of the decade. Considering that small bank mergers do not typically generate community comments as often as large bank mergers, less frequent exams significantly loosened the main accountability mechanism for this class of banks.

Proponents of CRA countered GLBA's CRA weakening with one provision designed to increase accountability for banks that sought to become financial holding companies (FHCs). FHCs can own non-bank subsidiaries and affiliates such as insurance companies and securities firms. Before being allowed to become FHCs, the banks would need to have at least a Satisfactory CRA rating.[474] While well intentioned, this provision would not have much force in practice since about 98 percent of banks have passed their CRA exams over the last several years as described in Chapter 2. A more direct method of stimulating more reinvestment financing would have been to apply CRA to the non-bank entities a bank would be acquiring or establishing. The votes for this approach were not available when GLBA was passed. However, even a mostly symbolic nod to CRA such as the FHC provision reminded stakeholders that CRA had Congressional allies who would work for improving the law in subsequent years.

CRA modernization bills that aim to fix GLBA flaws don't pass but establish blueprints for reform

Right on the heels of the passage of GLBA, two Midwest Representatives, former Rep. Thomas Barrett of Wisconsin and Luis Gutierrez of Illinois, approached NCRC to develop a CRA modernization bill that would not only defang CRA sunshine but would also rectify the shortcomings in GLBA by applying CRA broadly throughout the financial industry. These two lead sponsors of the bill were joined by 29 co-sponsors in the July 2000 introduction of the Community Reinvestment Act of 2000.[475] In July of 2001, the Congressmen re-introduced the bill, which had 36 co-sponsors. Rep. Thomas Barrett eloquently described the rationale behind the bill stating:

"CRA will become less effective if it is not updated to keep pace with the rapid changes that are occurring in the financial services marketplace as a result of the Gramm-Leach-Bliley Financial Modernization Act of 1999. The Community Reinvestment Modernization Act of 2001 will ensure that the hundreds of thousands of Americans, most often minorities and the working poor, will continue to have access to capital and credit. The bill we are reintroducing today will update CRA to match the increased market powers the Financial Modernization Act creates. It will make banks accountable again by updating CRA to cover all loans and lenders. This not only includes mortgage companies, but also insurance companies, investment firms and other affiliates of banks that will increasingly be offering loans and basic banking products in the new financial world. The bottom line is that CRA is good for business. It not only levels the playing field to make sure that all creditworthy Americans have access to capital and credit, it makes good business sense."[476]

Congressmen Barrett and Gutierrez were thinking beyond one of the original rationales for CRA as applied to banks. This rationale was that in return for banks receiving federal deposit insurance, they had an obligation to serve all communities. Like Barrett and Gutierrez, the original authors of CRA also were thinking more broadly and understood that an affirmative obligation can and should be applied to other private sector entities playing key roles in our economy. Author and former Senate Banking staff member Robert Kuttner stated that his colleague Kenneth A. McClean "found the language in nineteenth century legislation on grain elevators that you have an obligation to serve the public needs and convenience. There is a long legacy of different kinds of legislation that created an affirmative obligation for a private actor to do something."[477] Along the same lines, NCRC President and CEO Jesse Van Tol asserted, "Banking is a privilege, not a right. Conceptually, there are a lot of entities in some shape or form that are privileged to do their businesses by the government and in exchange they ought to produce a community benefit."[478]

For many years, discussions about applying CRA to other parts of the financial industry stalled since federal guarantees and subsidies did not seem as visible for other parts of the industry. However, this perspective changed dramatically during the 2008 financial crisis. Institutions' financing of abusive lending was a major cause of the crisis and the government had to bail out the culprits. A dramatic illustration that non-banks would be rescued by the federal government occurred when Bear Stearns was the first non-bank to access credit via the Federal Reserve Discount window during the crisis.[479]

Eugene Ludwig, a former Comptroller of the Currency, recently stated, "If you're supported by the federal government, economically — and everybody is to some degree or another, and that is particularly obvious right now — then in particular, you have a broader set of responsibilities, it seems to me. To perhaps put a finer point on this, where the [Federal Reserve] is using its tools to support a business, or an investor in a business, it is using the government safety net, and this should particularly convey upon the recipients' additional societal obligations."[480]

While it is plausible to apply an obligation to serve all communities to several private entities, a financial institution is distinct from other companies in that a financial institution invests and safeguards individual and community wealth. When financial companies' abilities to use people's wealth is unchecked, socially undesirable consequences such as monopolization and manipulation result, as argued by former Supreme Court Justice Louis Brandeis in the early 20th century.[481] In contrast, under robust regulatory oversight involving a community reinvestment obligation and public accountability, financial institutions are more likely to use other people's money in socially optimal manners.

Curbing discriminatory behavior remains a compelling motivation for CRA as applied to banks and is also a motivation for applying CRA to non-bank financial institutions. Greg Squires conducted several studies in the 1990s documenting racial disparities in access to homeowners' insurance. In addition, Squires reported that "the National Association of Insurance Commissioners (an organization of state insurance commissioners who regulate the insurance industry) concluded in an analysis of 33 cities in 20 states that there is considerable evidence that residents of urban communities, particularly low-income and minority neighborhoods, face greater difficulty in obtaining high-quality homeowners insurance coverage through the voluntary market, when compared to residents of other areas."[482] More recently, ProPublica and Consumer Reports found that the disparities in premiums between African American and White neighborhoods for automobile insurance in California, Illinois, Texas and Missouri were higher than can be explained by differences in risk.[483] In addition, Emily Flitter documented that people of color of all income levels had more difficulty than Whites receiving payments for their claims involving damage to their homes from insurance companies.[484]

Although discriminatory behavior in the financial industry is not the root of all racial or income disparities in wealth, it is certainly one of the major factors. Narrowing the significant disparities thus remains another compelling reason to apply CRA broadly across the financial industry. The Urban Institute calculated that families near the top of the wealth distribution had six times the wealth of those in the middle of the distribution in 1963 but now have twelve times the wealth. Viewed through a racial lens, the average White family had seven times the wealth of an African American family and five times the wealth of a Hispanic family by 2016, a disparity that persisted since 1963.[485] Moreover, the Pew Research Center found that a slight majority of Americans have some stock holdings mostly through 401(k)s and other retirement savings but the amount invested in stock varies widely by income (a median investment of $8,400 for those with incomes under $35,000 compared to $138,700 for those with incomes of $100,000 and higher). Moreover, about 61 percent of White households owned stock compared to about 30 percent for Hispanics and African Americans.[486]

As the authors of CRA modernization bills reasoned, if community reinvestment obligations remain confined to banks, CRA will cover a shrinking segment of the financial industry and its success in addressing disparities in wealth and revitalizing communities would be diminished. Speaking in the late 1990s, former Comptroller Ludwig stated, "At the end of 1996, for the first time, the dollar volume of mutual funds exceeded the dollar volume of bank deposits."[487] By 2017, global non-bank assets totaled $52 trillion, up dramatically from $30 trillion in 2010.[488]

The significant number of resources in non-banks include trillions of dollars in business and assets. Insurance companies collected $1.3 trillion in premiums in 2021, with property and casualty insurance accounting for about half of this amount.[489] The U.S. mutual fund industry had $27 trillion in total assets.[490] Finally, independent mortgage companies have out-competed banks in recent years, making more than half of all home loans, according to NCRC research.[491]

CRA modernization bills strengthened CRA as applied to banks and applied CRA to non-banks

The CRA Modernization Act of 2000 and 2001 sought to strengthen CRA as applied to banks by making the CRA exam more rigorous and deleting the harmful aspects of CRA sunshine. In recognition of racial disparities in lending, the bills directed the federal bank agencies to examine lending in neighborhoods of "different racial characteristics" in addition to low- and moderate-income neigh-borhoods.[492] To further protect people of color, the bill directed the federal agencies to lower ratings if they detected significant amounts of predatory lending.[493] The bill's authors inserted this provision because as early as 2000, advocates had raised alarms about high cost subprime lending targeted towards communities of color. It was important to ensure that banks were not engaged in that lending.

This was also the first bill in several years to update data report-ing requirements in order to bolster CRA exams and help weed out abusive lending. The CRA Modernization Act would enhance the HMDA data to include "information on loan pricing and terms, including interest rates, bona fide discount points, origination fees, financing of lump sum insurance premium payments, balloon pay-ment, and prepayment penalties."[494] It was also the first bill to call for the reporting of demographic characteristics of small business loan applicants including the race and gender of the small business owner and the revenue size of the small business.[495] The HMDA enhancements and small business reporting would make their way into the 2010 Dodd Frank Wall Street Reform and Consumer Pro-tection Act.[496]

The CRA Modernization Act also increased the breadth of CRA exams by requiring all affiliates of banks that lend or offer banking services to be included on CRA exams.[497] The bill directed the agencies to conduct evaluations and assign ratings to each state and metropolitan area in which a bank has branches. In addition, evaluations and ratings were to cover areas where banks had .5 percent of the total amount of loans, regardless of whether they had branches there.[498] This provision intended to encompass the increasing share of lending occurring beyond bank branches. The market share of less than 1 percent might seem small but when I did research for NCRC member organizations, this market share often equated to 50 or even 100 loans, which seemed to merit a separate CRA assessment in order to hold banks accountable to meeting needs in their communities. To counter CRA grade inflation, the ratings system would be adjusted by introducing Low- and High-Satisfactory ratings as possible overall ratings.[499]

The CRA Modernization Act repealed the reduced frequency of exams for smaller banks under $250 million. It also softened CRA sunshine by just requiring the disclosure of the initial text of CRA agreements by banks and did not require disclosure based on the exercise of free speech and participation in the CRA process by community organizations.[500]

As early as 2000, the authors of the CRA Modernization Act recognized that independent mortgage companies had a significant market share and should be covered by CRA. The Act established an examination regime similar to those for banks which highlighted scrutiny of a mortgage company's retail lending to LMI borrowers and people of color in areas in which a mortgage company had more than .5 percent of the total loans in a geographical area. Examiners were to analyze whether the mortgage companies offered flexible loan terms and conditions to facilitate lending to underserved communities while at the same time lowering ratings if evaluations turned up evidence of predatory lending. Exams were to evaluate the number of community development investments in affordable housing and community development as well as assessments of community development services including homeownership counseling.[501]

The CRA Modernization Act introduced a novel sanction for ratings below Low Satisfactory. A mortgage company receiving failed ratings would not be permitted to sell their loans to Fannie Mae and Freddie Mac, cutting off an important method for these companies to acquire more capital with which to make more loans. Before implementing this sanction, however, the regulatory agency (the bill had designated this agency to be the Department of Housing and Urban Development) would provide an opportunity for the company to execute an agreement with the agency for compliance with CRA. If the mortgage company experienced sanctions, it could still make loans insured by the Federal Housing Administration (FHA). The provision of the bill calling for a sanction offered a chance for contrition and corrective action before the sanction was imposed. In the case of companies failing to execute a restorative agreement, the sanctions did not completely shut off business by maintaining an outlet to the FHA so that the company could improve on its next CRA exam.[502]

To more fully increase wealth building in underserved communities, the CRA Modernization Act also applied CRA to securities companies and insurance firms. The bill would evaluate retail activities in much the same way for these companies as it would for banks. In the case of securities and insurance companies, the exams would assess the distribution of retail customers including those in LMI neighborhoods. Community development investments in affordable housing and economic development would also be assessed.[503] As described by Liz Cohen and Rosalia Agresti in the case of securities companies, "Investment banks could create funds for and provide direct investment in businesses owned by low-income individuals and minorities or businesses located in low-income and minority communities. Broker-dealers could sell shares in these funds or the actual debt and equity securities issued. Investment banks and broker dealers could provide training and technical assistance for individuals, entrepreneurs, and small businesses. They could locate facilities in underserved areas."[504]

Insurance companies likewise have expertise in investing and could develop similar vehicles to benefit LMI neighborhoods. In order to acquire data for CRA exams, the CRA Modernization Act would impose data collection reporting requirements similar to HMDA for insurance companies and securities firms.[505] These bill provisions were inspired by experiences on a state level. A few states had experimented with HMDA like data for insurance companies.[506] California has also imposed data collection regarding community development investments for insurance companies.[507]

One of the final and important codas of the CRA Modernization Act was to require banks seeking to become financial holding companies to apply to the federal bank agencies. The agencies would be required to consider the riskiness of the proposed mergers and the CRA record of the entities involved. The general public would have an opportunity to submit comments on the applications.[508] This would correct a flaw of GLBA which allowed banks to establish financial holding companies and get into the business of insurance and securities without an application and public input.

The next CRA modernization bill to be introduced was the Community Reinvestment Modernization Act of 2009. The lead sponsor was Rep. Eddie Bernice Johnson of Texas. A former staff member of Rep. Barrett's office became a staff person for Rep. Johnson after Barrett left Congress to become Mayor of Milwaukee, Wisconsin. He then worked with NCRC to update the CRA modernization bill. This bill had more co-sponsors at 60 than the previous ones.[509] The provisions were similar to the modernization bills of 2000 and 2001 with a few enhancements. The CRA modernization bill of 2009 retained the improvements to HMDA data and mandated the creation of small business and farm loan data including demographics of the applicants.[510] In light of the subprime loan crisis and the Great Recession, enhancements to HMDA data included information on loan delinquency and defaults so that the public and the federal agencies could identify lenders with high loan failure rates and take appropriate action.[511] Upon the introduction of the bill, Johnson stated, " In recent months, we have seen the catastrophic effects that unsound loans can have on families and communities. Today we take another step toward ensuring that financial institutions lend responsibly, while continuing to encourage them to invest in all the communities in which they operate. The Community Reinvestment Act has a long record of benefiting low- and middle-income neighborhoods and the banks and thrifts that lend in those neighborhoods. Expanding CRA to cover all financial institutions will make this good law even better."[512]

Like its predecessors, the CRA Modernization Act of 2009 applied CRA to mortgage companies, securities firms, and insurance companies. However, it went one step further and applied CRA to credit unions. The CRA exam for credit unions was to be like those of banks with one exception. Some credit unions have a field of membership that consists of customers affiliated with an institution like a church or an employer. In those cases, the assessment area would be the credit union's common bond or its field of membership. Other credit unions cover specific geographical areas; for these credit unions, assessment areas delineation would mirror that of banks.[513] The state of Massachusetts has a state CRA law and has been examining credit unions for several years.[514] The CRA Modernization Act of 2009's credit union provision was influenced by Massachusetts's experience.

The CRA modernization bills of 2001, 2002, and 2009 did not make it to the floor of the House of Representatives and were not scheduled for votes in the relevant House Committees. A large constituency exists for these bills and includes hundreds of community-based organizations, sympathetic Mayors and Governors, and progressive minded churches and other religious institutions. This constituency helped generate 60 co-sponsors for the 2009 bill. However, the other side includes the financial industry lobby. A CRA modernization bill takes on all the lobbies of the banks and non-banks. Credit unions have strong lobbying organizations as well. Not even the financial crisis and Great Recession in the late 2000s created an environment ripe for CRA modernization. The financial industry at large had failed to serve communities in a safe and sound manner. In return for a rescue, it would have been eminently reasonable to impose an affirmative obligation across the industry to serve communities in a safe and sound manner.

It is hard to state conclusively why CRA modernization bills could not advance, but a comparison of the presence of banks and financial institutions compared to community-based organizations can shed some light. Every Congressional district seems to have a community bank, a credit union, or some other financial institution. As much as the reinvestment movement has tried, coalitions of community-based organizations including NCRC do not have the same presence across Congressional districts. NCRC and its members, for example, have traditionally been clustered on the east coast, the west coast, and in some areas of the Midwest such as Illinois and Chicago, the home base of NPA and the Woodstock Institute. In addition to unequal presence in Congressional districts, banks and financial institutions have more extensive executive and managerial staff than the thinner staff of community organizations, which are fewer and under-resourced. While my supposition is that the benefits outweigh the costs of CRA for financial institutions as well as society as a whole, the more resourced and staffed financial industry will feel costs more acutely and be a position to better articulate them consistently and repetitively to Congress than community groups can articulate the benefits of reinvestment. Thus, the stalemate in legislative action. While community-based organizations have staved off the most harmful proposals for weakening CRA, it has been hard to significantly expand the law.

The best that could be done was to include enhanced HMDA data requirements and the introduction of race and gender data for small business and farm lending in the Dodd-Frank Wall Street Reform and Consumer Protection Act of 2010 as described above. Staff from the Treasury Department told me that they consulted with the CRA Modernization bills and pulled the data provisions from the bills. Improved data disclosure at least provides opportunities for CRA bills at a later date if the data indicates persistent disparities in access to financial services by race, gender or income. Indeed, the passage of HMDA in 1975 helped spur the passage of CRA in 1977 since HMDA documented disparities by demographics of neighborhood as documented in Chapter 4.

The early version of the Dodd-Frank Act included a provision to shift CRA oversight from the federal bank agencies to the newly established Consumer Financial Protection Bureau (CFPB).[515] Authorizing one agency to implement CRA likely would have been an improvement. The federal bank agencies were slow to enact needed changes in the CRA regulation, in part, because trying to obtain agreement among three or four of them is quite difficult. The decision-making at the CFPB would have been quicker. However, the bank lobby did not like this change, perhaps because they were accustomed to their regulatory agencies or were concerned that a new agency would implement tougher or unpredictable CRA exams.

CRA modernization activity on the Senate side was quiet until the arrival of Senator Elizabeth Warren. Starting in 2018, the Senator introduced the American Housing and Economic Mobility Act in successive Congressional sessions including in 2021 and most recently in 2024.[516] This ambitious bill funded the expansion of the affordable housing supply, created a downpayment program for first time homebuyers, enhanced fair housing protections to include outlawing discrimination based on sexual orientation and gender identity, and modernized the Community Reinvestment Act (CRA). The Senator asked NCRC to draft the CRA section and asked us to focus on improving CRA as applied to banks and to expand CRA to independent mortgage companies.

§203, Strengthening the Community Reinvestment Act of 1977, bolstered CRA by increasing opportunities for community participation when banks were merging and when banks barely passed their CRA exams.[517] Using the approach in previous CRA modernization bills, §203 applied CRA at a bank holding company level, meaning that CRA exams would evaluate the activities of banks and their affiliates that lend.[518] The bill would institute five ratings with a rating called Sufficient that indicated the bank barely passed its exam. In order to avoid the pitfalls of the current CRA law, the bill would also allow the agencies to add ratings and institute a point system if the five ratings in the bill did not curb CRA ratings inflation or blurred distinctions in bank performance.[519] The bill mandated that assessment areas covered at least 75 percent of total bank or mortgage company lending, including lending beyond branches and offices.[520] Critically, the bill addressed racial disparities in access to credit and capital by directing the federal agencies to engage in data analysis, designate underserved areas with low levels of lending, and examine bank activity in these areas. NCRC research had concluded that underserved census tracts had a high percentage of people of color.[521]

A new feature called Improvement Plans was introduced to increase community input when a bank performed in a lackluster manner in an assessment area.[522] When a bank received a rating of Sufficient or lower in an area, it could still pass overall but had performed poorly in the area. If it was not directed to improve in the area, it could continue to neglect the specific area since it passed its exam. Accordingly, §203 required the bank to draft an Improvement Plan indicating how it would achieve at least a Satisfactory rating in the area(s), submit the plan to its regulatory agency, which would subject the plan to a public comment period. Thus, the Improvement Plan requirement was an attempt to reduce inconsistencies in performance and to engage the communities that the bank had overlooked in enhancing the bank performance in those communities.

The 2024 version of the bill bolstered public input by requiring a public hearing in conjunction with a CRA exam for banks with assets of more than $50 billion.[523] This provision harkens back to the recommendations of National People's Action (NPA) outlined in Chapter 3 during the early years of CRA to increase public input and accountability. More recently, community-based organizations have difficulties influencing CRA exams of these very large banks. Community organizations lack the resources of agency examiners and are unable to influence overall ratings by conducting comprehensive analyses across several geographical areas in numerous states. However, inconsistencies or weaknesses in performance in certain geographical areas may receive more notice by agency examiners if community organizations from those areas can marshal convincing evidence and testimony during hearings. As a result, chances could increase that examiners and banks address these inconsistencies during examinations.

Along the same lines, §203 enhanced the merger application process by making more robust the legal mandate requiring banks to demonstrate public benefits. Specifically, a merging institution would be required to develop a community benefits plan, similar to a community benefits agreement (CBA), that would contain measurable goals for "future amounts of safe and sound loans, investments... and services in low- and moderate-income communities and other underserved communities."[524] The banks would be required to consult with community-based organizations and other stakeholders in developing these plans.[525]

The former head of the House Committee on Financial Services, Rep. Maxine Waters introduced the Making Communities Stronger through the Community Reinvestment Act in September of 2022, which like Senator Warren's bills, sought to bolster CRA by increasing community input and by expanding coverage of lending activities. In response to advocates' concerns that some banks were partnering with non-bank companies to make high cost and abusive consumer loans, the bill would require CRA exams to scrutinize lending activity conducted by partnerships among banks and non-banks. The exams would assess the affordability and sustainability of these loans to ensure that banks were meeting credit needs safely and soundly.[526]

In addition, the bill would require banks to establish consumer advisory committees that would consist of community group representatives and other stakeholders and would advise the banks on the extent to which they were meeting credit needs of people of color, LGBTQ+ communities and other underserved communities. The number of community advisory committees would depend on the asset size of the bank and its geographical reach.[527] This provision is akin to the community advisory committees created in the wake of CBAs and help in the implementation of CBAs as well as creating a more real-time dialogue with banks so they can respond to evolving community needs.

Conclusion

The GLBA law was a vision of free market proponents that assumed the competitive deficits of the U.S. financial system would be solved by further consolidation and economies of scale. At best, this is a proposition that could in some circumstances make lending more efficient. At worst, this type of law furthers anti-competitive behavior, resulting in inferior service and higher prices. For LMI and other underserved communities, lending remains a high-touch operation in which branch staff use non-automated underwriting techniques. This type of relationship-based lending is best conducted by smaller institutions rather than national behemoths relying more on machine learning and non-branch-based lending. In response to GLBA, CRA proponents attempted to retain community responsiveness by strengthening CRA as applied to banks and increase resources for reinvestment by expanding CRA to non-bank lenders, insurance companies, and securities firms including those that merged with banks. The proponents of CRA also tried to alter the CRA sunshine provision which was designed to discourage community groups from participating in the CRA process and therefore thwarted one of the core purposes of CRA, which was to make banking fairer by empowering community-based organizations.

Congress did not adopt CRA expansion but did attach data enhancements to the home and small business data in the Dodd Frank Act. Data disclosure lays the foundation for further community reinvestment reform efforts and law by exposing continued disparities in access to financial services and providing insights into how to narrow these disparities. At the same time, the federal bank agencies refrained from implementing CRA sunshine in a manner that would club community groups into submission. On the contrary, community groups continued to work with sympathetic members of Congress on ways to recommend structural methods such as advisory committees to increase community input and to better hold banks accountable to communities as they became larger.

7

A Lawsuit and a Regulatory Reversal

A logical approach to writing about a law, including a fair lending law, would be to track its legislative changes chronologically and then review regulatory adjustments required by passed legislation amending the law. CRA, however, defies this logical approach. Since its passage in 1977, amendments to the law were relatively few. Even the weakening amendments of the GLBA in 1999 did not necessitate momentous regulatory rulemaking. Thus, the legislative and regulatory CRA tracks have operated separately from each other for the most part. It is possible that CRA bills that did not pass influenced subsequent regulatory reform. While we lack concrete evidence of this, lawmaker bills can influence the thinking of the bank agencies and lawmakers themselves comment on proposed regulatory changes. For example, some proposed bills that sought to reduce CRA requirements may have influenced the regulatory agencies to make CRA exams for smaller banks streamlined. In contrast, the CRA modernization bills may have influenced the regulatory agencies to expand the geographical reach of CRA exams and to improve data collection to hold banks more accountable for safe and sound lending and investments in traditionally underserved communities.

As Congress was considering but not passing CRA bills in the 2000s, the agencies undertook various regulatory reforms. During the administration of President George W. Bush, the agencies proposed and implemented reforms that streamlined exams for smaller banks, which ended up lessening their accountability to engage in reinvestment. The four agencies at the time split, with one of them implementing a damaging change and the other three adopting a less damaging reform but a reform that nevertheless drew opposition from community based organizations. The agency that split from its counterparts eventually rescinded its different CRA rule.

Then during the Donald J. Trump administration, the Office of the Comptroller of the Currency (OCC) split again from the Federal Reserve Board (FRB) and the Federal Deposit Insurance Corporation (FDIC). The proposed OCC rule was opposed by banks and community organizations. The organization that employed me, NCRC, sued the OCC, asserting that the rule was contrary to the purpose of the CRA statute

The Bush streamlining lessens requirements for smaller banks

Administrations guided by free market principles focus on reducing regulatory costs on banks, particularly smaller banks. However, CRA enables markets to work better by reducing market failures including imperfect information flows and discriminatory behavior as discussed in Chapter 2. Nonetheless, while some differences in CRA exams are appropriate for banks of various sizes, a reform proposal can veer too far in lessening accountability by unnecessarily eliminating exam elements that assess lending, investment, or service records. On August 2, 2005, the FRB, OCC, and FDIC issued a final rule that narrowed CRA exam requirements for a new category of banks, called intermediate small banks (ISB) banks. The final rule stated, "The joint final rule addresses regulatory burden imposed on small banks with an asset size between $250 million and $1 billion by exempting them from CRA loan data collection and reporting obligations. It also exempts such banks from the large bank lending, investment, and service tests, and makes them eligible for evaluation under the small bank lending test and a flexible new community development test."[528]

While these changes appear to increase flexibility and reduce burden, digging beneath the surface uncovers less accountability, which is likely to cause declines in reinvestment activity. In particular, the newly minted intermediate small banks were no longer required to submit publicly available CRA small business data. These banks remain important small business lenders, particularly in smaller cities and rural counties. Without access to publicly available data, community groups and other stakeholders lack effective tools for holding them accountable to lending to underserved small businesses or farms in LMI census tracts. NCRC made clear in its comment letter the extent of the loss. The letter stated that if the data deletion occurred, a lack of transparency would impact a significant share of the lending marketplace in several states. Using the CRA small business data available prior to the 2005 final rule, NCRC stated, "Mid-size banks (or intermediate small banks) in Kansas issued 9,439 small business loans or 35.8 percent of the total when excluding credit card lenders. Likewise, mid-size banks in Idaho, Arkansas, and South Carolina issued 25.4 percent, 20.9 percent, and 16.5 percent of the small business loans, respectively. In the ten states sampled, the median market share of mid-size banks was 14.5 percent of the loans issued and the mean market share was 18.4 percent."[529] NCRC further asserted that the data submission requirements for intermediate small banks (ISB) were not burdensome as they had been successfully reporting this data since 1996.

Another detrimental aspect of the final rule was that the new community development test no longer examined the branching patterns of Intermediate Small Banks (ISB) banks on a consistent basis. Branches are vital for traditionally underserved populations to access loans and deposit accounts. As of the time of the final rule, NCRC documented that 1,508 ISB banks would no longer be examined for branch placement in census tracts of varying income levels.[530] Subsequently, Silver and Marsico found that a sample of almost 100 ISB banks revealed that more than half of the new exams did not discuss the distribution of branches across census tract categories.[531] Data on branch location remains readily available via FDIC databases on the FDIC website for all banks so reporting this data does not reflect a burden for these banks.[532] Instead, deletion of the service test with its examination of branching and services provided to LMI census tracts reduces examination of bank services and increases the possibilities that some banks will respond by providing fewer services to residents in LMI tracts.

Instead of deleting these aspects of ISB exams, the agencies could have committed to tailoring their exams by focusing on comparisons between ISB banks rather than their much larger peers if ISB banks were disadvantaged in component tests by comparisons with larger banks. In fact, it was not clear that they were disadvantaged. Ironically, the lending test comparisons would have likely favored ISB banks since they specialize in serving the smallest businesses. NCRC's comment letter revealed that in a sample of ten states, ISB banks issued a significantly greater percentage of loans to the smallest businesses with revenues under $1 million in revenues than their larger peers.[533]

The Office of Thrift Supervision (OTS) went further in reducing regulatory costs for lending institutions. The other agencies thought the OTS went too far and jeopardized CRA's benefits and reinvestment activity. Thus, the OTS issued its own separate rule at around the same time. First the OTS, re-defined small thrifts (or savings and loan institutions) as those with assets of less than $1 billion.[534] This means that thrifts with assets between $250 million to $1 billion were only examined for their lending activities in contrast to ISB banks in this asset range overseen by the FRB, OCC, and FDIC that had lending and community development financing examined. Thus, the OTS change for smaller institutions was reaching farther than that of its counterpart agencies. In addition, large thrifts with assets above $1 billion in assets could choose their own weights for their lending, investment, and service tests. In contrast, large banks with assets above $1 billion had tests that weighed the lending test at 50 percent, the investment test at 25 percent, and the service test at 25 percent. Allowing thrifts to choose their own weights created CRA exams and ratings that were inconsistent and could not be compared across agencies. In addition, a thrift's ability to choose its own weights allowed it to discount the impact of weaknesses in its performance on one or more of its component tests towards its overall rating.

The OTS couched its changes in terms of providing greater

flexibility to thrifts. It stated, the "final rule provides flexibility for savings associations evaluated under the large retail institution test to opt to be evaluated with the same or greater emphasis given to either investments or services than at present."[535] Despite this reassuring explanation, Silver and Marsico found that the median total of community development (CD) lending and investment of a sample of thrifts before and after the changes declined from $6.2 million to $5.7 million, or about $500,000 less for each thrift. In addition, the thrifts that decreased the weight of their investment test had a median decrease of about $249,000 in their investments.[536] The OTS changes were too much for that agency to countenance in future years. In 2007, the agency, under new leadership, rescinded its rule and aligned its rule with the other three agencies.[537]

The OCC did not learn from the OTS blunder prompting NCRC to sue

After the OTS' mistake of acting alone, the OCC fell into the same trap. The Trump Administration appointed a former banker, Joseph Otting, to be the Comptroller of the Currency. Despite misgivings voiced by the banking industry as well as community groups, Mr. Otting proceeded with a counterproductive proposal that would likely decrease reinvestment in LMI communities. The other two agencies did not join his proposal. Despite Mr. Otting personally calling bank CEOs and trying to convince them that his proposal had been mischaracterized, the banks were not persuaded.[538] Even after these unsuccessful calls in June of 2020, the OCC issued a revision to its CRA regulation. Part of the introduction stated:

> Although commenters disagreed with the approach outlined in the proposal, the agency ultimately agreed with the minority of

commenters who expressed support for the proposed framework. The lodestar for this new CRA framework is increased transparency, objectivity, and consistency in application, which will help the OCC achieve the objective of the CRA—to encourage banks to meet the credit needs of their entire communities, including LMI individuals and areas.[539]

In my career at NCRC, I did not recall another instance of a final rule accompanied by a preamble admitting that the agency was going against the wishes of the majority of the stakeholders commenting on a proposed rule.

The OCC rule generated industry and community organization opposition because its attempts to over-simplify compliance with CRA would re-direct bank reinvestment activities away from the greatest needs and would not accurately measure bank compliance with CRA. The focal point of the final rule was a CRA evaluation measure which was a ratio of the dollars of CRA activities divided by deposits. As a highly weighted measure on CRA exams, it would drive banks to find large dollar activities that were not necessarily the most responsive to needs. For example, many localities have needs for lower dollar mortgages for LMI borrowers or micro loans of small dollar amounts for very small businesses. Banks, however, would have incentives to find large scale deals for massive infrastructure projects in order to increase the dollars in the numerator of the CRA evaluation measure. Several stakeholders felt that the priority for CRA was to focus on the smaller scale home and small business lending lacking in too many LMI neighborhoods rather than CRA to be re-oriented to larger scale infrastructure projects that usually do not need as much of a CRA incentive for receiving financing.

As discussed in Chapter 4, the CRA evaluation measure was

inconsistent with Proxmire's change to the original CRA bill. In response to concerns of credit allocation, the Senator dropped the requirement that banks indicate the ratio of loans to deposits they anticipated would be in their primary service areas. Now, five decades later, the OCC implemented a similar ratio that would be a major determinant of a bank's CRA rating. To make matters worse, the OCC declined to establish thresholds or specific ratios that would correspond to various CRA ratings because the OCC indicated it lacked the data to establish thresholds. This was a tacit admission of the arbitrariness and complexity of the CRA evaluation measure which the agency ironically touted as making CRA compliance more objective and transparent. The OCC said it would try to collect data and establish thresholds during a future rulemaking. This was contrary to the usual practice of backing up proposals, especially new ones that departed from decades of practice, with careful data analysis regarding the proposal's impacts.[540]

The OCC's ratio approach renewed concerns about credit allocation, especially if the thresholds for the ratios turned out to be inflexible and did not account for sudden changes in economic conditions that made achieving them difficult. It is best to steer clear of concerns of credit allocation by creating a series of performance measures as the agencies did in their 1995 rule so that banks did not have to hit particular thresholds on a few measures but instead could compensate with better performance on some of them that would offset worse performance on others.

The Community Bankers Association (CBA) wrote that "a balance sheet-based metric would fail to provide sufficient consideration for lending activities like LMI mortgage and small business loan programs, which are crucial to many communities, but do not result in the large dollar volumes favored under the Measure."[541] Likewise the Independent Community Bankers Association (ICBA) asserted that "The use of nationwide performance benchmarks (in the CRA evaluation measure) may not be sufficiently well-suited to assess the performance of community banks."[542] The ICBA continued that that the nationwide approach the OCC used to generate benchmarks for the CRA evaluation measure could not adequately address economic conditions or other contextual factors in a smaller bank's geographical service area.[543] Other comment letters cited that a bank's ratio may not pass the required levels because house prices are relatively low in many non-coastal areas of the country.

The final rule added essential infrastructure and community facilities to the regulatory definition of community development.[544] The definition of essential infrastructure was broad, including roads, bridges, tunnels, mass transit, water supply and distribution and sewage treatment. Likewise, the term community facilities was wide-ranging and included hospitals and public safety facilities.[545] In contrast, the current regulation does not explicitly include infrastructure, which means that the final OCC rule elevated the importance of these items in contrast to the current regulation. Magnifying the concerns about an emphasis on infrastructure, the final rule removed the emphasis on primarily benefit (more than 50 percent of the dollars benefiting LMI people or communities) and instead allowed community development activities to partially benefit (less than a majority of the dollars) LMI people and communities.[546] In practice, this could mean more frequent financing of large-scale infrastructure projects such as bridges since bridges were an explicit regulatory category and since they could partially benefit LMI people. Combined with the CRA evaluation measure, the OCC final rule would have likely encouraged banks to aggressively pursue infrastructure projects with tangential benefits for LMI people and communities.

In addition, the OCC's final rule constrained community input on CRA exams. The final rule emphasized public comments about local area needs and opportunities that examiners would use when conducting performance context analysis. Oddly, the OCC did not explicitly state whether an examiner would consider comments on the CRA performance of a bank, which, after all, is the bottom line in terms of helping to determine the rating for a bank.[547] As discussed in previous chapters, the authors of CRA sought to empower community groups and to provide them with opportunities to influence banks' responsiveness to community needs. The OCC was moving in the opposite direction in its June 2020 rule. In contrast to the OCC 2020 rule, the current CRA regulation requires banks to keep a public file that includes public comments on the performance of the bank in meeting community needs.[548]

Filing a complaint against the OCC on June 25, 2020, in the United States District Court, Northern District of California, San Francisco Division, the California Reinvestment Coalition (CRC) and NCRC alleged that the OCC:

> Acting alone and without the support of the other federal regulatory agencies that implement the CRA, the OCC issued a Final Rule that guts the Act and eviscerates the backing it provides to the LMI communities and communities of color that have long suffered from discrimination by financial institutions. The Final Rule will siphon significant amounts of lending, investments, and bank services away from LMI communities. It will allow banks to receive credit for activities that do little or nothing to help those communities and that may in fact harm and displace the residents of these communities. By broadening the regulation's geographic criteria and applying a one-size-fits-all formula, the

Final Rule ignores local needs and allows banks to disregard a large number of communities in favor of ones where it may be more financially advantageous to concentrate their investments. And in implementing a ratio-based approach and removing the right of the public to comment on bank performance, the Final Rule will result in banks passing over smaller, more beneficial projects, and will diminish or eliminate opportunities for community engagement and input—long the linchpin of successful community reinvestment efforts.[549]

The complaint continued,

"... the Final Rule also represents a failure by OCC to engage in the "reasoned decisionmaking" required by the Administrative Procedure Act (APA). In rushing its Final Rule through the administrative process, OCC provided little or no data or analysis to support its new approach—to a degree that even many banks criticized the measure because of the uncertain effects it will have on their operations."[550]

The OCC was at odds with the other agencies. The complaint included quotes from the other agencies about the OCC's lack of transparent data analysis in support of the rule.[551]

For example, the complaint quoted Martin Gruenberg, a member of the FDIC's Board of Directors as asserting that the proposed rule was "a deeply misconceived proposal that would fundamentally undermine and weaken the Community Reinvestment Act." He said that OCC's single-metric proposal amounted to a "'count the widgets' approach that does not take into account the quality and character of the bank's activities and its responsiveness to local needs." Gruenberg further noted that the "OCC had itself acknowledged a lack of data and analysis to support its new approach; that it would allow banks to entirely ignore many of its assessment areas and still receive a "passing" grade; that it would dilute the CRA's focus on LMI communities; and that it would undermine bank engagement and dialogue with local community stakeholders."[552]

The OCC responded by filing a motion to dismiss the case, asserting that CRC and NCRC as coalitions of community-based organizations did not have standing to sue because they could not prove injuries as a result of the OCC's final rule. In a decision issued in late January of 2021, Judge Kandis Westmore dismissed the OCC's challenge and allowed the case to proceed. The judge reasoned:

> Both (NCRC and CRC) are membership associations, together comprising more than 900 community reinvestment organizations, community development financial institutions, minority- and women-owned business associations, and social service providers. Plaintiffs and many of their members depend on CRA-qualifying grants and loans from OCC regulated entities to provide lending, financial counseling, homeownership assistance, and other critical forms of investment in LMI communities. Additionally, Plaintiffs expend substantial resources to negotiate with banks to obtain commitments to support the credit needs of LMI communities and communities of color,…and comment on banks' CRA performance and merger applications.[553]

The judge continued that the OCC issued a final rule just six weeks after the close of the comment period, did not publish research in support of its rule, and that both the FDIC and Federal

| Ending Redlining through a Community-Centered Reform of the Community Reinvestment Act

Reserve Board refused to join the rule.[554] The judge repeated assertions by community-based organizations that new community development activities such as financing essential infrastructure that would be allowed to only partially benefit LMI communities could divert needed bank financing from LMI communities.[555] In rejecting the OCC's contention that the plaintiffs had no standing, the judge declared:

> One example is that NCRC's Housing Counseling Network comprises organizations that receive grants directly from banks to fund their services. Plaintiffs allege that if banks can achieve a passing CRA score through other means that only "partially" benefit LMI communities, a bank can suspend smaller-dollar grants for housing counseling in LMI communities. It is enough to allege that these core activities will now have to compete with investment opportunities that could not previously receive CRA credit.[556]

Thus, Judge Westmore allowed the case to proceed. However, the Acting Comptroller, Michael J. Hsu, in mid-December 2021 rescinded the 2020 OCC rule so that the OCC could now join the other two agencies in promulgating a careful and well developed CRA rule.[557]

Conclusion

The first two decades of the twenty-first century were tumultuous times for the regulations implementing CRA. For the first time in CRA's history, the federal agencies implementing CRA split, ending their decades-long commitment to adopting uniform, interagency CRA regulations. The OTS split first, adopting a CRA regulation and examination regime with which the other agencies did not agree. After a few years, the OTS, under a new director, rescinded its harmful regulation. This should have been a warning that when the agencies do not consider and adopt revisions to their CRA regulations on an interagency basis, hasty regulations can be adopted by one or more of the agencies. However, the agencies did not heed this lesson and warning. During the Trump administration, the OCC developed a regulation at odds with CRA's legislative intent and practice. As a result, bank trade associations joined community organizations in opposing it. A community organization lawsuit was in process until the Biden administration assumed office and embarked on a new rulemaking, which the next chapter will review.

8

Will a Promise of Progress Endure?

The lawsuit against the OCC continued until President Joe Biden's administration appointed another head of the agency which rescinded the OCC rule. After hurtling towards a splintered CRA regime with distinct regulations for banks overseen by different agencies, the federal bank agencies regrouped and carefully developed an interagency proposed rule during a multi-year process. The Federal Reserve System took the lead when it issued an Advance Notice of Proposed Rulemaking (ANPR) in September of 2020 and took public comments for a period of four months.[558] Then, two years later, the agencies used the ideas in the Fed's ANPR as the foundation for their proposed rule, which they released and asked for public comments during a three month period from May to August of 2022.[559] In total, the general public and interested parties had several months to officially make comments as well as countless other opportunities over a multi-year period to influence a proposed rule that itself was developed and revised meticulously. This was in sharp contrast to the rushed OCC rule.

On October 24, 2023, the agencies issued a final rule that was very close to the proposed rule. Overall, it was the most significant change in the CRA regulations in 28 years since the final 1995 rule. When almost three decades transpire before updating a regulation, the changes need to be bold if they are to make up for lost ground, particularly as the internet flourished and banking also changed technologically. The agencies were up to the task, making some important and positive changes to parts of the regulation. They succeeded in making the retail lending test more rigorous, a change that has the potential to decrease CRA ratings inflation and therefore motivate banks to make more loans in underserved and low- and moderate-income communities. They updated geographical areas on CRA exams to take into account lending through the internet and other non-branch means. Capturing more loans on the lending test is another aspect of the reform that promises to increase lending to LMI populations. They increased data collection and public reporting requirements that hold the potential to further increase bank services and investments to left-out communities.

However, the agencies did not fill some large gaps. They did not expand the reach of CRA exams to consider a bank's record of serving people of color or communities of color in a systematic way. As discussed in Chapter 4, the impetus for CRA was redlining against communities of color. While Senator Proxmire and his staff left out an explicit mention of race in order to increase the chances of CRA passage, it was clear that they intended the law to serve redlined and underserved communities. There are methods to increase the attention of CRA exams to all underserved communities, including communities of color, that the agencies missed on this round of reform. The agencies did include CRA consideration of Special Purpose Credit Programs (SPCPs) that can be designed to serve people and communities of color experiencing documented difficulties in access to credit. While this is an advance, it is in part of the exam that can only earn banks positive consideration, meaning if banks are likely to pass exams without establishing SPCPs, some or many may skip over SPCPs.

On balance, the agencies constructed a new CRA regulation and exam regime that can be built upon. The gaps, though significant, are not fatal to the endeavor of increasing access to credit and capital. Community groups probably will need to fight efforts to weaken the new regulation and to push the new regulation to better serve all communities, including communities of color. Banks of good will, of which there are many, should continue working in partnership with community organizations and oppose efforts to weaken the regulation while offering reasonable suggestions for improving any new and inadvertent inefficiencies which increase their costs without helping them serve LMI or communities of color.

When the FDIC board voted to adopt the CRA rule, Chairman Martin Gruenberg stated, "CRA's simple premise – that banks have an affirmative obligation to serve the local communities in which they do business – is as powerful and relevant today as it was in 1977. Since its enactment, CRA has become the foundation of responsible financing for low– and moderate–income communities in the United States. This final rule will significantly expand the scope and rigor of CRA and will assure its continued relevance for the next generation."[560]

Not all senior officials at the three banking agencies agreed with

Chairman Gruenberg's assessment. The vote of the FDIC board resulted in three members in favor and two opposed. Likewise, the vote of the Board of Governors of the Federal Reserve System was six in favor and one opposed. Expressing the views of the opposition, FDIC board member Travis Hill stated, "But the more complex a rule is, the less likely it is that bankers, the public, and examiners fully understand it; the more time and cost is spent on training, consultants, vendors, lawyers, compliance systems, IT tools, and more training; and the less likely it is that the rule is applied in a consistent and intended manner over time. At some point, the costs of added complexity outweigh the benefits of added precision and granularity, and I think this rule has blown far past that point."[561]

Who is correct: FDIC Chairman Gruenberg or Board member Hill? I believe that Chairman Gruenberg has the more convincing perspective as the description of the final rule below will illustrate. The agencies conducted comprehensive research and analysis on the benefits of the final rule and made several changes designed to respond to concerns about undue complexity, including leaving out of the rule additional measures that advocates had promoted. At the same time, concerns expressed by Hill should continue to be addressed through periodic review and revision of the final rule so that the CRA regulation becomes both more efficient and equitable over time. This chapter now turns to major aspects of the rule and analyzes the advances of the final rule as well as shortcomings from the perspectives of equity and efficiency. After a review of exam structure, the shortcomings are discussed first, followed by a review of the advances. This chapter will not cover all aspects of the final rule but will focus on major themes and issues.

Change in exam structure mostly positive but scrutiny of some aspects of bank activity lessened

The 2023 final rule (printed in early February of 2024 in the Federal Register) maintained the basic structure of CRA exams of most types of banks with the exception of a modest change for large banks. Large banks with assets above $2 billion will have the most rigorous exams consisting of four tests: the retail lending test, the retail services and products test, the community development finance test, and the community development services test.[562] The current exams for large banks as described in Chapter 2 consist of three tests: the lending, investment, and services test. The exam structure moved to four component tests to accommodate two changes: 1) an analysis of community development lending was moved from the lending test to the new community development finance test that also includes community development investments, and 2) a qualitative analysis of the innovation and flexibility of loan products was moved from the retail lending test to the new retail services and products test which will also include a qualitative assessment of deposit products for the largest banks with assets of more than $10 billion. The retail services and products test will also analyze of the distribution of bank branches, remote service facilities and for certain large banks, digital delivery. Overall, the change in exam structure is positive in that it will accommodate more rigorous quantitative analysis, particularly for retail lending. However, there are aspects such as a possible diminution of the importance of investments and qualitative analysis of bank products that concerned stakeholders should monitor.

Intermediate banks with assets between $600 to $2 billion will have a retail lending test and a streamlined community development test.[563] This is much the same as their current tests, except that the lending test for intermediate banks will have borrower and census tract metrics that are the same as for large banks.[564] Small banks with assets below $600 will continue to have just a lending test.[565] All banks will continue to have a strategic plan option under which they substitute a plan describing measurable goals for their lending, investing, and service activities that would have been scrutinized under the exams that corresponded to their asset levels.[566] Lastly, limited purpose banks that do not regularly offer retail lending and other services will be subject to a community development finance test.[567]

Federal agencies lessen exam requirements for several banks risking less reinvestment from those banks

In a move that was motivated to respond to the concerns of bank trade associations, the agencies reduced exam rigor for approximately 994 banks. The agencies changed the asset thresholds for specifying intermediate banks from the previous range of $376 million to $1.5 billion in effect during 2023 to a new asset range of $600 million to $2 billion.[568] This will have the effect of moving the designation of 778 banks from intermediate to small banks. Small banks, unlike intermediate banks, do not have a community development test that looks at their loans and investments that finance affordable housing, economic development projects, or community facilities.[569] As a result the amount of community development financing of these banks is likely to decline. In a comment letter to the agencies on their proposal to adjust the asset thresholds, NCRC stated that a study it had conducted a few years prior estimated that intermediate banks in the current asset range had financed about $1 billion in community development on an annual basis.[570] Removing a community development test from a significant subset of intermediate banks can dramatically reduce the $1 billion in annual financing, which most likely is disproportionately directed to smaller cities and rural areas where these intermediate banks are disproportionately headquartered.[571]

At the same time, the asset threshold change will reclassify about 216 large banks into intermediate banks.[572] While these banks will still have a community development test, albeit a streamlined one, they will no longer have a retail services and products test that assesses the distribution of their branches including the number and percentage of branches in LMI communities. Branches remain important points of access to banking for LMI populations, including very small businesses and first-generation home buyers. This change will likely reduce access to banking and credit for the customers of these banks.

It is possible that the more rigorous exams for large banks including the community development test, and the retail services and products test may compensate for the reduction in CRA requirements for the banks now subject to the less comprehensive exams. Under increased scrutiny from more robust exams, large banks may make more community development financing, branches, and bank services available to LMI communities. However, even if this occurs, the distributional impacts are likely to remain deleterious since the smaller banks that have reduced requirements are more likely to be in small cities and rural areas which are parts of the country that are traditionally underserved and have less access to large banks. The agencies extol the benefits of tailoring CRA exam requirements to the size of banks and reducing costs for smaller banks. However, in this case, exam requirements were reduced for hundreds of banks that had been undergoing the more rigorous exams since the 2005 regulatory changes, or almost two decades ago. There is scant evidence that these banks had been impaired in any significant way by these exam requirements. In fact, the CRA exams may have spurred them to find more profitable financing and service opportunities. This was a mistake from an equity and efficiency perspective. The agencies and stakeholders need to monitor this change and seek ways to compensate for any future harm.

Merger application requirements untouched by the final CRA rule with both positive and negative implications

The final CRA rule left in place the existing merger application requirements described in detail in Chapter 3.[573] That chapter described how agency reviews of merger applications involve scrutiny of past CRA performance and consideration of a bank's future or prospective ability to serve the convenience and needs of communities. This review of future public benefits had prompted a number of banks to strike Community Benefits Agreements (CBAs) with community organizations that committed the banks to hundreds of billions of dollars in future amounts of loans, investments, and services to traditionally underserved communities.

Chapter 3 detailed the agency hesitancy about these agreements with the agencies occasionally hinting at support but other times including a footnote in their approval orders that these agreements are not required by the CRA statute or implementing regulations (Chapter 5 described how the agencies in the 1995 reforms flirted with CBAs but ultimately did not address them specifically in the regulation). Advocates had hoped that at least the footnotes in the approval orders would disappear and be replaced with language that indicated that CBAs could assist banks meet their legal requirements to demonstrate future benefits as a result of mergers. Moreover, advocates had hoped that CRA exams would assess banks' progress in meeting the goals in CBAs after their mergers with possibilities of either ratings enhancements or downgrades depending on their progress or lack thereof in meeting the CBA goals. This would be akin to the strategic plan option. But unfortunately, the final regulation did not address CBAs in the context of merger reviews, CRA exams, or as part of the strategic plan option. The strategic plan option became more detailed, with a combination of goals and performance tests, so it is unclear the extent to which banks will utilize this option.[574] Perhaps, goal setting under CBAs can form the basis for some goal setting under the new strategic plans in future years.

At the same time, the agencies declined to diminish merger application requirements. Some banks desired to weaken merger reviews by allowing automatic approvals of applications if banks passed their CRA exams. Since 98 percent of banks pass their exams as documented in Chapter 2, these "safe harbor" proposals would eviscerate the merger review process. Even banks that score outstanding should undergo a rigorous review of their merger applications as the agencies acknowledged in their 1995 regulatory reform discussed in Chapter 5. CRA exams can be two years old or older, meaning that more recent performance could be different. In addition, banks with the highest rating can still exhibit uneven performance across states and localities which should be addressed.

The agencies in the final rule acknowledge that the convenience and needs factor in merger applications is prospective while CRA exams are a retrospective examination of bank performance, implying that CRA exams alone cannot be relied upon to assess the future abilities of the merging banks to meet community needs. According to the agencies, "In some cases, the CRA examination might not be recent, or a specific issue raised in the application process might not be reflected in the CRA rating (although it might be generally relevant to a CRA evaluation), such as a bank's progress in addressing weaknesses noted by examiners or implementing commitments previously made to the reviewing agency."[575] The agencies are elevating the importance of issues raised by the general public during the application process as well as whether banks addressed weaknesses noted in their previous exams. Agency acknowledgment of this signals to community organizations that they should remain active in the application process and during CRA exams to maximize the chances of the agencies or the banks addressing unresolved issues. CRA is a continual obligation imposed on banks to meet community needs; thus, members of the public should be continually commenting to the agencies about banks' record in serving their communities.

As described in Chapter 3, one of the three agencies, the FDIC, made a change in its policy regarding mergers to provide implicit recognition of CBAs. Without referring to CBAs explicitly, the FDIC's policy statement on mergers now suggests that the FDIC may review the records of banks adhering to commitments made during the merger application process. It is unclear what corrective action the FDIC may require if a bank is not meeting goals in a CBA. However, this is a step by one of the agencies that community organizations hope they can build upon in the future.

CRA's consideration of race is lacking

The proposed rule did not expand CRA exam scrutiny of bank activity in communities of color or adopted any proxy procedures, such as examining activities in underserved census tracts that are disproportionately communities of color. The agencies proposed that CRA exams would display data tables on lending by race and ethnicity, but the tables would have no impact on the final ratings.[576] The final rule stipulates that the race and ethnicity lending data will be published on agency websites instead of in the exams.[577]

The lack of exam consideration of race does not respond to persistent and stubborn racial and ethnic disparities in lending. A NCRC report concluded that "In 2007, 24.2% of home purchase originations were to (Black, Indigenous, People of Color) BIPOC borrowers, and in 2020 that figure was just 26.6%, a 2.4% increase in 13 years."[578] This study also found that for an African American, the average loan amount was $259,220 and the average property value was $285,118, leaving African Americans with the lowest average equity at closing of $25,546 in 2020. Whites, in contrast, had average equity at closing of $72,655, almost three times the amount for African Americans.[579] Using 2022 HMDA data, the Consumer Financial Protection Bureau (CFPB) issued a report with findings like NCRC's. The CFPB found that African Americans and Hispanics had higher denial rates, lower median credit scores, and higher median interest rates than Whites and Asians.[580] The flat level of lending combined with significant disparities in equity will not curb longstanding inequities unless policy and practice pushes in a different direction.

Incorporating race in CRA exams is controversial and will be resisted by industry stakeholders. In late fall of 2023, the Illinois Department of Financial and Professional Regulation (IDFPR) proposed regulations implementing a state CRA law that applies CRA to banks, mortgage companies, and credit unions chartered by the state. In a precedent setting move, the IDFPR sought to establish Illinois' CRA as the first CRA law in the country at any level that would consider race on CRA exams. The state would have commissioned a study identifying racial and ethnic disparities in lending in geographical areas in Illinois. The IDFPR would then consider a bank's record of lending, investing, and offering community development activities by race and ethnicity in geographical areas with significant racial and ethnic disparities when assessing whether a lending institution should earn an Outstanding rating.[581] While NCRC and allies had urged the IDFPR to evaluate performance to racial and ethnic groups experiencing disparities in determining ratings below Outstanding as well, the IDFPR's final rule would have represented an important advance. Unfortunately, a state legislative committee that reviews proposed regulations in Illinois asked the IDFPR to strip out the disparity study after industry backlash.[582] In response, advocates worked with sympathetic lawmakers in 2024 to pass a bill requiring the disparity study and allowing IDFPR to use findings of the study to influence its CRA exams.[583] This experience illustrates the difficulty but not impossibility of adopting disparity studies that would direct CRA assessments of reinvestment activity to communities and people of color.

On a federal level, bank agency disparity studies would also be consistent with the Fair Housing Act that directs federal agencies including the bank agencies to take affirmative action to implement the Fair Housing Act's prohibition against discrimination. The Fair Housing Act also directs the Department of Housing and Urban Development to conduct studies documenting housing discrimination and to publish the results of the studies.[584] Identifying racial, ethnic, and gender groups by metropolitan area or rural county experiencing ongoing discrimination or significant disparities in access to lending and bank services would seem to be a logical first step in combating the disparate treatment.

As well as shying away from disparity studies pointing to geographical areas where bank performance by race and ethnicity should be scrutinized, the federal agencies declined to adopt NCRC's proposal to conduct data analysis to determine which census tracts are underserved.[585] CRA exams would then assess bank lending, investment, and services to underserved tracts. This is an approach similar to current CRA rules under which the agencies designate certain tracts in rural areas as underserved and distressed and then assess bank community development activities in these tracts.[586] In addition, the 2023 final rule would also allow CRA examiners to assess bank retail lending as an additional qualitative factor in these rural tracts.[587] Despite building upon the procedures for rural underserved tracts, the agencies declined to adopt NCRC's proposal for designating additional tracts in urban and suburban areas as underserved. This is a significant equity loss because a NCRC report had identified underserved tracts based on low levels of lending on a per capita basis; 57 percent of the residents of these underserved tracts, on average, were people of color.[588] If the agencies had adopted an underserved tracts approach, they would have hewed to an original legislative CRA objective described in Chapter 4 of increasing bank access in underserved communities and would have also addressed shortages of safe and sound loans and investments in communities of color.

The agencies also decided not to enhance the transparency of the fair lending reviews that accompany CRA exams. NCRC had suggested that since the agencies would be providing publicly available data tables describing lending by race and ethnicity, the fair lending reviews should explicitly probe further in geographical areas where a bank has either particularly low percentages of loans to people of color or high denial rates. The fair lending reviews should describe the methodology such as econometric analysis or matched pair testing that further analyzed the disparities appearing in the data tables. The agencies responded to this request by stating that "Moreover, although the agencies appreciate suggestions to enhance the rigor of fair lending examinations, such examinations are outside the scope of this rulemaking."[589] This is a puzzling response since the agencies reiterated that the fair lending review will continue to penalize banks through possible downgrades if they discriminate, arbitrarily exclude LMI census tracts from assessment areas, or violate consumer protection laws.[590] Why wouldn't the agencies be more transparent about their work on the fair lending review, connect the review to the new data tables on race and ethnicity, and enhance the public's confidence in the seriousness with which the fair lending review exposes discriminatory and illegal behavior?

One area in which the agencies explicitly encouraged lending to underserved populations including people of color and businesses owned by people of color was recognizing Special Purpose Credit Programs (SPCPs) as responsive lending products evaluated by the new Retail Services and Products Test.[591] Authorized under the Equal Credit Opportunity Act (ECOA), SPCPs are lending programs created by banks that focus on lending to people of color and other underserved populations as documented via data analysis.[592] However, the part of the new CRA test that assesses SPCPs can only positively influence a CRA rating. In other words, if a bank thinks it will pass its exam, it could opt to skip creating SPCPs. If the evaluation of the responsiveness of products could increase **or** decrease scores on the Retail Services and Products Test, banks would have more of an incentive to establish SPCPs and other responsive products. Nonetheless, if the new CRA exams are rigorous, a large number of banks may seek bonus points and adopt SPCP programs to assure passage.

The agencies explain their tepid approach to race by stating, "The agencies have also assessed other relevant legal and supervisory considerations, including, in particular, the constitutional considerations and implementation challenges associated with adopting regulatory provisions that expressly address race and ethnicity when implementing statutory text that does not expressly address race or ethnicity. Based upon these considerations, the agencies have determined not to include additional race- and ethnicity-related provisions other than what is adopted in this final rule."[593]

Yet, it is possible that consideration of race in the manner suggested by NCRC could survive strict scrutiny in a court of law. In the affirmative action case involving higher education in the summer of 2023, Chief Justice Roberts stated that "Any exception to the Constitution's demand for equal protection must survive a daunting two-step examination known in our cases as "strict scrutiny."[594] Roberts further described strict scrutiny as: 1) the government possessing a compelling interest to address the issue and 2) the government programs or policies are narrowly tailored to achieve a specified remedy. Glenn Schlactus, Partner at Relman Colfax, a prominent civil rights law firm, affirms that in the context of government affirmative action contracting, the Supreme Court has accepted, "remedying the effects of past or present discrimination" as a compelling interest. Schlactus further described a disparity study identifying a specific underserved population in a specific geographical area as narrowly tailored to an identified group experiencing differential (less) access to lending due to past or present discrimination.[595] Referring to part of the Roberts ruling in which the Chief Justice says that action to remediate wage discrimination is permissible,[596] Schlatus says "Race conscious remedies have long been permitted to address specifically identified racial discrimination. This is a good analogy for curing the continuing effects of discrimination in the world of credit." In addition, the other option for increasing racial equity of identifying underserved tracts is a "race neutral alternative" accepted in case law, he adds.[597]

It appears the federal bank agencies would have solid legal

grounding to adopt a more robust approach to increasing access to credit and banking services for people and communities of color. Although adding race and ethnicity as an evaluation factor on CRA exams is controversial, a multitude of alternative approaches exist making it possible for the agencies to adopt one or more approaches that would achieve acceptance from many stakeholders and may convince others to withhold judgment until results are evaluated after a few years.

Agencies should have addressed segregation more directly

Previous chapters described the origins of CRA advocacy in Chicago as concerted efforts to prevent predatory real estate agents and discriminating lenders from precipitating White flight from neighborhoods which would then flip to predominantly African American ones with plummeting property values, lack of lending, and increasing poverty. Chicago was the birthplace of CRA advocacy, but real estate blockbusting and increasing neighborhood segregation afflicted communities across the country. In her recent book, Laura Meckler describes decades-long efforts by neighborhood residents to maintain integration in Shaker Heights, a suburb of Cleveland. In the late 1950s and early 1960s, neighborhood residents had to combat bank redlining when banks declined Whites as well as African Americans in neighborhoods experiencing racial transition.[598] The discrimination victimized everyone, Whites as well as people of color, who wished to maintain integration. Against similar odds, Richard and Leah Rothstein's *Just Action* describes valiant community efforts to maintain integration in Philadelphia, including creating a neighborhood association in Mount Airy that persuaded Whites not to panic sell and that welcomed African Americans.[599]

Despite the concerted efforts of multiple stakeholders in communities across the country, segregation remains entrenched. The Brookings Institution found modest increases in racial integration but still overwhelming and persistent segregation over the decades. For example, predominantly African American neighborhoods had an average percentage of Whites of 31 percent in 2018, virtually the same as in 2000. Moreover, income segregation compounds racial segregation. Brookings also revealed that 80 percent of low-income African Americans and 75 percent of low-income Hispanics lived in low-income neighborhoods in contrast to just 50 percent of low-income Whites.[600]

A study authored by Jones, Squires, and Nixon demonstrated the benefits of integration on health outcomes. Neighborhoods with high levels of poverty often confront their residents with poor quality housing and other environmental hazards. Furthermore, amenities such as quality grocery stores are not present, contributing to poor health outcomes. The authors assessed whether inclusionary zoning programs (in which developers are either encouraged or required to produce a specified percentage of affordable housing units for modest income residents in multifamily or single-family developments) helped improve health outcomes when this housing was located away from communities with concentrated poverty. Sampling 500 cities (430 without inclusionary zoning and 70 with this zoning), the authors discovered that inclusionary zoning was associated with lower blood pressure and cholesterol, while holding several other socioeconomic factors constant.[601] This study suggests that if CRA better fostered integration and supported policies like inclusionary zoning, health outcomes and other quality of life indicators would improve for low- and moderate-income people. This would provide overall societal benefits such as higher work productivity and lower health costs.

To examine whether CRA exams promoted integration, I sampled several CRA exams of the ten largest banks by asset size in metropolitan areas undergoing significant levels of gentrification (lower income neighborhoods experiencing an influx of affluent households) and metropolitan areas with significant levels of poverty. A survey of 63 metropolitan areas experiencing gentrification identified just three bank financed projects that included affordable housing for lower income people or small business development in gentrifying neighborhoods. Likewise, another survey of 56 metropolitan areas with high levels of neighborhoods with concentrated poverty found just 2 exams that featured mixed-income housing, but the overall distribution of incomes was disproportionately lower income in the housing developments.[602]

In response to the paucity of CRA exam attention to integration, community-based organizations urged the agencies to include pro-integrative efforts explicitly in the regulatory definition of community development. The CRA tests including the lending and community development tests would then systematically examine and rate the breadth and depth of pro-integrative housing and small business finance. The exams would assess whether the banks were financing low- and moderate-income housing in middle- and upper-income urban and suburban communities as well as affordable housing in gentrifying communities.

CRA exams could complement public sector efforts fostering integration. State and local jurisdictions receiving Department of Housing and Urban Development funding are required to develop plans to promote integration under the affirmatively furthering fair housing (AFFH) requirements.[603] These plans could include public and private sector housing programs that combine loans with subsidies such as downpayment assistance to enable low- and moderate-income families to reside in integrated neighborhoods. CRA exams could scrutinize the extent to which banks are offering home loans in conjunction with public sector housing programs that increase integration.

In their final rule, the agencies shied away from exam criteria that would regularly assess integration efforts across the component tests. In addition, the rule did not explicitly cite bank participation in AFFH programs as responsive or impactful, earning banks favorable consideration on the community development or other tests. The agencies implemented incremental changes that will promote integration, but it is doubtful that a future survey along the one I conducted would find significantly higher percentages of affordable housing or economic development projects that strive to preserve a racial or income mix in neighborhoods. Under the final regulation, future CRA exams would recognize community development and affordable housing projects supporting homeownership and rental housing for LMI households in high opportunity areas as responsive and impactful. High opportunity areas are most likely middle- and upper-income because they are defined as those in which the cost of housing is high and affordable housing opportunities are few.[604] In addition, the final rule includes consideration of rental housing as affordable if tenants with up to 80 percent of area median income can afford the rents and if the housing is in census tracts in which the median rent is affordable for tenants with incomes up to 80 percent of the area median.[605] This definition includes middle- and even high-income census tracts with rental housing affordable to LMI tenants.

While the two instances of promoting integration in high

opportunity areas and in non-LMI tracts are positive, the final rule opts for examples of pro-integrative activities as opposed to a more comprehensive approach assessing the extent of pro-integrative activities. In addition, the final rule rarely mentions the imperative of integrating neighborhoods; a final rule preamble is important in that the policy considerations it emphasizes sends messages to examiners, banks, and community stakeholders about the standards CRA exams will establish. This final rule does not establish a priority for integration and will not encourage banks to regularly seek out integrative projects. Advocates desiring more attention on integration should comment to the agencies and on bank CRA exams to increase attention to the areas of the rule that promote integration.

Reducing CRA ratings inflation: Significant progress on lending test of the large bank exam with hints of increased rigor on the other tests

As described in Chapter 2, about 98 percent of banks pass their CRA exams. For someone not acquainted with CRA, it would be easy to conclude that CRA is a weak law that would not succeed in pressuring banks to increase their lending, investing, and services in LMI neighborhoods and formerly redlined areas. Yet, as Chapter 2 also describes, sophisticated statistical studies conducted over several years have documented that CRA has pushed banks to increase their home and small business lending in LMI communities while maintaining the safety and soundness of their lending. However, if CRA ratings were more rigorous and revealed more distinctions among the performance of banks, CRA likely would be more successful in increasing bank reinvestment activities.

The bank agencies were most successful in boosting the rigor of the lending test because they were able to use publicly available data on a bank level to predict how their new methodology would impact lending test ratings. They were simultaneously seeking a ratings regime that would reveal finer distinctions in performance while being reasonable in terms of banks being able to pass if they made concerted efforts. The lending test has a series of performance measures including the percent of loans to LMI borrowers and the percent of loans to LMI neighborhoods. Current exams also compare a bank's percent of loans to these borrowers against the percent of loans made by all other lenders in a geographic area (the market benchmark) and the percent of the families that are LMI (the community benchmark). Current exams leave it up to the examiner to make judgments about how well the bank's percent of loans compares against the market and community benchmark. While several examiners did a careful job in these assessments, the amount of examiner discretion in the current system created inconsistencies in ratings and some CRA ratings inflation.

To rectify this, the agencies created thresholds specifying how the comparison between a bank's percent of loans against the community and market benchmarks corresponds to ratings. For example, in order to receive an Outstanding rating on the retail lending test, a bank's percent of loans to low-income borrowers needs to be 115 percent of the market's loans to low-income borrowers. For example, if all banks in the area made 10 percent of their loans to low-income borrowers, a particular bank would need to issue at least 11.5 percent of their loans to achieve an Outstanding rating in lending to low-income borrowers. Alternatively, the bank can meet or exceed the threshold for Outstanding on the community benchmark.[606] Outstanding on the community benchmark for low-income borrowers is 100 percent of the community benchmark.[607] In this geographical area, assume that 9 percent of the families are low-income. This means that the bank would need to make at least 9 percent of its loans to low-income borrowers. The agencies choose the lower of the thresholds for the two benchmarks for determining the rating. In this case, the 9 percent threshold for the community benchmark is the lower threshold. So instead of needing 11.5 percent for Outstanding as demanded by the market benchmark, the bank can hit 9 percent or the threshold on the community benchmark.

For the lower ratings, the thresholds are logically lower. To achieve a Low Satisfactory rating, for instance, the bank's percent of loans to low-income borrowers would need to be 80 percent of the market or 60 percent of the community benchmark. Continuing with the above example, the community benchmark is once again lower. Nine percent of the families are low-income and 60 percent of nine percent is 5.4 percent. The bank would need to make 5.4 percent of its loans to low-income families to score Low Satisfactory on lending to low-income families.

In response to industry concerns that the thresholds were too high in the proposed rule, the agencies lowered a number of thresholds. The threshold for the market benchmark, for example, was lowered from 125 percent to 115 percent for earning an Outstanding rating. The agencies reasoned that the final threshold needs to be above the average or 100 percent for the market because to achieve Outstanding, the bank should be offering a higher percent of loans to a borrower group than the market (all lenders, as a group). Industry was still concerned that if enough banks wanted to push for Outstanding, the market average would ratchet up over time to higher and higher percentages that would eventually entail unsafe and reckless lending. The agencies tested their thresholds and reported that in geographical areas with high percentages of loans to low- or moderate-income borrowers, the community benchmark set at 100 percent would be lower than the market benchmark. Thus, banks would not need to make higher and higher percentages of loans compared to the market in order to score Outstanding.[608]

On the other end of the scale, the agencies stated that passing the retail lending test by scoring at least Low Satisfactory would be readily attainable. The threshold for the market benchmark of 80 percent for the rating of Low Satisfactory ensures that the bank can pass by issuing a share of loans that is below average for the market, but still judged as reasonably serving credit needs. Moreover, the agencies posit that it would be possible for many banks in a particular area to be below average but still at or above the Low Satisfactory threshold since the market includes non-bank lenders that may not be performing as well as banks.[609]

The agencies also stated that examiners will consider "additional factors" and performance context in unusual circumstances. This includes markets with relatively few LMI tracts (which can occur in rural areas) or in which a bank has a such a high market share that it has a disproportionate influence on the market benchmark (making it hard to exceed the market threshold since its lending levels can drive the average lending rates in the market). A list of additional factors is enumerated in the regulation and can be used to adjust lending test ratings in exceptional circumstances.[610] As the new exams are rolled out, community organizations and other concerned stakeholders should monitor CRA exams and ensure that the use of these additional factors are clearly and thoughtfully described on exams and are not employed in a widespread manner that ends up replicating CRA ratings inflation.

The retail lending test would create ratings for several borrower and census tract categories for home, small business, small farm lending, and for automobile lending in the case of banks with sizable numbers and percentages of automobile lending. The borrower and census tract categories would include: low-income borrowers, moderate-income borrowers, low-income census tracts, moderate-income census tracts, small businesses or farms with less than $250,000 in annual revenue, small business or farms with revenues between $250,000 and $1 million.[611] These categories are more detailed than the current exams, which combine low- and moderate-income borrowers and tracts and do not have the category of the smallest businesses/farms below $250,000 in revenue.

The agencies appropriately reasoned that CRA exams should measure lending to a variety of borrowers and businesses to ensure that banks are meeting a wide variety of credit needs in a locality. Moreover, there are enough categories so that weak performance on some categories can be compensated with stronger performance on other categories – this is an approach recommended in Chapter 5. Finally, the agencies employ a weighting scheme based on the share of the population or businesses for each income or business category in determining a final rating for all the categories considered together.[612] The contribution of a particular geographical area to an overall rating is likewise determined by a weighted average of the percentage of a bank's retail loans and deposits in each geographical area scored by the exam.[613] The weighing methods therefore ensure that the largest population groups, census tract categories, and geographical areas with the most loans and deposits contribute the most to a rating and that a bank is not unduly penalized for not hitting the mark to a smaller subset of families or communities.

Using historical data from 2018 through 2020, the agencies estimate that the great majority or about 90 percent of banks subject to the new retail lending test would pass with a Low Satisfactory or higher rating on the test. The estimated distribution would be about

10.5 percent rated Outstanding, 47.2 percent rated High Satisfactory, 33.2 percent rated Low Satisfactory, 9 percent rated Needs-to-Improve, and .2 percent rated Substantial Noncompliance.[614] If this or a similar ratings distribution occurs when the new exams are administered, the agencies would have succeeded in revealing meaningful distinctions in performance without being overly punitive. The great majority of banks pass but at the same time, about one third of them barely pass with Low Satisfactory and about 9 percent fail. The ratings distribution should motivate about 40 percent of the banks to work harder since passing is realistically achievable. More effort by this subset of lagging banks means more loans in traditionally underserved communities.

Community-based organizations would have preferred the proposed thresholds instead of the thresholds the agencies finalized in October of 2023. For example, the proposed threshold of 125 percent for Outstanding performance means that a bank needs to be approximately 25 percent higher than the aggregate or, roughly speaking, the median percentage of lending in the market. Outstanding should be reserved for banks that are significantly better than their peers; 25 percent higher seems significantly better. In contrast, the final threshold of 115 percent does not seem to be as effective to identify or distance Outstanding banks from their peers. However, the ratings distribution estimated by the agencies for the final thresholds does appear to identify a sizable number of banks in each ratings category, including Low Satisfactory, making the ratings more meaningful. This is an area of the final rule that the agencies and all stakeholders should monitor as the new CRA exams become available to make sure that ratings are indeed reflective of differences in performance.

It must be remembered that the final overall ratings will not have the High or Low Satisfactory category unlike the ratings on the component tests. However, the final rating for a bank will be accompanied by a score. Banks with Satisfactory ratings can score from 4.5 to 8.5. Those with scores closer to 4.5 likely were Low Satisfactory on most of their component tests, while those closer to 8.5 were High Satisfactory on their tests.[615] This score will now be public, increasing banks' accountability and motivation to work harder by making more loans and investments.

Critics of the new CRA regulations including board members of the Federal Reserve System and FDIC voting against the final rule argued that the agencies have created unrealistically difficult CRA exams and that as a result banks will either pull back their lending or concentrate their efforts in few geographical areas. In addition, others will be pushed to make unsafe and unsound loans.[616] However, as described in Chapter 2, evidence exists that a subset of banks are under-performing, and that market failure results in suboptimal lending levels in LMI neighborhoods and communities of color. Nonetheless, prudent CRA policy would entail monitoring lending and market developments after the new CRA exams are introduced and then adjusting if the tests are unrealistic or remain too lenient. The best course of action is not to be inflexible and pre-judging but to be an open-minded practitioner willing to enact any necessary adjustments.

Like the new retail lending test, the retail services and products test for large banks establishes performance measures and bench-marks but does not create thresholds for assigning ratings. Since branches are a major means for LMI populations to access banking and credit, this test measures the percentage of a bank's branches in LMI census tracts against the percentage of branches of all banks in LMI tracts and the percentages of households and small businesses in LMI tracts.[617] While choosing appropriate market and community benchmarks, the agencies declined to establish thresholds for them like those of the lending test. The data available to the agencies for testing thresholds for the branch evaluation was not as detailed as the data testing lending test thresholds. However, a lack of thresholds opens the possibilities of subjective and inconsistent judgments on the part of examiners.

As an alternative to thresholds, the agencies could have established clearer guidelines than those currently. For example, following the general rule in the lending test, the agencies could have specified that to earn an Outstanding rating on the distribution of branches across tract income categories, the bank needs to offer a higher percentage of branches in LMI tracts than other banks and a percentage of branches that is equal to the percentage of households and businesses in LMI tracts. Similarly, to earn Low Satisfactory, the percentage of branches would be below the percentage of peer bank branches and households and businesses but not substantially below. This would be an improvement over current guidance that offers vague descriptions such as Outstanding is earned if a bank's "service delivery systems are readily accessible to geographies and individuals of different income levels in its assessment area(s)." [618]

Other aspects of evaluating bank services are also ambiguous regarding measurements and the levels of service that correspond to various scores or ratings. An important example of this is how to consider bilingual and translation services at branches or online, which will be evaluated by the new retail services and products test.[619] This is critical for populations including Asians and Hispanics that have limited English speaking and reading proficiency. It is also an issue for people with disabilities such as those with hearing and sight impairments. Will a bank need to provide bilingual and translation services at all branches or offer higher levels of these services in traditionally underserved areas in order to perform at a Satisfactory or Outstanding level. It might not have been possible to answer all these questions in finalizing the rule, but the agencies should recommit to revisiting this issue as the new CRA exams unfold and soliciting the views of traditionally underserved populations as to what levels of accommodations correspond to which scores and ratings.

The agencies indirectly concede the legitimacy of the criticism of unclear measurements by stating, "The agencies note that, while examiner judgment is an important part of the CRA evaluation process, the agencies will endeavor to minimize unnecessary subjectivity and increase consistency among examiners by providing updated guidance, training, and standards applicable to evaluations under this test while also attempting to guard against ratings inflation."[620] While appreciated, this approach would have been improved upon if guidance could have been issued in conjunction with the final rule. Some sampling of current CRA exams would have helped the agencies establish reasonable guidelines.

Recognizing the importance of on-line banking, the agencies will also evaluate the extent of the availability of checking and savings accounts offered digitally over the internet by census tract income category.[621] Although banks with assets over \$10 billion and other large banks that lack branches will need to provide data to the agencies concerning digital delivery,[622] the agencies are not committing to comparing banks to each other based on the percentage of products offered digitally in LMI tracts.[623] This should change in order to make exams more objective and consistent.

As stated above, the retail services and products test will also have a component called retail banking products evaluation that will include an evaluation of the responsiveness of credit and deposit products to the needs of LMI borrowers. Microbusiness loans (as discussed in Chapter 3), small dollar mortgages that facilitate lending to LMI populations by using alternative credit histories (as opposed to credit scores) as well as deposit products that have reduced fees and overdraft penalties would generally score well on this part of the test.[624] As important as these products are, the agencies opted to make this part of the test optional in the sense that it can only contribute positively to a rating by adding bonus points. The agencies explain that they "are sensitive to concerns raised by some commenters that the final rule should not operate in a way that regulates or otherwise requires banks to provide certain deposit products." The agencies note that "evaluations of deposit product... does not regulate or set the prices of a bank's product offerings and associated fees."[625]

Yet, an evaluation of the extent of flexible and responsive products is a regular component of current CRA exams. Current exams review product terms and conditions and occasionally calculate the percentage of loan products that are innovative and flexible. In the final rule, the agencies state that they will consider the percentage of deposit products that are responsive. Overall, however, a more comprehensive approach that is rated like other parts of the exam would seem to be justified by CRA's mandate to provide credit and deposit services in a safe and sound manner. An evaluation of whether bank products are affordable and sustainable to LMI populations is also important considering that LMI populations lacking access to traditional banking have too often been at the mercy of abusive and unscrupulous lending institutions – usually lightly regulated nonbanks but also banks in some instances.

The credit and deposits products evaluation should have included the possibilities of negatively as well as positively influencing a rating. An abusive product, for example, can be legal but can exhibit high delinquency and default rates. Why wouldn't that be negatively considered just like affordable products could be positively considered. This would not be dictating products to banks since a lower rating is not an agency prohibition against a product but an indication that a bank will not score well on a CRA exam if it offers usurious and unaffordable products. An evaluation of product quality with possible penalties as well as rewards would ensure the products are safe, sound, and responsive within the intent of the CRA statute.

Another test for large banks, the community development finance test, likewise introduced performance measures that would be used consistently across large bank exams. However, like the retail services and products test, the performance measures would not be accompanied by thresholds or guidelines, risking too many subjective examiner judgements. As stated in Chapter 2, community development lending and investing finances large scale projects that have a more sizable impact on neighborhoods than individual home or small business loans. While retail lending is critical, an individual home loan will not have as an immediate or large-scale impact like a loan or investment for a supermarket or a health care clinic. A neighborhood can only become viable if it has access to community development financing just like it needs access to home and small business loans. Thus, the measures for community development financing need to be carefully constructed to leverage significant amounts of community development finance.

One component of the community development finance test would be a ratio of community development loans and investments divided by deposits in a metropolitan or non-metropolitan area. This is an improvement from the current exams that use inconsistent ratios such as community development finance divided by assets or community development financing divided by Tier I capital.[626]

A non-constant ratio makes it difficult to compare banks against each other and determine which banks are outperforming their peers. Furthermore, the examiners usually do not try to make peer comparisons, which is an important part of determining a rating for a bank on various tests. To rectify this, the new regulation will compare a particular bank's ratio against all other banks in the geographical area.

For metropolitan areas, the exam will also consider a nationwide average of a ratio of community development dollars divided by deposits in metropolitan areas; exams covering a rural county or counties will consider a nationwide average of a ratio of community development dollars divided by deposits in non-metropolitan or rural counties.[627] The rationale for considering a nationwide average is to adjust for metropolitan or non-metropolitan areas that are highly competitive and have high ratios of community development divided by deposits and areas that are relatively lacking in community development and have lower ratios. In competitive markets, an examiner may place more weight on the national average since local ratios may be unrealistically high. Conversely, in depressed markets with lower ratios, the examiner may place more weight on the local ratio since it may not be possible to achieve the higher national ratio. While comparing both local and national average ratios against a particular bank's ratio has merit, a lack of thresholds or guidelines could result in some lenient examiners choosing the lower ratio to compare against the bank's ratio regardless of the demographic and economic conditions in a locality.

One approach to the two comparator ratios would be to weigh them. In more competitive markets, comments on the proposed rule to the agencies suggested that an examiner could use a weighted average that consisted of a 60 percent weight for the national ratio and a 40 percent weight for the local ratio.[628] The reverse could occur in depressed markets. Then after a weighted average is calculated, an examiner would determine a rating on this component based on how far above or below the bank's ratio was above the blended peer comparator ratio. Guidelines could describe a procedure like this or at least require examiners to show their work rather than just stating what the rating is. An absence of justifications and documentation of analysis occurs too often in current exams; instead, a reader can encounter recitations of numbers and a rating without explanations.

The agencies responded to comments about thresholds by explaining, "While the agencies also believe that consistency could be improved using thresholds in the Community Development Financing Test, current data limitations preclude the agencies' ability to explore including thresholds in the test at this time. The agencies note that they could consider thresholds in future rulemaking once they have accumulated data and have experience applying the metrics and benchmarks. For now, the agencies intend to issue guidance to further clarify how they will apply the Community Development Financing Test."[629]

Accompanying the quantitative components of the community development test is a qualitative review that consists of impact and responsiveness factors. These include whether an activity targets a census tract or county experiencing high levels of poverty. The agencies explain that they "will provide a summary of a bank's impact and responsiveness review data, such as the volume of activities by impact and responsiveness review category, and incorporate the impact and responsiveness review into the performance conclusions and the written performance evaluation."[630] In other words, a more quantitative examination of the qualitative factors will include considering the volume of community development financing by impact category (such as community development financing in high poverty areas) that is particularly responsive to needs. Nevertheless, as the agencies accumulate more data and experience, they will need to establish additional guidelines that make clearer the relationship between the volume of responsive financing and a score or rating for that part of the test. For example, does more than 50 percent or 75 percent of the financing being in responsive categories correspond to an Outstanding rating? Without more thresholds in the future, exams could become inconsistent and subjective. Also, projects that involve smaller dollar grants that have large impacts such as homeownership counseling could be overlooked if the qualitative and quantitative measures are not carefully balanced on CRA exams.

The agencies are correct that additional data will help inform the development of more precise thresholds. In this vein, it is positive that the new community development finance test will require large banks to submit data that provides the agencies and stakeholders with the ability to conduct analysis and test various thresholds. It is important, however, for the agencies to commit to another rulemaking after the passage of a few years. In the interim, the agencies must develop further guidance along the lines discussed above. In general, this revision of the CRA regulation made significant strides in laying the foundation for more objective and consistent exams. However, in a number of component tests, the quantitative and qualitative analysis remains incomplete due to the absence of data that can be remedied in a few years. To complete the job of realizing the full potential of CRA, future rulemaking is needed. At the very least, guidelines developed in consultation with industry and community-based organizations should establish more precise measures and thresholds.

The overall weight of qualitative factors on the community

development finance test or other tests is left to the discretion of the examiner.[631] This discretion may result in inconsistencies across exams and a selective overemphasis on qualitative factors for banks with poor quantitative performance in a manner that would inflate ratings. NCRC had recommended an overall weight of 40 percent for the qualitative factors.[632] The examiner must also describe in clear detail why the qualitative performance is or is not responsive to needs. Too often, these descriptions on current exams can be cursory.[633] For example, affordable housing that was energy efficient, located near transit, helped integrate a neighborhood, was highly accessible to people with disabilities, had solar panels, a childcare center or a health care facility in its lobby would be more responsive than one that lacked one or more of these attributes. While an examiner cannot tally these details for all community development, particularly in the case of large banks, the examiner can carefully choose a sample of community development projects across various assessment areas (such as large cities and rural counties) in a state and further probe for the qualitative aspects of performance. It would be productive if the agencies engage community-based organizations and banks in developing guidance for the qualitative criteria and their weight and in reviewing the new CRA exams after the 2023 rule is fully implemented in 2026.

Calvin Bradford, Senior Research Fellow at the Woodstock Institute, emphasizes the importance of qualitative measures explaining that they are needed to consider differences in needs across geographical areas and differences in bank capacities. He stated, "It is the soft measures that are in many ways the most important in encouraging creativity and rewarding banks for doing good things. For example, large banks help smaller banks with back-room stuff like underwriting and don't get credit for that."[634]

For large banks, a new community development services test will assess the extent to which banks offer services and engage in activities that facilitate the provision of banking and financial services to underserved populations. One type of service could be the provision of technical assistance recommended by Bradford to smaller banks including Community Development Financial Institutions (CDFIs) and low-income credit unions.[635] Another of these key activities is homeownership and housing counseling that prepare community members for applying for loans and then managing the finances of homeownership. As described in Chapter 1, these services are critical for first-time and first-generation homeowners like Sabrina Walls. Moreover, if banks continue to close branches, populations unfamiliar with homeownership will have increased chances of success if they have financial coaching in lieu of access to staff at bank branches. Thus, the community services test should promote counseling and banks working with community-based nonprofit organizations like Meg Guerra's described in Chapter 3 in providing it. The final community services development test, as a separate test, has a critical role in promoting a high touch, community-friendly model for home and small business ownership.[636] The agencies must ensure that the qualitative factors are well developed such as demonstrating the success of counseling in terms of clients in sustainable ownership. Moreover, the agencies erred in allowing CRA points for financial counseling that benefits all income levels, not just low- and moderate-income community members, who need it the most as documented by lower rates of banking and homeownership.[637]

Finally, in the case of limited purpose banks and strategic plans, the agencies eliminated a loophole that had permitted some banks with significant retail lending operations to opt not to have retail lending examined. Chapter 2 had discussed the high incidence of

Outstanding ratings on exams of limited purpose banks and those that opted for strategic plans. In some cases, an elimination of the retail lending test may have made it easier to achieve an Outstanding rating when in fact, the bank was not doing a good job making responsible retail loans to LMI borrowers. The agencies recognized these possibilities of exam manipulations and stated, the new limited purpose test, "should not become a means for banks to avoid an evaluation of their retail lending products that would otherwise be subject to an evaluation under the Retail Lending Test." For that reason, the agencies have revised the definition of "Limited purpose bank.... to only include banks that do not offer the types of loans evaluated under the Retail Lending Test or otherwise provide the loans solely on an incidental and accommodation basis."[638] Likewise, if a bank opting for the strategic plan would normally be subject to the retail lending test, it must either retain the performance measures used in the retail lending test or propose goals for retail lending instead.[639]

Agencies strive to promote holistic community development featuring community-based organizations

Clear agency instructions of what activities count on CRA exams must accompany any set of quantitative performance measures. CRA exams will not promote sustainable and ecological revitalization of underserved or distressed neighborhoods if banks receive credit in a willy-nilly fashion for a wide range of activities, several of which can harm the neighborhood environment or livability. Accordingly, the agencies sought to clarify and expand the list of activities that banks should finance to help generate vibrant neighborhoods. The agencies also sought to target the activities to LMI neighborhoods and encourage banks to work in partnership with community-based organizations.

In an effort to provide more flexibility as well as better targeting, the final rule generally allows banks to receive credit for community development financing anywhere in the country provided that a majority of the dollars of the financing benefits LMI people or census tracts.[640] Currently, banks confront more restrictions on serving geographical areas beyond their bank branches. The final rule loosens these restrictions provided that the community development is targeted to traditionally underserved communities. In addition to benefiting LMI people or tracts, the community development activity will be considered impactful and responsive to needs if it is directed to Native American land areas, persistent poverty areas and areas with low levels of community development financing.[641] Advocates had been concerned that eliminating geographical restrictions on community development financing would encourage banks to roam the country finding the easiest places in which to finance community development. Instead, if implemented carefully, the final rule can instead direct financing to places in dire need of financing such as Native American reservations that are now often skipped over by banks since most banks do not have branch-based assessment areas covering reservations; many reservations have few bank branches as described in the interview of Dave Castillo in Chapter 3.[642]

In addition to improved targeting, the final rule enhances the list of activities considered as community development. This includes the usual and important categories of affordable housing and economic development focused on small business growth, but also community facilities, community infrastructure, disaster preparedness and weather resiliency, and neighborhood-based revitalization and stabilization.[643] While a number of these activities already count under the current CRA rules, the agencies sought nevertheless to clarify that these activities counted and also to broaden the types of activities counting under each of the categories. For example, under disaster preparedness and weather resiliency, the final rule discusses financing flood control systems, green space, community solar projects, and energy efficiency upgrades to heating, ventilation, and air conditioning (HVAC) systems.[644] Under community facilities, the agencies list libraries, childcare facilities, parks, hospitals, healthcare facilities, and community centers.[645] Similarly, under community infrastructure, banks could finance broadband, telecommunications, mass transit, water supply and distribution that benefit LMI and other categories of underserved census tracts.[646]

Community supportive services "contribute to the health, stability, or well-being of low- or moderate-income individuals."[647] This includes workforce development and job training programs. This is an important category for people with disabilities. While the preamble to the rule discusses the recommendations of advocates for people with disabilities, the final regulation does not explicitly mention them in conjunction with job training. The agencies remind readers of the final rule that any lists in the final regulation are not exclusive and that additional community supportive services will be included in an illustrative list of qualifying activities.[648] It is hoped that people with disabilities receive sufficient attention in this illustrative list since banks will place more of a priority on funding workforce development and job training for people with disabilities if they are included in the illustrative list.

When describing community development activities that benefit LMI populations, the agencies sought to clarify activities that would not count such as revitalization initiatives that displace long-time LMI residents. The agencies use the language of "forced or involuntary relocation" to cover instances in which residential buildings are demolished leading to forced relocation or when buildings are rendered uninhabitable leading to involuntary relocation.[649] Community-based organizations and stakeholders should be vigilant and ensure that these protections are indeed enforced by CRA examiners not giving credit to revitalization activities that do not benefit LMI people and lead to their displacement.

Indeed, the agencies recognize that community development activities are more likely to confer long-term benefits on community residents if they involve input from the community and bank partnerships with community-based organizations. Under the final rule, revitalization and stabilization activities that include re-use of vacant buildings or restoration of a main street business district are to be conducted by a bank working with either a public sector agency or a mission-driven nonprofit organization.[650] Regarding working with a nonprofit organization, the agencies explain, "mission-driven nonprofit organizations will provide another mechanism to ensure a nexus between an activity and community needs in a particular geographic area, given these organizations' knowledge and record of working within, and with residents of, targeted geographic areas."[651]

On the other hand, while several public agencies can pursue revitalization efforts in a good faith effort to benefit all neighborhood residents, other public agency efforts can have detrimental, or displacement, impacts on LMI residents. There is no guarantee that the emphasis on banks working with local public agencies in revitalization activities will be beneficial in the ways intended by the agencies, but hopefully the emphasis on also working with community-based organizations and ensuring that the majority of the dollars benefit

LMI people will guide most examiners to making sound choices about which public sector projects should earn CRA credit.

The agencies are also creating a category of community development that features banks working with mission-based and community-based financial institutions dedicated to serving LMI and other underserved communities and populations. These institutions include minority depository institutions (MDIs), women depository institutions (WDIs), low-income credit unions (LICUs), and community development financial institution (CDFIs). In establishing this category, the agencies further endeavored to increase bank responsiveness to needs. They state that "the agencies believe that MDIs, WDIs, LICUs, and CDFIs often have intimate knowledge of local community development needs and opportunities, allowing them to conduct highly responsive activities."[652] The interview of Namoch Sokhom and his work for a CDFI in Chapter 3 reinforces the importance of this agency decision.

Another instance of empowering community-based organizations includes the encouragement of new activities that are either new to a particular bank or new to a geographical area. The final rule considers new activities to be responsive and impactful. In the final rule, the agencies state that they "believe that this impact and responsiveness factor will facilitate bank-community partnerships to identify new strategies for addressing community development needs, especially those not adequately addressed by existing products."[653] Illustrating the intention of this responsiveness factor, the final rule cites a bank in a partnership with a community-based organization to acquire land and create shared equity affordable housing.

The care with which the final rule takes to enumerate and elaborate on community development activities and the responsiveness of those activities to needs will hopefully create CRA exams that are better able to leverage a high volume of community development financing valuable for communities. Currently and in the case for the new exams, one common form of community development financing is mortgage-based securities (MBS). MBS are bank investments in security instruments consisting of loans to LMI borrowers. Investments in MBS, mostly by large banks, help other banks make loans to LMI borrowers because the banks originating the loans can move the loans off of their books and acquire capital with which they can make more loans. However, MBS markets are well developed and if CRA exams encourage excessive MBS investments, the other types of community development activities described here remain underfunded. Thus, it is encouraging that the agencies make a concerted effort to outline the many types of non-MBS community development financing opportunities. Moreover, one new community development investment metric for large banks over $10 billion in assets which consists of community development investment dollars divided by deposits will not count MBS in the numerator.[654] This will hopefully also spur a greater variety of non-MBS community development investments, including those in which bank-community based partnerships are integral.

Assessment area expansion an integral reform so that CRA can keep pace with banking

For decades, community organizations had been exhorting the agencies to update assessment areas, the geographical areas on CRA exams, so that CRA exams can adapt as access to banking becomes less tied to branches due to the internet and other non-branch forms of product delivery. While up to 80 percent of lending still occurs in geographical areas with branches, high profile lending institutions are disrupting branch-based lending by lending through the internet.

For fear of losing out in the competition, other banks are starting to follow.[655]

I prepared a report for NCRC a few years ago that found that while most of the lending conducted by the largest 50 banks by asset size were in geographical areas with their branches, some notable exceptions were likely to be copied in future years. For instance, State Farm Bank, FSB is an affiliate of the insurance company. Insurance agents nationwide sell products including mortgage loans. About three percent of State Farm's home loans were in the thrift's one assessment area, Bloomington, Illinois, which is where the headquarters is located. State Farm does not have branches. A lesser-known bank, Everbank, headquarted in Jacksonville, Florida, had fifteen branches located in Florida. However, it gathered deposits via the internet and had a national network of brokers and correspondents with whom it does business. Just 7 percent of its home loans were in its Florida assessment areas. The OCC 2012 exam did not attempt to conduct examination of lending outside of the assessment areas.[656]

My study also found evidence of CRA ratings inflation when CRA exams covered less than a majority of a bank's loans. This makes intuitive sense since banks can ignore meeting needs of LMI populations in areas where they are not rated and can focus on smaller number of areas where they are rated. The eleven banks in which the percent of home loans covered by assessment areas was less than 50 percent were more likely to be rated Outstanding on the lending test than all banks in the sample – the banks with less assessment area coverage received an Outstanding on the lending test 36 percent of the time as opposed to all the top 50 banks that received the top rating 23 percent of the time.[657] A major reason to combat ratings inflation by increasing exam rigor and expanding assessment area coverage is to boost lending to LMI borrowers and communities.

As described in Chapter 2, bank lending levels to LMI communities are higher when geographical areas are covered by assessment areas than when they are not.

In their final rule, the agencies appropriately update assessment areas to cover lending occurring beyond branches. Large banks with more than 20 percent of their lending outside branch networks and 150 home loans or 400 small business or farm loans in a metropolitan area(s) or rural county or counties without their branches will be required to designate these areas as retail lending assessment areas (RLAAs).[658] The agencies calculated that about 23 percent of home lending and 39 percent of small business lending outside of facility-based assessment areas (FBAAs or areas with branches on CRA exams) would be covered by RLAAs.[659] This is a reduction from the proposed rule of 50 percent for home lending and 62 percent for small business lending.[660] The reduction in RLAA coverage was due to the agencies increasing the loan count thresholds in response to push back from the industry. While community advocates would have preferred a higher percentage of lending evaluated on a local basis in RLAAs, the RLAA component of CRA exams will nevertheless require local metropolitan or rural county examination where banks are making concentrations of loans outside of branches. Indeed, the banks would need to work harder because the agencies estimated that performance in about 20 percent of RLAAs would have been rated Needs-to-Improve.[661] Yet, the agencies calculated that overall failure rates for banks were considerably lower, meaning that RLAAs were a spur to improving performance, particularly for banks seeking an Outstanding rating, but were not unduly punitive in terms of driving up failure rates to unrealistically high levels.

In response to comments challenging the legality of RLAAs,

the agencies responded that the CRA statute requires banks to meet needs in their entire community. Moreover, while the statute explicitly refers to evaluations at a metropolitan and state level where branches are located, the statute does not limit evaluations to these areas.[662] Moreover, the agencies affirmed that "retail lending assessment areas would accord with CRA's focus on a bank's local performance in helping to meet community credit needs, promote transparency by providing useful information to the public and banks regarding their performance in specific markets, and improve parity between banks that lend primarily through branches and those banks with different business models."[663]

RLAAs are complemented by Outside Retail Lending Assessment Areas (ORLAAs). The final rule requires the large bank retail lending test to evaluate loans outside of FBAAs and RLAAs on a nationwide level in ORLAAs. ORLAAs are metropolitan areas or rural counties outside of FBAAs and RLAAs in which the bank has made additional loans. This is a major advance. In other words, for the first time, CRA exams for large banks will now capture all home, small business, and small farm lending activity, which will now be examined in FBAAs, RLAAs, and ORLAAs. The evaluation is also sensitive to bank business models. Since most banks are predominantly branch-based and the agency's methodology elevates the importance of lending in FBAAs, FBAAs would receive most weight, followed by RLAAs.[664] Exam methods for weighting scores in FBAAs and RLAAs place most weight on those areas with higher percentages of deposits and loans, which will usually be FBAAs for traditional branch-based banks. Lending in ORLAAs will generally receive the least weight in determining a rating; this seems fair since ORLAA lending can be dispersed across several states and most banks will have the least ability to direct this lending to LMI communities.[665] Overall, the agencies appear to have struck an appropriate balance to ensuring that all lending is evaluated under an exam regime that is the most rigorous for geographical areas where banks have the most capacity to direct their lending to traditionally underserved communities.

Intermediate banks will not have RLAAs but those that make the majority of their loans outside of FBAAs will be required to be evaluated not only in FBAAs but also in ORLAAs.[666] Although community-based organizations had advocated for RLAAs for intermediate banks, capturing their loans in ORLAAs will be important, particularly for these banks that adopt an on-line lending model.

Covering the majority of bank loans by assessment areas is necessary but not sufficient to ensure that banks serve needs across a variety of geographical areas. On current CRA exams, rural counties and smaller metropolitan areas tend to count less towards the overall rating and have less detailed examinations.[667] This approach is not consistent with ensuring that credit needs in all communities are met. To remedy this, the agencies proposed and adopted a requirement that large banks with ten or more FBAAs and RLAAs must receive at least a Low Satisfactory rating, the lowest passing rating, in 60 percent of their FBAAs and RLAAs.[668] Community-based organizations had wanted a higher pass rate of 70 percent or more, noting that under a 60 percent threshold, a large bank can fail in 40 percent of its assessment areas and still pass. Nevertheless, this is the first time that the CRA regulation has imposed a passing requirement based on specified percentage of assessment areas. As the new CRA regulation is implemented, stakeholders will assess the extent to which this new requirement boosts bank reinvestment in smaller cities and rural communities.

Public engagement enhanced but full potential of public engagement not realized

One of the most important, if not the central goal, of CRA is to improve the engagement of the public with both banks and agencies so that CRA's mandate that banks serve community needs is best fulfilled. The CRA regulations should establish a regular and thoughtful process for dialogue among the stakeholders. When considering the final rule, two aspects of public engagement are key: (1) are processes and logistics for public input enhanced so that it is easier for the public to engage banks and agencies, (2) do the quantitative and qualitative methods for assessing bank performance on exams facilitate or frustrate public input.

As discussed in Chapter 3, the agencies have inconsistent procedures for facilitating public input. For some of the agencies, the public can submit comments on CRA exams and merger applications over the internet. For other agencies, the task is more difficult and involves phone calling and emailing an agency in the hopes of figuring out to whom to send comments. Moreover, the agencies are inconsistent regarding their timeliness in responding to public queries. One approach that the agencies in the final rule discuss is creating a portal for submitting comments for agencies that do not have an existing internet option.[669] However, this is a possibility and not an agency commitment to do so. Instead, the agencies should have declared whether it is a portal or some other method that the public will have an easy way to submit comments and that agency officials will respond to questions from the public in an expeditious manner (preferably within 48 hours). A lack of an ironclad commitment to an approach that is standardized and straightforward for facilitating public comment is a disappointment in implementing a law whose effectiveness relies on public engagement.

On the positive side, the agencies will post notices on their websites of upcoming exams for a six-month time period thirty days before the start of each quarterly exam period. Moreover, public comments on a bank's CRA performance must be published on bank websites.[670] The agencies also should have pledged to post the comments on their websites. As discussed in Chapter 2, examiner accountability would be increased for responding to comments if the bank agencies themselves posted comments from the public on their websites. Positively, the agencies' changes foster a more transparent process, which makes it more puzzling why the agencies did not standardize a method for submission of comments or answering questions. For example, if an exam or merger application did not consider a comment from a member of the public, that member may want to ask questions probing why and how to increase the chances that future comments will be explicitly considered.

A public-friendly process must be complemented by examination methods that facilitate a public's understanding of the exam's methodology so that they can most effectively tailor their comments that would then be more likely to be considered by examiners. The quantitative benchmarks and the weighting of the benchmarks, particularly on the retail lending test, became more complex, possibly making it harder for members of the public to comment on quantitative performance. As a former employee of NCRC, which regularly provided technical assistance to community organizations, I can attest that most community groups understand the importance of data analysis but a minority of them undertake the analysis. In many cases, NCRC (myself included as one of the research and policy staffers) would do the analysis for them and help them understand key results. This was true under the current CRA examination regime and will probably remain so under the new regime.

However, the examples described above, such as a bank scoring an Outstanding rating on the metric of loans to low-income borrowers if they are 115 percent above the all-lender percentage is a calculation that can be readily understood by members of the public. With some training, more people will hopefully use these metrics. In addition, by injecting more certainty into scores corresponding to specific performance on the metrics, the new exams will likely stimulate more people to perform analyses in their own geographical areas. They may be motivated to do so because of the new rule for several large banks requiring passing in 60 percent of their assessment areas in order to pass overall. This rule may empower community organizations and embolden them to analyze performance and comment on bank performance in their communities. Each community becomes more important because failure in a handful of areas may imperil a bank's overall rating. This is as it should be: CRA requires banks to serve all communities, not just some of them.

Just as if not more importantly, the qualitative aspects of performance, particularly on the community development tests provide an important avenue for community input. When a bank engages in a large-scale economic revitalization or housing project, does this project benefit long-term neighborhood residents or fuel eventual displacement of modest income residents and people of color. The qualitative criteria emphasizing benefits to LMI populations provide a key means for neighborhood residents to express their views to examiners about these critical issues. It could lead to some banks changing their approach, for example, regarding affordable housing and undertaking projects that set aside more units for LMI residents. The qualitative criteria could also encourage banks to layer beneficial aspects of projects on top of each other, for instance, creating energy efficient housing and community development featuring green space, renewable energy, and weatherization.

While qualitative criteria on the community development test have significant influence on the rating for that test, these criteria are only positive factors (not possible downgrades if they are absent) on the retail services and products test. The bonus points approach most likely dilutes the power of community input on the affordability and sustainability of bank products. This is an area that should be revisited by the agencies after a few years of experience with the new exams.

The agencies missed an opportunity for significantly increasing public input and the effectiveness of that input by not adopting a community group proposal regarding an improvement plan requirement. Under this requirement, banks that score poorly would submit a public improvement plan with measurable goals of how they will achieve a Satisfactory or Outstanding performance. Specifically, if a bank scored Low Satisfactory or less on a component test or overall at an assessment area level or Needs-to-Improve or Substantial Noncompliance overall at the institution level, the bank would submit an improvement plan subject to public comment. This would reduce the binary aspect of CRA – a bank passes or fails – and would help make CRA a more continuous dialogue among stakeholders of how a bank can better serve all its communities. Unfortunately, the agencies declined to adopt this recommendation and instead noted that a bank which received less than a Satisfactory overall rating would need to add to its public file how it will improve its performance.[671]

Importantly, the agencies did not make public input more difficult as the aborted CRA rule by former OCC Comptroller Otting would have. The final rule made advances but left out some important and relatively simple methods like an iron-clad commitment to making it easier to comment on exams. Moreover, the relationship between exam methodology and public input must always be kept in mind as the new rule is implemented.

Agencies enhance data on CRA exams but most of the new data is not readily available in public databases

Community input is also facilitated if CRA exams are supplemented by publicly available data that is generated through the process of banks submitting data to the federal agencies that the agencies require as part of the CRA evaluation. Under the final rule, new data that the banks must report include information on deposit accounts by census tract income category, data on deposit accounts considered responsive to needs of LMI customers, automobile lending data for major automobile lenders, and data on community development loans, investments, and services.[672] However, except for the data on community development loans and investments, the other new data will not be available publicly in excel or other formats for downloading. Public access to data is key for holding banks accountable. For example, under the final rule, the public will have access to CRA disclosure statements and aggregate statements on community development financing that will allow members of the public to compare a bank against its peers annually on a FBAA and metropolitan area-level regarding their level of community development finance and the types of needs financed such as affordable housing and economic development.[673] Considered in the context of the demographic and economic conditions of a locality, the data will help members of the general public prod banks performing worse than their peers to step up their financing in localities that need more affordable housing or economic development or other aspects of community revitalization.

In contrast, the other new data such as those on deposit accounts will only be available on CRA exam tables. Since the agencies produce exams about once every two or three years, annual comparisons among banks will be difficult using data from CRA exams. Moreover, when data cannot be obtained in electronic form, the public needs to create its own databases in a labor-intensive manner by manually inputting data from exams into spreadsheets (I have done this hours-long task for samples of 50 to 100 banks). This clunky means of accessing bank data limits its effectiveness as accountability mechanisms. After experience with the new rule for a few years, the agencies might be more amenable to advocate requests to develop more publicly available datasets with the new CRA data.

Finally, the agencies will be presenting HMDA data, which has been collected for decades, in new ways on their websites.[674] In response to concerns about racial equity, the agencies are striving to increase the transparency of data on lending by race and ethnicity. In the proposed rule, the agencies had proposed including HMDA data tables on lending by race, ethnicity, and income in the banks' CRA exams. In response to industry objections that these new tables would be misleading since CRA exams would not rate lending performance by race and ethnicity, the agencies will now display these tables on their websites and will provide annual notices to the public regarding the availability of these tables.[675] While a strong case can be made that the data should be on CRA exams, if the agencies present the data in an informative and easy-to-understand manner on their websites, they will be increasing transparency and accountability of banks. As discussed in Chapter 2, the CFPB disseminates HMDA data to the public, but mostly in a raw data format that only a subset of the public skilled in data analysis can readily access. The agency has declined so far to provide summary tables of distinct types of lending by race, ethnicity, and income that can be converted into excel and that would expand public use of the data. It would be a somewhat ironic but positive development if the bank agencies once again produce accessible tables that used to be provided for years by the Federal Financial Institutions Examination Council.

Industry lawsuit against the final rule amounts to a basic objection to CRA

About three months after the federal bank agencies finalized their CRA rule, the American Bankers Association (ABA) led a lawsuit co-filed with other trade associations and chambers of commerce against the final rule. In a press release accompanying the filing of the lawsuit, ABA President and CEO Rob Nichols asserted, "We strongly support and appreciate the goals of the Community Reinvestment Act, but in this exceedingly complex rulemaking, the agencies have created a CRA evaluation framework that unlawfully exceeds what Congress authorized and fails to recognize banks' demonstrated commitment to fully serving their communities. Even more troubling, the Final Rules risk undermining the very goals of CRA by creating disincentives for banks to offer certain products or lend in geographies outside of their branch network."[676]

One of the major complaints in the lawsuit concerned the creation of RLAAs. Because RLAAs are assessment areas with concentrations of lending beyond bank branches, the lawsuit alleges that the agencies exceeded their statutory authority because assessment areas can only be geographical areas encompassing bank branches. The lawsuit cites the statute's statement of purpose that makes a reference to meeting needs in local communities.[677] However, the very first phrase in the purpose statement maintained that "regulated financial institutions are required by law to demonstrate that their deposit facilities serve the convenience and needs of the communities in which they are chartered to do business."[678] This affirmation implies that banks are to serve all communities that their charter allows them to serve. The reference to "deposit facilities" is statutory shorthand for bank charters broadly and is not confined only to refer to branches.[679] Moreover, Section 2903 of the statute mandates that CRA exams assess performance in the "entire community," not just areas where branches are.[680] If a bank is chartered to do business in a particular state, is it reasonable for the bank to say that it will only adhere to its CRA obligations in a couple of cities where it has branches but not in surrounding counties with no branches but high volumes of the bank's loans?

It is doubtful that Senator Proxmire would agree with this interpretation nor would the ABA witness that testified at the CRA hearing asking for more flexibility to serve rural areas beyond the big cities as reviewed in Chapter 4. The ABA suit also maintains that since the statute refers to evaluations in states and metropolitan areas where banks have branches, then evaluations beyond the branch footprint are disallowed.[681] Yet, as Chapter 4 also reviews, the Riegle-Neal Interstate Banking and Branching Efficiency Act in 1994 added this language to the statute as banks were expanding across state lines. It would seem the intent is less to confine exams around bank branches but more to require that exams ensure reinvestment in all states, metropolitan areas, and rural counties that banks are serving as banks became interstate institutions. This would suggest that efforts to allow CRA exams to catch up with the evolution of banking including mobile and non-branch means of service should be regarded favorably.

In his recent book regarding judicial methods for examining federal law and the Constitution, Former Associate Justice Stephen Breyer remarks:

> Congress cannot write statutes that precisely address every possible application of each phrase to all circumstances. Life is too unpredictable. Congress will almost inevitably write words that overshoot or undershoot their mark. Congress can often ameliorate this human circumstance by writing more abstract, general words instead of detailed, precise phrases. But it can do this if, and only if, courts cooperate by considering legislative purposes when the courts interpret statutes.[682]

The Congressional purpose and legislative history of CRA would support the agency decision to examine bank activity in all geographical areas where banks are undertaking a significant amount of activity to ensure that banks are serving community needs.

The complaint states that RLAAs would be unreasonable and burdensome because "Banks also will be required to cultivate relationships in new assessment areas to facilitate the identification and pursuit of sound low- and moderate-income lending opportunities, or to purchase low- and moderate-income loans."[683] However, a central purpose of CRA is to encourage banks to develop business relationships and partnerships including with nonprofit organizations that would help them serve LMI populations. In RLAAs where banks have figured out how to make high volumes of loans, is it conceivable that banks would have no business partnerships that they could further utilize so they can reach all markets and groups of borrowers? The complaint's arguments undercut the quote about supporting CRA since the lawsuit implies that the work of CRA is burdensome and not beneficial to banks, let alone the community. In fact, the complaint continues by saying that banks will just reduce their lending beyond their branches so they would not incur RLAA designations and evaluations.[684] How plausible is it that they would just give up money-making opportunities to competitors because of a CRA requirement? Instead of basing a lawsuit on dubious assertions, it would be preferable if the ABA would support the position of advocates that for CRA to work best, it must be applied to all lending institutions including non-bank mortgage companies. Any costs would be reduced because they would be spread out more evenly across the entire lending industry.

The meaning of community is changing – at least for the banks that continue to close their branches and increase their mobile and online banking. Virtual deposit gathering activity will likely generate large numbers of deposit customers residing beyond a branch network. A significant number of these virtual customers will apply for and receive loans; these customers with both deposits and loans could remain concentrated in specific geographical areas. It would seem appropriate following the complaint's logic on coupling deposit taking and lending in CRA exams to include these geographical areas without branches in evaluations. Additionally, advocates desire that de-coupled deposit and lending activity also should be evaluated so that the statute's mandate that a bank meet needs in all communities be realized. Nevertheless, the ABA objects to evaluation and data collection of deposit activity on the grounds that it is too costly, disregarding benefits of improving CRA exams and identifying and increasing profitable opportunities of expanding business underserved communities.

It is contradictory that the complaint objects to the agencies requiring CRA exams to assess activity beyond branch-based assessment areas. As Brad Blower of Inclusive Partners, LLC points out, the bank trade associations stated in their comment letters that banks should receive favorable CRA consideration for community development activities outside of their assessment areas.[685] But if the agencies considered some activities but not other activities such as retail lending outside of branch-based assessment areas, the exams would become arbitrary and capricious – a quality the bank trades oppose in their complaint. Instead of covering all important activities, the exams would only cover some of them. That would be unfair to communities.

The ABA's complaint estimates that the first-year implementation costs would be $600 million or more than six times the OCC's estimate of $91 million.[686] First-year implementation costs include start-up costs such as creating new data gathering tools which are not incurred in subsequent years. The complaint is likely overestimating costs because of its first-year focus and because it refers to a survey of 100 banks without describing the survey questions asked or the methodology for calculating costs.[687] The brief filed by the federal bank agencies in the lawsuit states that additional costs are minimal. The brief states that, "Put in the context of the banks' overall expenses, the estimate of these compliance costs are mere hundredths or thousandths of a percentage point of the affected banks' aggregate total noninterest expenses."[688]

Since the lawsuit is focused on costs, it shies away from estimating benefits in terms of reinvestment in LMI communities including ones still experiencing redlining. Chapter 2 included a rough estimate of how benefits just in terms of increases in home lending in LMI tracts overwhelmed initial agency estimates of costs. While the complaint makes a valid point that the agencies' cost benefit analysis could have been more comprehensive, an even better approach for the ABA would have been to cooperate with the agencies to develop a robust cost benefit analysis including surveys of benefits as well as costs over the period.[689] An evenhanded and comprehensive cost-benefit analysis with multiple stakeholder input from the community as well as banks would likely lead to a different conclusion than one in a lawsuit that does not describe its cost-benefit methodology.

The ABA complaint attempts to clinch its argument by stating that the final rule is arbitrary and capricious. It states that, "the CRA requires periodic evaluation of a bank's CRA performance, but the Final Rules leave banks guessing about what areas will be assessed, which products will qualify for CRA evaluation, and what market benchmarks they must meet in order to earn a "Satisfactory," much less an "Outstanding," rating.[690] The complaint explains that banks need data in order to figure which areas will be RLAAs, which of their products will be evaluated across its assessment areas, and how they compare against their peers which is necessary for determining their likely rating. The exams would be completed before the data needed by the banks would become available, forcing the banks to guess in their own CRA analysis, according to the complaint.[691] However, this phenomenon occurs now under current exams. Data including home lending involves a time lag under which data for the most recent year becomes available late the following year. Because of the lag in the public availability of industrywide data, banks, like the public, often do not know how they stack up to their peers in home lending in the last year of the CRA exam cycle. Currently, banks and the public use historical data for the preceding two or three years as guides about bank performance in the last year of their exam.

This has proven workable for banks during the last three decades of CRA exams given the 98 percent pass rate described in

Chapter 2. It would be workable under the new regime as well. This argument does not prove capriciousness because CRA over the last three decades would then be capricious. Finally, it is inconceivable that banks could not use their own internal data to have fairly certain predictions regarding where they would have RLAAs and which products would be evaluated in which assessment areas.

The complaint states that Congress does not desire the agencies to modernize CRA including creating RLAAs because it has rejected the CRA modernization bills that have been introduced over the years.[692] At the same time, however, Congress has rejected bills put forward by CRA opponents that would repeal or significantly weaken CRA. Congressional opponents of CRA have admitted over the years that they did not have the votes for repeal.[693] The complaint's line of reasoning implies the agencies should not do anything since the most expansive pro-CRA bills nor the most aggressive anti-CRA bills did not pass. What the agencies attempted to do was make reasonable compromises that they knew would not totally please banks or community groups, but that would make CRA more effective and less frustrating by making it more transparent and objective. In this light, the ABA complaint is counterproductive as it is designed to deter meaningful action to rectify the vestiges of discrimination and improve the life chances of all communities.

Conclusion

CRA rulemaking must proceed in a data driven process with interagency coordination and ample opportunity for public input. The agencies developed their 2023 interagency final rule based on extensive data analysis, particularly regarding the development of the scoring system for the lending test. In addition, interested members of the public could comment during several months in the comment period associated with the Federal Reserve's ANPR and the proposed rule. Moreover, a nearly three-year period occurred during the Federal Reserve's ANPR and the interagency Notice of Proposed Rulemaking (NPR) during which stakeholders had access to regulatory officials to engage in conversations about the rulemaking and their preferred approaches.

The history of CRA regulatory rulemaking illustrates that when a single agency proceeds with a rule on its own, the result is often harmful of the statutory goals of CRA. As described in the previous chapter, the OTS' unilateral revisions in the mid-2000s resulted in decreases in bank reinvestment activity. Similarly, the OCC's final 2020 rule would have skewed CRA activity away from a focus on community needs.. While the dollar amount of activity may have increased due to a faulty performance measure, it is probable that substantial amounts of any increased activity would have had either marginal benefits for traditionally underserved communities or harmful impacts associated with large infrastructure projects that were not well conceived because they did not involve input from the impacted communities.

In contrast, the 2023 final rule, while imperfect, is a solid foundation for future rulemaking and adjusts the scope of CRA exams so that they are better able to assess the reinvestment records of banks that have undergone tremendous technological and business model changes. In addition, the agencies have more than two years to implement the rule (from October 2023 until January 2026 when the rule becomes effective).[694] This provides opportunities to improve the rule by clarifying issues in agency guidance and other documents including how to use some of the performance measures that do not have thresholds like those in the retail lending test. Banks and community groups have opportunities to provide input on guidance materials developed by the agencies.

When evaluating a new rule, a useful yardstick is not whether the new rule is perfect but whether it is likely to increase bank reinvestment activity and whether it establishes a solid foundation for future rulemakings to augment the positive aspects of the rule. By this yardstick, the 2023 rulemaking succeeds and is the most transformative rulemaking since 1995. It established objective performance measures, especially for the large bank lending test, but also for the retail service and products test, and the community development tests. The retail lending test has the most detail regarding the thresholds and performance ranges that banks must obtain to receive Outstanding and Satisfactory ratings. While the other tests have performance measures, these tests remain under-developed in the sense that examiners probably have too much discretion in how to interpret the results of bank performance on the measures, possibly leading to subjectively, ratings inflation, and inconsistencies across exams.

However, the agencies have pledged to write additional guidance which hopefully will clarify how performance on the other exam metrics will be judged. Moreover, the agencies will consider additional reforms in possible future rulemakings to performance measures and the possible development of thresholds as well as more precision on the qualitative measures. The job for advocates and other stakeholders is to hold the agencies to these promises and push for future rulemaking or additional guidance if in future years, CRA exams are not living up to their potential. This is particularly important if aspects of exams such as only positive consideration regarding the affordability and sustainability of lending and deposit products proves to be a shortcoming in holding banks accountable for offering responsible and responsive products. In addition, the impacts of streamlining that stripped community development and service tests from hundreds of banks needs to be assessed and compensated for if parts of the country experience declines in reinvestment activity in coming years.

What must be greatly appreciated is that the reforms in assessment areas for large banks ensure that all home, small business, and small farm lending and investment activity will be evaluated for the first time. This is a huge advance, especially considering that more banks will be engaging in hybrid product delivery using branches and non-branch means while many others will be moving away from branches in the coming years. Since shortly after the 1995 rulemaking, community organizations have been advocating for these types of changes in assessment area procedures.

In terms of empowering members of the public and making it easier for community groups to offer input on CRA exams, the agencies receive mixed reviews. There is no good reason why an easy-to-use portal over the internet (or other method) could not be developed on an interagency basis to facilitate community group comments and questions. The agencies must also promise professionalism in terms of answers being responded to promptly. As currently constituted as of this writing, the agencies, by and large, are dedicated to the proposition that CRA will work best only if the community at large is engaged as one of the most important stakeholders in the CRA process. Finally, clarity in the quantitative measures plus elevation of the importance of qualitative measures should further sharpen and focus public comments, making them more effective.

An evaluation of the final rule would not be complete from the community group perspective if it did not mention that the rule did reach far enough in consideration of lending, investing, and services in communities of color. The agencies should have at least developed proxies for examining activity in communities of color such as underserved census tracts. As discussed in Chapter 4, NPA and others were advocating for this in 1970s and the hearings leading up to the passage of CRA in 1977 included a focus on underserved communities. Promotion of Special Purpose Credit Programs (SPCP) in CRA exams is a positive development but not a sufficient response, particularly since SPCPs will be considered in a part of the retail services and products test that only earns positive consideration. The agencies have opened the door on racial equity; community groups will continue knocking and hope to further open the door in future years, especially after the case law hopefully swings back in favor of addressing the pernicious impacts of past and current discrimination.

The unevenness of any final regulation is the result of compromises the agencies strike among the competing interests of community groups and banks. The agencies adopted exam features that are not rigorous enough from the perspectives of community organizations in part because they responded to concerns about burdens and costs from the industry. While community advocates do not usually agree with assertions regarding the degree of burden posed by CRA exams, some compromise is necessary to create enough acceptance from all stakeholders. Furthermore, the most effective way to revisit these compromises and to update complex regulations is to revisit rules periodically every five years or so. Allowing 28 years to elapse between the most significant regulatory changes in 1995 and 2023 frustrates stakeholders and lessens the ability of CRA exams to keep pace with evolution in technology and bank practices.

Unfortunately, even the most thoughtful revision to a regulation is not immune from political or legal challenge in today's polarized environment. In addition to the February 2024 lawsuit against the final CRA rule, the industry filed a lawsuit in the spring of 2023 against a final rule implementing Section 1071 small business and farm loan data that would be used on CRA exams.[695] As of this writing, the industry is appealing District Judge Crane's decision in favor of the Consumer Financial Protection Bureau and its implementation of Section 1071.[696] The industry trade associations have embarked on a campaign to delay or derail the most significant CRA reform since 1995. The trade association's comment letter and lawsuit couch these concerns in an overall criticism of inadequate agency presentations of data and supporting rationale for the proposed changes. However, an objective comparison between the development of the interagency proposal with the OCC final rule described in the previous chapter would conclude that interagency rule had carefully developed reasoning which the OCC rule lacked. Moreover, contrary to the ABA's assertions, stakeholders essentially knew what the final rule would contain and had an opportunity to influence its development over a multiple year period.

In contrast to the ABA lawsuit, the NCRC lawsuit against the OCC was based on the belief that the OCC final rule was contrary to the purpose and intent of CRA as well as the legislative history of CRA which rejected a simplistic ratio approach adopted by the OCC. Moreover, the great majority of stakeholders opposed the OCC final rule, but the OCC declared in its preamble to the final rule that it would proceed anyway. That seems to define an arbitrary and capricious approach in contrast to the 2023 interagency rule.

As stakeholders, both banks and community groups have a responsibility to proceed in a reasonable manner. Lawsuits should be used as a last resort and only in exceptional circumstances like the case of the OCC final rule, which officials of the other federal agencies also criticized. An over-reliance on the judicial system undermines attempts of regulatory rulemaking to be transparent, fair, and solicitous of public input. It ultimately undermines the CRA statute and efforts to eradicate redlining.

A more constructive approach would be to monitor the implementation of the 2023 final rule and to provide input to regulatory agencies often. Stakeholders should also support periodic and incremental adjustments to the final rule such as agency review and possible revisions every five years. In that manner, an important regulation has the best chance of achieving necessary and calibrated refinements.

The final 2023 rule, despite its flaws, offers a foundation for both community groups and bankers to build a better CRA examination regime and increase profitable and responsible lending, investment, and services in all communities and particularly the ones that have not fully recovered from decades of discrimination. It is hoped that stakeholders can come together in a cooperative spirit to seek improvements in the equity and efficiency of the final rule, but first, concerned stakeholders will now need to wait the fate of the industry lawsuit to know whether this needed reform to the CRA regulation is upheld or whether the agencies need to start anew.

After taking Avenue's First-time Homebuyer Education class and receiving downpayment assistance, Amedie Robinson purchased a home in Houston's Near Northside community. The 2023 regulatory CRA reform sought to elevate housing counseling and flexible lending on CRA exams.

Photo credit: Tom Callins and Avenue

9

Next Steps for CRA: Recommendations for Lasting Impact

John Taylor, NCRC's first President and CEO, affirmed that "Access to credit and capital is a civil right and should be recognized as such."[697]

Taylor's bold statement is insightful and more nuanced than appears on the surface. Access to credit is one of the prerequisites for our country to realize the ideals expressed in the Declaration of Independence as promoting life, liberty, and the pursuit of happiness. If communities suffer redlining, they are also likely to experience other forms of discrimination and thus are more prone to becoming impoverished; their residents will lack the necessities of life including adequate jobs, shelter, and food. As the stories of Freddie Grey and Sabrina Walls make clear, CRA should be thought of as a civil or human rights law that can literally make the difference between a quality life or death. At the same time, no individual has an inalienable right to credit, particularly if the person is not credit worthy and ready for a loan. However, on a neighborhood level, CRA acts as a civil rights law by making redlining or discrimination against neighborhoods illegal. And as documented in Chapter 1, redlining was one of several structural and institutional factors placing communities of color and modest income communities at significant disadvantages. Removing redlining is therefore necessary for communities to enable their residents to enjoy life, liberty, and the pursuit of happiness.

If we put communities first and empower neighborhood residents, we will be more successful in ending redlining, stopping housing discrimination, and revitalizing neighborhoods. The forces of systemic discrimination extend beyond the financial industry so applying a community centered CRA throughout the financial industry will not eradicate impoverished neighborhoods. However, it is my bet that expanding a community centered CRA across the financial industry will result in more neighborhoods being reinvigorated in a manner that benefits residents instead of displacing them. The victims of redlining know firsthand what the credit needs of their neighborhoods are, and they have a long-term stake in the success of their neighborhoods. Not involving them as a central focus of reinvestment is not only wrong, but also counterproductive.

Community must be at the center and empowered – the victims are not the villains

So, what does a community centered CRA look like? First, it breathes more life into CRA exams and merger applications. Instead of stale technical documents with mountains of numbers and formulas, CRA exams and decisions on mergers should feature narrative and community views that put meaning into the quantitative analysis and helps explain banks' weaknesses and strengths in reinvestment. Federal agencies must clearly communicate to communities and their organizations the process for commenting on CRA exams and merger applications. They must make logistical details clear including deadlines and where and to whom to send comments. The agencies must take the comments seriously and indicate how their analysis incorporates the comments. They should provide final CRA exams and orders on mergers and other bank applications to those who commented. This is not done consistently now. More public hearings should be held on merger applications. Agency courtesy and professionalism must become part of an ethos that communities matter and that they will be listened to and respected for their key insights into how to fulfill CRA's mandate that banks serve their needs.

CRA exams and merger orders must cease being blunt and binary. Often, they have the feel of a bad novel that lacks complexity. The only story is that either the bank passed or failed its exam or that its application has been approved or rarely rejected. However, there is more nuance than that in CRA. CRA exams should reflect a dialogue between historically disenfranchised communities and a financial industry that had and has a powerful impact on their fate. One should think of CRA as a bargaining session where all participants are respected and accommodated. If a bank passes its exam, it is still unlikely that it does not have weaknesses on which to improve. The CRA regulation should require improvement plans subject to public comment for assessment areas in which a bank has scored Low Satisfactory or less. Likewise, CRA exams in a new section called expectations for improvement should discuss the extent to which bank products and programs respond to needs and opportunities as articulated by the community. If there are clear lending, investment, or service weaknesses identified in these parts of an exam, a bank should be expected to improve upon them in the next exam or else a rating in certain assessment areas, component tests, or overall should be impacted.

Merger orders should likewise facilitate dialogue and solutions benefiting banks and communities. CBAs arising from mergers or in the normal course of business can also form the basis of CRA strategic plans. The agencies should employ conditional approvals more frequently. In addition, substantive issues raised by the community should be revisited in subsequent CRA exams.

Opponents of CRA will periodically cast communities as villains instead of victims. They will allege that community organizations are merely trying to "shakedown" banks. They will try to reinvigorate CRA sunshine. Disclosure of the initial CBA agreements and improved data disclosure and review on CRA exams are better means than former Senator Gramm's sunshine to ensure that all parties – community organizations and banks – are held to high standards for delivering quality community development financing and services.

While promoting public input on CRA exams is imperative, CRA experience to date suggests that the most prevalent form of public input is negotiating CBAs or influencing banks to adopt community benefit plans. At this point, CBAs are an informal part of the CRA process. They may remain so for some time. However, it is vital that the agencies treat them with more respect and cease the practice of issuing footnotes in merger approval orders that CBAs are not required by the CRA statute. Instead, approval orders could acknowledge that they are one way banks can demonstrate their legal requirement that mergers benefit the public in terms of banks being better able to meet community convenience and needs. As

Chapters 2 and 3 document, CBAs have increased bank lending and reinvestment. In this context, why not encourage them?

CBAs are not without their critics. Some worry that CBAs do not represent all communities since CBA negotiations may not involve all groups in all geographical areas served by banks. Others such as former Senator Phil Gramm worry that CBAs may result in banks funding fraudulent or ineffective activities. Gramm's CRA sunshine law aims to curtail a central part of CRA, which is ascertaining community needs by involving community groups and the public at large in the CRA and merger application process. Instead of Gramm's sunshine requirement, transparency of CBAs can be maintained by a requirement for disclosure of the CBAs and the agencies placing the CBAs on their websites. In addition, as discussed in Chapter 6, regulatory agencies and CRA examiners can judge the quality of CRA-related grants, loans, investments, and services stimulated by CBAs and encourage banks to continue those that are effective and discourage those that are not. Finally, not all discussions during the bank merger application process need to result in CBAs. Community input can also inform robust bank plans submitted on their merger applications about how specifically they will satisfy their public benefit requirements. These plans, however, need to have measurable outcomes and be more specific than the vague promises that have often appeared on merger applications over the years.

The controversy over CBAs is reminiscent of the controversy over the rise of labor unions and labor-management contracts. It would seem that these contracts over the decades have provided for increases in the safety and standard of living of workers. They provide for increased worker participation and empowerment. Yet, these contracts are imperfect instruments that can appear to be one-sided or excessive at times regarding the benefits or costs for one of the parties involved. As CBAs evolve, they too should be viewed through this lens. Increases in transparency and follow-through by all the parties including banks, community organizations, and agencies should hopefully improve their equity and efficiency.

CRA exams must be comprehensive and robust

CRA requires banks to respond to a variety of community needs. Accordingly, it must have a variety of well-constructed quantitative and qualitative performance measures and component tests that measure the extent to which banks respond to needs. As discussed in Chapters 5 and 8, several performance measures are fairer for banks as well as communities. Banks can often compensate for weaker performance on some measures with stronger performance on others and thereby pass their exams. Indeed, CRA legislative development and regulatory rulemaking as discussed in Chapters 4 and 5 have rejected simplistic performance measures that focus on just one or a few ratios as more akin to credit allocation.

Large banks must undergo exams that assess their retail lending and services and community development financing. Traditionally underserved communities cannot successfully revitalize if they only receive a subset of these activities like retail home purchase lending but not others such as economic development financing that reinvigorates businesses on Main Street. The agencies erred by reducing the requirements for comprehensive exams for intermediate banks. These banks now have less robust retail tests since they do not publicly report small business lending and their branching patterns are not consistently analyzed on CRA exams. Instead of reducing exam coverage, agencies can respond to concerns of comparing smaller banks to larger ones by focusing exams for the smaller banks on peer comparisons of banks with similar asset sizes, particularly on the community development finance tests that can involve complex financing for larger banks.

Exams will have reduced effectiveness if they lack publicly available data for their analysis. Publicly available data is also needed by community groups that will conduct their own analyses, thereby providing an accountability check on examiners' analyses as discussed in Chapters 3 and 8. Over time, more data needs to be become publicly available including more robust data which I hope is provided by Section 1071 in the case of small business lending and in the updates to the CRA regulation in the case of community development financing data.

While many banks still lend mostly via their branches, others are serving their communities via the internet or other non-branch means. The authors of the 1977 law did not foresee the internet but they understood that even in the 1970s, some banks were becoming national in scope and thus CRA exams needed to have the ability to assess their reinvestment activities beyond areas in which they have their branches. It is consistent with the original legislation for the agencies to examine bank activity beyond their branch network and establish assessment areas beyond branch networks.

A looming and unresolved issue in CRA examination and practice is race and CRA. Redlining often focused on communities of color. The political environment of the 1970s helped explain the absence of an explicit mandate for CRA to serve communities of color. The political and legal environment remained challenging in the regulatory rewrite in the 1990s and remains so today. However, CRA always had a focus on underserved and redlined communities. It is consistent with this focus to identify underserved census tracts and require CRA exams to assess bank activity in these tracts. Many of these tracts are communities of color. This can be supplemented by CRA exams recognizing and evaluating bank Special Purpose Credit Programs (SPCPs) that identify via data analysis underserved people and communities, which could include people of color in various metropolitan areas and rural counties across the country.

Lastly, CRA has one major enforcement mechanism, that is the merger application process. CRA ratings and performance influence decisions on mergers. However, this leaves out enforcement for the multitude of banks that are not merging. Enforcement options for these banks include the proposed improvement plan requirement that addresses inconsistencies in performance. The agencies could also adjust the fees they assess banks for supervision based on their CRA performance. Furthermore, previous CRA modernization bills denied certain privileges such as selling loans to Fannie Mae and Freddie Mac unless a poor performing lender submitted a plan for improving its performance as discussed in Chapter 6. The federal government could also deny poorly performing banks con-tracting opportunities with agencies until they improve their CRA performance.

No matter how well the recent CRA reform adjusts to changes in banking or achieves improvements in objective assessment of per-formance, CRA exams are likely to remain imperfect. Enforcement and ratings rigor has waxed and waned as this book has pointed out. CRA exams need to have checks and balances just as any system of democratic government must. The agencies need to increase public comments by creating an easier process for commenting and keeping a publicly available record of comments. As Chapter 3 demonstrates, case studies have shown that public comments on CRA exams have improved bank performance in subsequent years. The agencies should improve the chances of comments having positive impacts by keeping a publicly available record of them, which enables the public to increase accountability by observing how examiners and banks respond to them and facilitating more research on the connection between public participation and CRA performance.

Another way to correct weaknesses in CRA exams is to provide opportunities for community groups and other stakeholders to negotiate CBAs during merger applications to correct anything overlooked by CRA exams, particularly for the largest banks.

Data on CRA performance in all aspects of reinvestment from retail lending to community development financing must be robust and publicly available so that the public can offer their own views on CRA performance. Publicly available data is another check on CRA exams in that stakeholders can engage in data analysis and provide input into whether the CRA exam is rigorous. The more transparent and participatory the CRA enforcement system, the more it is likely to achieve heightened levels of reinvestment.

State level CRA laws can pave the way for innovation

We should not wait or solely rely on Congress or the federal bank agencies to improve CRA. The Consumer Financial Protection Bureau (CFPB) identifies eight states that apply versions of the federal CRA to banks and in some cases to non-bank lenders including mortgage companies and credit unions.[698] A number of these state laws have novel features such as additional protections against the loss of affordable housing that federal CRA should emulate. Advocates should use states as laboratories of democracy and continue pushing for more states to adopt CRA laws including applying CRA to non-banks that the federal government has not yet done. This may in turn apply pressure on Congress to expand CRA to more financial institutions.

CRA must be applied to all parts of large banks and broadly throughout financial industry

The largest banks in the country have sizable non-bank financial subsidiaries and affiliates including investment banks, mortgage companies, and insurance firms. CRA should be applied to all these entities in order to leverage increases in safe and sound lending to and investing in traditionally underserved communities. In addition, CRA should be made more rigorous for the largest banks in the country. In the early days of CRA, NPA had suggested hearings accompanying CRA exams.[699] Hearings could readily be part of CRA exams for the largest 50 or 100 banks. NPA and other advocates found that it was hard in the 1970s to hold the largest banks accountable for responding to local needs. This is even more true today. Hearings could be another way to elevate the importance of local needs across the footprint of the national banks and ensure that CRA exams assess banks' responsiveness to these needs. Improvement plans could also help smooth out performance by requiring the largest banks to improve in geographical areas including smaller cities and rural areas where their performance lags.

As well as applying CRA to all parts of banks, this book has made the case for applying CRA exams to insurance companies, securities firms, independent mortgage companies, and credit unions. Reinvestment stands a better chance of succeeding by applying a CRA requirement to all parts of the financial industry. Banks were not the only entities with a past that included redlining or abusive lending. As discussed in Chapter 2, nonbanks participated in these nefarious practices and should, therefore, contribute their significant resources to a program of reinvestment.

In addition, Fannie Mae (Fannie) and Freddie Mac (Freddie) continue to have outsized influence in the industry since they purchase sizable number of loans from banks and non-bank lenders. They are subject to affordable housing goals, but these goals are national level goals that mandate that these entities purchase designated percentages of loans that were made to LMI borrowers and underserved communities.[700] There is no local accountability. NCRC has urged the regulatory agency, the Federal Housing Finance Agency (FHFA), to examine Fannie and Freddie purchasing activity across metropolitan areas and rural counties. The FHFA could identify a subset of urban and rural areas that Fannie and Freddie are underserving and mandate improvements in these areas. The improvements could be incremental in that Fannie and Freddie could be required to improve in 30 percent of these areas (or higher if the performance was particularly poor for one of the enterprises) over a two- or three-year period and then address the remaining areas over future years.[701] So far, the FHFA has not adopted this or a similar approach. Alternatively, the FHFA could make data on Fannie's and Freddie's performance on a county and metropolitan level publicly available so that stakeholders can engage Fannie and Freddie in addressing local weaknesses in performance identified by the data analysis. Since redlining is a local phenomenon, the FHFA should meaningfully supplement national goal setting with local accountability mechanisms. This would also make it easier for banks and non-bank lenders to serve underserved communities. If the FHFA does not elevate the importance of local performance, then Congress should consider this reform.

CRA beyond the financial industry

As maintained by Chapter 1, the tragedy of systemic discrimination cannot be solved by one law applying to one industry. CRA is not a failure if it does not revitalize all impoverished neighborhoods. As important as it is to apply CRA across the entire financial industry, that reform would unlikely be enough. We need to think about additional industries and spheres including the public sector that has its own history with exclusive zoning and other racist policies.

Jesse Van Tol, President and CEO of NCRC, maintained:

> People underestimate the size of the problem, so you have a problem that was hundreds of years in the making, that involves some of the darkest parts of American history, the stealing and destruction of wealth, particularly for Black people and people of color generally. The problem is multifaceted in its creation, and it has to be multifaceted in its solutions. There are CBAs in a development context. The community benefit requirement is built into the Affordable Care Act for hospitals. The concept is really this: there are a lot of entities that are privileged in some way, shape, or form to do their business by the government, and in exchange they should produce a community benefit.[702]

As Fishkin and Forbath discuss, progressives, New Deal liberals, and other reformers have emphasized that when government grants a charter to a private business, the private business must be beholden to the community. Likewise, when Senator Proxmire and his staff drafted the CRA statute as reviewed in Chapter 4, they insisted that banks, which thrive by using their customer's money, must provide a community benefit. Over the decades, policymakers and economists have debated whether businesses must only answer to their stockholders or a broader array of stakeholders including workers and the local community. Those policymakers advocating for stakeholders suggest that private companies should have mechanisms for soliciting the input of stakeholders including slots on the board of directors for workers and community members as well as advisory committees composed of these stakeholders. Lastly, reformers have emphasized that a lack of democratic input in the private sector imperils political democracy. Forbath and Fishkin state that we must "build a regime of corporate governance that is compatible over the long run with democratic government."[703]

When thinking about charter obligations, one industry that should produce community benefits includes nonprofit hospitals. In exchange for a nonprofit tax exemption, the Affordable Care Act of 2010 imposed a requirement that these hospitals conduct a Community Health Needs Assessment (CHNA) every three years and then implement strategies to respond to identified needs. A hospital must define a community it serves including medically underserved communities, low-income, or minority communities. Medically underserved communities do not receive adequate medical care and exhibit high incidences of health problems such as those documented in formerly redlined communities discussed in Chapter 1. The hospital is to identify barriers including the cost of health care and environmental factors contributing to poor health outcomes. Just like CRA requirements, the hospital must solicit the views of the underserved community. The CHNA then develops strategies to combat these barriers.[704]

The CHNA requirement has leveraged resources, but its full potential remains unfulfilled. An example of a CHNA inspired program is ProMedica's support for free and reduced-breakfast and lunch programs for low-income children in its service areas of Ohio and Michigan. The hospital's CHNA had identified food insecurity as a factor contributing to poor health outcomes.[705] Another Midwest hospital, Morris Hospital, serving 18 rural counties identified lack of transportation as a health barrier. Since the inception of its transportation program, the hospital has supported 140,000 rides to medical facilities.[706] Overall, however, the Lown Institute has documented that nonprofit hospitals have not contributed their fair share to charity over the years. It calculated a fair share deficit of over $14 billion in 2020.[707] Perhaps, advocates can combine their CRA and CHNA work and partnerships to further leverage more resources for holistic approaches to community revitalization.

The real estate development industry has featured the development of CBAs since the 1990s (according to Van Tol, NCRC started using the term CBA for CRA agreements in order to encourage connections to other agreements in other industries). The rationale for these CBAs is that the developments often receive tax subsidies and in return they should benefit the surrounding communities. At the same time, CBAs seek to prevent harm associated with development such as displacement of lower income residents. CBAs are often negotiated between community organizations and real estate developers and sometimes also involve local city governments. Benefits arising from CBAs include living wage requirements, local hiring goals, affordable housing, childcare centers, and other community facilities.[708] PowerSwitch Action offers several recommendations for strong CBAs that are quite similar to CBAs in the CRA context and include oversight committees with community representation and measurable goals to monitor CBA performance.[709] An example of a successful CBA is the Pittsburgh Hill District CBA that included $1 million for the development of a grocery store and funding for a job referral and training center.[710]

The grocery store example is relevant for CBAs with real estate developers and with banks since food deserts are a significant problem in lower income neighborhoods and a pressing credit need is financing grocery stores. This points to a need to coordinate efforts of all the stakeholders – cities, developers, and lenders – using the tools of CBAs and CRA. Community organizations should work jointly on CBAs that apply to banks and developers so that redevelopment, particularly large scale redevelopment in urban or suburban areas, do not displace modest income people and provide them with the ability to remain in affordable housing and operate small businesses in areas undergoing redevelopment.

Another overlooked opportunity for coordination is the affirmatively furthering fair housing requirement (AFFH) arising from the Fair Housing Act. AFFH requires local jurisdictions to identify barriers to integration and develop strategies to overcome these barriers. The AFFH plans can focus on racial inequities in access to transit, job opportunities, affordable housing, and/or to affordable loans.[711] Often, the plans will identify segregation and unequal access to credit as pressing problems but will not then recommend that CRA be employed in a way to provide more home lending and homeownership or rental opportunities in integrated communities. NCRC recently commented on the proposed AFFH plan of the Washington DC region and recommended strengthening it by using CRA in an integrative manner.[712] To tackle the multifaceted problems identified by Jesse Van Tol, CRA-inspired synergies among legal requirements, public policy, and private sector actors must be further developed in transparent manners highlighting community input.

Conclusion

The road to reinvestment, recovery, and repair will be long and arduous. Centuries of discrimination and disinvestment not only inflicted deep wounds on people of color and people with modest incomes. It also harms all of us by creating a divided country stunted in its economic and cultural development because it limited the possibilities and life chances of a significant segment of its population. For every two steps forward in our collective effort to repair the self-inflicted wounds, there might be a temporary step backward as we sort out disagreements and recommit ourselves to overall social wellbeing. But if we keep stepping forward in a persistent and determined manner, the future could be brighter for all of us.

The struggle to achieve progress is aptly illustrated by the bank trade association lawsuit against the final 2023 interagency revision to the CRA regulations. As this book is being finalized, we do not know what the fate of the industry lawsuit will be. Will the agencies prevail or will they need to go back to the drawing board and draft a new regulation? If the latter is the case, this will be a staggering step backward, but the scrappy advocates and sympathetic bankers that I know will not be deterred and will continue pushing for a reinvigorated CRA no matter what new forms that may take. Hopefully, the thoughts and recommendations I offer in this book will help guide any needed reform to CRA to make it a community-centered, inclusive, and successful reinvestment effort.

Undoubtedly, the recent election also will affect the future of CRA. Republican Administrations have not been as sympathetic to CRA as Democratic ones. However, a CRA infrastructure consisting of departments within banks and nonprofit community-based organizations has developed over 40 years and produces profitable lending and investment opportunities. This infrastructure has a vested interest in CRA and will promote it. For example, some banks have defended CRA when it has been under attack. As a result, administrations that are not sympathetic to CRA have not tried to eliminate it but weaken it via regulatory revisions. This may very well occur again as the incoming Trump administration revisits the update to the CRA regulation promulgated during 2023. CRA will always remain contested ground but so far, enough stakeholders have combined to defend and promote CRA, ensuring its survival and opportunities for it to be strengthened at a future time. I am cautiously optimistic that CRA will not only weather storms but will eventually come out stronger.

The genius of CRA is that on the surface its requirement is simple: banks must serve all communities, including and especially the redlined ones. Yet behind this surface simplicity is a profound quest for repair, transparency, and empowerment of disenfranchised communities. For our restorative quest to succeed, communities must be invited to participate in reinvestment initiatives and engaged with respect and humility. Several banks in the process are transformed into institutions that remain profit seeking but take a more holistic view of their success in that they will ultimately only prosper if they help pull up their communities and do so in responsible and safe and sound manners. This ethos needs to be spread throughout our society and institutions. Serving all communities fairly and equitability in an accountable manner and in a way that empowers communities will make our country a more hospitable, harmonious, and prosperous place.

Josh Silver

Currently a consultant and Senior Fellow at the National Community Reinvestment Coalition (NCRC), Josh Silver's 30-year career at NCRC involved protecting and strengthening the Community Reinvestment Act (CRA), fair lending laws, and data disclosure laws to hold financial institutions accountable for fair and responsible lending. He was also a development manager for two years at Manna, Inc., a local nonprofit housing developer based in the District of Columbia. Before NCRC and Manna, Josh was a research associate at the Urban Institute in the District of Columbia.

He has a master's in public affairs from the Lyndon B. Johnson School of Public Affairs at the University of Texas at Austin and a bachelor's from Columbia University in New York City.

He splits his time in Morris, CT near a lake and in Bethesda, MD with his wife, Kathy Bakich, and cat, Daphne. His daughter, Michelle Silver, is currently pursuing a career in arts management and musical theater in London, United Kingdom.

Acknowledgments

Just as it takes a village to raise a child, it takes a community to write a book. I am indebted to my professional colleagues and research professionals for their invaluable assistance in writing this book. While I have been involved with the Community Reinvestment Act (CRA) for most of its adult life and have a good familiarity with the law and its practice, CRA is a complex law that cannot be fully grasped by any one individual. It has multiple facets addressing a wide variety of needs in urban and rural parts of the country from affordable housing to community development and increasingly to climate remediation. Thus, any writer needs to consult with multiple stakeholders to understand and describe the richness of this law. I do not have space to thank all the special people I have met on my CRA journey but if I do not mention you, you are in my heart and inspired this book.

I thank wholeheartedly my colleagues at NCRC including John Taylor, Jesse Van Tol, Kevin Hill, Adam Rust, Catherine Petrusz, Jason Richardson, and Bruce Mitchell. I benefited greatly from leaders of community-based organizations that I interviewed including Robert Dickerson, Kevin Stein, Meg Guerra, Namoch Sokhom, Denise Rodriguez, and Dave Castillo. I also gained insights and richness about fair lending law and regulation from technical experts including Stephen Cross, Glenn Schlactus, Calvin Bradford, Robert Kuttner, and Scott McKee. These experts, practitioners, and advocates span the decades of CRA experience.

The professionals at the Library of Congress are remarkable. I engaged a few of them virtually, and never had to go to the library because they were able to provide me with CRA-related documents from decades ago in virtual formats. I am also thankful for my compulsive nature as my files and records of three decades contained vital documents and research for writing this book.

The staff at Armin Lear are extremely knowledgeable and enthusiastic. I particularly want to thank Maryann Karinch, Armin Lear's publisher, for her thorough and prompt editing and her cheer.

We live in uncertain and contentious times. I was hoping the last part of my career would involve more consensus and bipartisan acceptance of CRA. I was hoping that stakeholders would view CRA more as a technical matter that needs periodic adjustments and less as a contentious fight that can often obscure the best and most practical solutions. Alas, this does not appear to be the case as a lawsuit filed against the most recent CRA regulation is pending as this book goes to press. The recent election also portends more review and revisiting of the regulatory revisions to CRA in 2023. I fervently hope that our better angels can prevail in the future so that all of us—banks, community organizations, and other stakeholders—can build upon this remarkable law in pragmatic ways that gives disenfranchised communities a seat at the table in revitalizing their neighborhoods. Ultimately, I dedicate this book to my family, my loving wife and daughter, because all our collective efforts are geared towards making this country and world fairer, peaceful, and habitable for all of our families and communities.

Selected Bibliography

Books

Breyer, Stephen. *Reading the Constitution: Why I Chose Pragmatism, Not Textualism*. New York: Simon and Schuster, 2024.

Castaneda, Ruben. *S Street Rising: Crack, Murder, and Redemption in D.C.* New York: Bloomsbury, 2014.

Chakrabarti, Prabal, David Erickson, Ren S. Essene, Ian Galloway, and John Olson, eds. *Revisiting the CRA: Perspectives on the Future of the Community Reinvestment Act*. Federal Reserve Banks of Boston and San Francisco, February 2009.

Conley, Dalton. *Being Black, Living in the Red: Race Wealth, and Social Policy in America*. Berkeley, California: University of California Press, 1999.

Fishkin, Joseph and William E. Forbath. *The Anti-Oligarchy Constitution: Reconstructing the Economic Foundations of American Democracy*. Cambridge, Massachusetts: Harvard University Press, 2022.

Flitter, Emily. *The White Wall: How Big Finance Bankrupts Black America*. New York, New York: One Signal Publishers, 2022.

Hyra, Derek. *Slow and Sudden Violence: Why and When Uprisings Occur*. Oakland: University of California Press, 2024.

Immergluck, Dan. *Credit to the Community: Community Reinvestment and Fair Lending Policy in the United States.* Armonk: M.E. Sharpe, 2004.

Immergluck, Dan. *Red Hot City: Housing, Race, and Exclusion in Twenty-First Century Atlanta.* Oakland: University of California Press, 2022.

Kirp, David L., John P. Dwyer, and Larry A. Rosenthal, *Our Town, Race, Housing, and the Soul of Suburbia.* New Brunswick, New Jersey: Rutgers University Press, 1997.

Marchiel, Rebecca. *After Redlining: The Urban Reinvestment Movement in the Era of Financial Deregulation.* Chicago: The University of Chicago Press, 2020.

Marsico, Richard D. *Democratizing Capital: The History, Law, and Reform of the Community Reinvestment Act.* Durham: Carolina Academic Press, 2005.

Meckler, Laura. *Dream Town: Shaker Heights and the Quest for Racial Equity.* New York: Henry Holt and Company, 2023.

National Commission on the Causes of the Financial and Economic Crisis in the United Sates. *The Financial Crisis Inquiry Report: Final Report of the National Commission on the Causes of the Financial and Economic Crisis in the United States.* New York: Public Affairs, 2011.

Rothstein, Richard. *The Color of Law: A Forgotten History of How Our Government Segregated America.* New York: Liveright Publishing Company, 2017.

Rothstein, Richard and Leah. *Just Action: How to Challenge Segregation Enacted Under the Color of Law.* New York: Liveright Publishing Corporation, 2023.

Stiglitz, Joseph E. *The Great Divide: Unequal Societies and What We Can do About Them.* New York, W.W. Norton and Company, 2015.

Journal articles

Barr, Michael S. "Credit Where It Counts: The Community Reinvestment Act and Its Critics." *New York University Law Review*, no. 103 (April 2005). Available via University of Michigan Law School, https://repository.law.umich.edu/law_econ_archive/art43/

Gonzalez, David J. X., Anthony Nardone, Andrew V. Nguyen, Rachel Morello-Frosch, and Joan A. Casey. "Historic redlining and the siting of oil and gas wells in the United States." *Journal of Exposure Science & Environmental Epidemiology.* January, 2023. https://doi.org/10.1038/s41370-022-00434-9

Friedline, Terri and Zibei Chen. "Digital redlining and the fintech market-place: Evidence from US zip codes." *The Journal of Consumer Affairs* Volume 55, Issue2 (Summer 2021). https://doi.org/10.1111/joca.12297

Jones, Antwan, Gregory Squires, and Carolynn Nixon. "Ecological Associations Between Inclusionary Zoning Policies and Cardiovascular Disease Risk Prevalence: An Observational Study." *Cardiovascular Quality and Outcomes,* 14, no. 9 (September 8, 2021). https://www.ahajournals.org/doi/10.1161/CIRCOUTCOMES.120.007807

Reid, Carolina, Guest Editor. "The CRA Turns 40." *Cityscape* Vol. 19, No. 2 (US Department of Housing and Urban Development, 2017). https://www.jstor.org/stable/e26328318

Silver, Josh and Richard Marsico. "An Analysis of the Implementation and Impact of the 2004-2005 Amendments to the Community Reinvestment Act Regulations: The Continuing Importance of the CRA Examination Process." *The New York Law School Law Review, 2008-2009*, Volume 53, Number 2, https://digitalcommons.nyls.edu/nyls_law_review/vol53/iss2/5/

Papers

Bostic, Raphael W. and Breck L. Robinson. "What Makes CRA Agreements Work? A Study of Lender Responses to CRA Agreements." Paper prepared for the Federal Reserve System's third biennial research conference "Sustainable Community Development: What Works, What Doesn't and Why." February 2003. https://www.federalreserve.gov/communityaffairs/national/CA_Conf_SusCommDev/pdf/bosticraphael.pdf

Calem, Paul, Lauren Lambie-Hanson, and Susan Wachter. "Is the CRA Still Relevant to Mortgage Lending?" Penn Institute for Urban Research, Philadelphia, September 2019. https://penniur.upenn.edu/uploads/media/Calem_Lambie-Hanson_Wachter.pdf

Castillo, Dave, Bruce C. Mitchell, Jason Richardson, and Jad Edlebi, "Redlining the Reservation: The Brutal Cost of Financial Services Inaccessibility in Native Communities." NCRC, Washington DC, December 2023, https://ncrc.org/redlining-the-reservation-the-brutal-cost-of-financial-services-inaccessibility-in-native-communities/

Conway, Jacob, Jack N. Glaser, and Matthew C. Plosser. "Does the Community Reinvestment Act Improve Consumers' Access to Credit?" Federal Reserve Bank of New York Staff Reports, No. 1048, January 2023. https://www.newyorkfed.org/medialibrary/media/research/staff_reports/sr1048.pdf

Dennis, Warren. L. "The Community Reinvestment Act of 1977, Its Legislative History and Its Impact on Applications for Changes in Structure Made by Depository Institutions to the Four Federal Financial Supervisory Agencies." Working paper No. 24, Credit Research Center, Purdue University, 1978. https://docplayer.net/47347583-The-community-re-investment-act-of-1977.html.

Ding, Lei and Carolina K. Reid. "The Community Reinvestment Act (CRA) and Bank Branching Patterns." Working Paper, WP 19-36, Federal Reserve Bank of Philadelphia, Philadelphia, September 2019. https://www.philadelphiafed.org/-/media/frbp/assets/working-papers/2019/wp19-36.pdf. https://doi.org/10.21799/frbp.wp.2019.36

Ding, Lei and Leonard Nakamura. "Don't Know What You Got Till It's Gone: The Community Reinvestment Act in a Changing Financial Landscape." Working Paper No. 20-18, Federal Reserve Bank of Philadelphia, Philadelphia, February 2020. https://www.philadelphiafed.org/community-development/housing-and-neighborhoods/dont-know-what-you-got-till-its-gone

Ding, Lei, Raphael Bostic, and Hyojung Lee. "Effects of CRA on Small Business Lending." Working Paper 18-27, Federal Reserve Bank of Philadelphia, Philadelphia, December 2018. https://www.philadelphiafed.org/community-development/credit-and-capital/effects-of-the-community-reinvestment-act-cra-on-small-business-lending or https://doi.org/10.21799/frbp.wp.2018.27

Joint Center for Housing Studies of Harvard University. "The 25th Anniversary of the Community Reinvestment Act: Access to Capital in an Evolving Financial Services System." Cambridge, March 2002. http://www.jchs.harvard.edu/research/publications/25th-anniversary-community-reinvestment-act-access-capital-evolving-financial

Liu, Feng, Young Jo, and Noah Cohen-Harding. "Data Point: 2022 Mortgage Market Activity and Trends." Consumer Financial Protection Bureau, Washington DC, September 2023. https://files.consumerfinance.gov/f/documents/cfpb_data-point-mortgage-market-activity-trends_report_2023-09.pdf

Michney, Todd M. "How and Why the Home Owners' Loan Corporation Made Its Redlining Maps." Digital Scholarship Lab, University of Richmond, 2023. https://dsl.richmond.edu/panorama/redlining/howandwhy

Mitchell, Bruce, Jason Richardson, and Zo Amani. "Relationships Matter: Small Business and Bank Branch Locations." NCRC, Washington, D.C, March 2021. https://ncrc.org/relationships-matter-small-business-and-bank-branch-locations/

Mitchell, Bruce and Josh Silver. "Adding Underserved Census Tracts as Criterion on CRA Exams." NCRC, Washington, D.C., January 14, 2020. https://ncrc.org/adding-underserved-census-tracts-as-criterion-on-cra-exams/

Mitchell, Bruce and Juan Franco. "HOLC "Redlining" Maps: The Persistent Structure of Segregation and Economic Inequality." NCRC, Washington, D.C., March 2018. https://ncrc.org/holc/

Munnell, Alicia H, Lynn E. Browne, James McEneaney, and Geoffrey M. B. Tootell, "Mortgage Lending in Boston, Interpreting the HMDA Data." Working Paper, No., 92-7, Federal Reserve Bank of Boston, October 1992. https://www.bostonfed.org/publications/research-department-working-paper/1992/mortgage-lending-in-boston-interpreting-hmda-data.aspx

Report by the Board of Governors of the Federal Reserve System, submitted to the Congress pursuant to section 713 of the Gramm-Leach-Bliley Act of 1999. "The Performance and Profitability of CRA-Related Lending." July 17, 2000. https://www.federalreserve.gov/boarddocs/surveys/craloansurvey/cratext.pdf

Richardson, Jason, NCRC, Bruce C. Mitchell, NCRC, Helen C.S. Meier, University of Wisconsin – Milwaukee, Emily Lynch, University of Wisconsin – Milwaukee, and Jad Edlebi, NCRC. "Redlining and Neighborhood Health." NCRC, Washington, D.C., 2020. https://ncrc.org/holc-health/

Richardson, Jason, Joshua Devine, Jamie Buell, and Dedrick Asante-Muhammad. "NCRC 2020 Home Mortgage Report: Examining Shifts During COVID-19." NCRC, Washington DC, January 2022. https://ncrc.org/ncrc-2020-home-mortgage-report-examining-shifts-during-covid/

Ringo, Daniel. "Revitalize or Stabilize: Does Community Development Financing Work?" Finance and Economics Discussion Series 2020-029. Board of Governors of the Federal Reserve System, Washington, D.C, 2020. https://doi.org/10.17016/FEDS.2020.029.

Silver, Josh "CRA Could Do a Better Job Promoting Integration." Housing Finance: A Series on New Directions, Poverty and Race Research Action Council, Washington DC, May 2021. https://prrac.org/pdf/racial-justice-in-housing-finance-series-2021.pdf

Silver, Josh. "CRA Performance Context: Why it is Important for Community Development and How to Improve It." NCRC, Washington D.C, April 2016. https://ncrc.org/ncrc-makes-recommendations-to-improve-performance-context-analysis-in-community-reinvestment-act-exams/

Silver, Josh. "The Community Reinvestment Act and Geography: How Well Do CRA Exams Cover the Geographical Areas that Banks Serve?" NCRC, Washington DC, April 2017. https://ncrc.org/wp-content/up-loads/2017/05/cra_geography_paper_050517.pdf

Silver, Josh. "The Purpose and Design Of The Community Reinvestment Act (CRA): An Examination Of The 1977 Hearings And Passage Of The CRA. NCRC, Washington D.C, June 2019, https://ncrc.org/the-purpose-and-design-of-the-community-reinvestment-act-cra-an-examination-of-the-1977-hearings-and-passage-of-the-cra/. A version of this article first appeared in Conference of Consumer Finance Law, Quarterly Report, Vol. 72, No. 4.

Silver, Josh, Archana Pradhan. and Spencer Cowan. "Access to Capital and Credit in Appalachia and the Impact of the Financial Crisis and Recession on Commercial Lending and Finance in the Region." Appalachian Regional Commission, Washington, D.C, 2013. https://www.ncrc.org/access-to-capital-and-credit-in-appalachia-and-the-impact-of-the-financial-crisis-and-recession-on-commercial-lending-and-finance-in-the-region/

Silver, Josh and Jason Richardson. "Do CRA Ratings Reflect Differences in Performance: An Examination Using Federal Reserve Data." NCRC, Washington, D.C., May 2020. https://ncrc.org/do-cra-ratings-reflect-differences-in-performance-an-examination-using-federal-reserve-data/

Zonta, Michela and Caius Z. Willingham. "A CRA To Meet the Challenge of Climate Change." Center for American Progress, Washington, D.C, December 2020. https://www.americanprogress.org/article/cra-meet-challenge-climate-change/

Zuluaga, Diego. "The Community Reinvestment Act in the Age of Fintech and Bank Competition." Policy Analysis, Number 875. Cato Institute, Washington, D.C, July 10, 2019. https://www.cato.org/sites/cato.org/files/pubs/pdf/pa-875-updated.pdf

Acronyms

Advance Notice of Proposed Rulemaking	ANPR
Affirmatively Furthering Fair Housing	AFFH
American Housing and Economic Mobility Act	AHEM
Birmingham Business Resource Center	BBRC
Community Benefit Agreement	CBA
Community Development Financial Institution	CDFI
Community Needs Assessment	CHNA
Community Reinvestment Act	CRA
California Reinvestment Coalition	CRC
Consumer Financial Protection Bureau	CFPB
Department of Housing and Urban Development	HUD
Department of Justice	DOJ
Dodd Frank Wall Street Reform and Consumer Protection Act of 2010	Dodd-Frank

Equal Credit Opportunity Act	ECOA
Fair Housing Act	FHA
Facility-based assessment area	FBAA
Farmworker Housing Development Corporation	FHDC
Federal Deposit Insurance Corporation	FDIC
Federal Financial Institutions Examination Council	FFIEC
Federal Housing Administration	FHA
Federal Housing Finance Agency	FHFA
Federal Reserve Board	FRB
Financial Holding Company	FHC
Financial Institutions Reform, Recovery, and Enforcement Act	FIRREA
Freedom of Information Act	FOIA
Gramm Leach Bliley Act of 1999	GLBA
Home Mortgage Disclosure Act	HMDA
Home Owner's Loan Corporation	HOLC
Illinois Department of Financial and Professional Regulation	IDFPR
Individual Development Account	IDA
Individual Taxpayer Identification Number	ITIN
Low- and moderate-income	LMI
Low-income credit union	LICU
Low Income Housing Tax Credits	LIHTC
Middle- and upper-income	MUI
Minority depository institution	MDI
Mortgage-backed securities	MBS
National Community Reinvestment Coalition	NCRC

Ending Redlining through a Community-Centered Reform of the Community Reinvestment Act

National People's Action	NPA
Office of the Comptroller of the Currency	OCC
Office of Thrift Supervision	OTS
Outside Retail Lending Assessment Area	ORLAA
Savings and loans	S&Ls
Small Business Administration	SBA
Special Purpose Credit Program	SPCP
Transportation Alliance Bank	TAB
Vermont-Slauson Economic Development Corporation	VSEDC
Washington Homeownership Resource Center	WHRC
Women depository institutions	WDI

Index

Ending Redlining through a Community-Centered Reform of the Community Reinvestment Act

Endnotes

Introduction

1   David Leonhardt, Amanda Cox, and Claire Cain Miller, "An Atlas of Upward Mobility Shows Paths Out of Poverty," *New York Times*, May 4, 2015, https://www.nytimes.com/2015/05/04/upshot/an-atlas-of-upward-mobility-shows-paths-out-of-poverty.html?searchResultPosition=1

2   Jason Richardson, Director, Research & Evaluation, NCRC Bruce C. Mitchell PhD., Senior Research Analyst, NCRC, Helen C.S. Meier, PhD, MPH, Assistant Professor of Epidemiology, University of Wisconsin – Milwaukee, Emily Lynch, MPH, Graduate Student Research Assistant, University of Wisconsin – Milwaukee, and Jad Edlebi, GIS Specialist, NCRC, *Redlining and Neighborhood Health*, (Washington, D.C., NCRC 2020). https://ncrc.org/holc-health/

3   Heather Cherone, "How Did Chicago Become So Segregated? By Inventing Modern Segregation," *WTTW News*, https://interactive.wttw.com/firsthand/segregation/how-did-chicago-become-so-segregated-by-inventing-modern-segregation

4   Richard Rothstein, "From Ferguson to Baltimore: The Fruits of Government-Sponsored Segregation," *Economic Policy Institute*, April 29, 2015, https://www.epi.org/blog/from-ferguson-to-baltimore-the-fruits-of-government-sponsored-segregation/#:~:text=In%201917%2C%20the%20U.S.%20Supreme,sell%20to%20whomever%20they%20wished.

5   Shelley v. Kraemer, 334 U.S. 1 (1948), https://supreme.justia.com/cases/federal/us/334/1/

6   Dan Immergluck, *Credit to the Community: Community Reinvestment and Fair Lending Policy in the United States* (Armonk: M.E. Sharpe, 2004) 93-95.

7   Immergluck, 93-95.

8   Sebastian Linde, Rebekah J. Walker, Jennifer A. Campbell, and Leonard E. Egede, "Historic Residential Redlining and Present-Day Social Determinants of Health, Home Evictions, and Food Insecurity within US Neighborhoods," *Journal of Internal General Medicine* 38(15) (November 2023) https://www.ncbi.nlm.nih.gov/pmc/articles/PMC10255945/

9   Richard and Leah Rothstein, *Just Action: How to Challenge Segregation Enacted Under the Color of Law* (New York: Liveright Publishing Corporation, 2023), 222–233.

10 In the mid-2000's, two books reviewing the history and policy of CRA were published. Immergluck (2004) and Richard D. Marsico, *Democratizing Capital: The History, Law, and Reform of the Community Reinvestment Act* (Durham: Carolina Academic Press, 2005). Chapter 2 will review studies published by the Federal Reserve System and other research but since the mid 2000's, there has not been full length books addressing CRA legislative and regulatory policy.

11 Rebecca Marchiel, *After Redlining: The Urban Reinvestment Movement in the Era of Financial Deregulation* (Chicago: The University of Chicago Press, 2020) 114-119, 135-145.

12 Wisconsin Historical Society, Senator William Proxmire Collection, "An oral history interview with Robert L. Kuttner," 30, accessed on January 24, 2024, https://content.wisconsinhistory.org/digital/collection/proxmire/id/3398/rec/34

13 Community Reinvestment Act (CRA), Code of Federal Regulations (CFR), Title 12, Chapter 30, § 2903(a), 1433, https://www.govinfo.gov/content/pkg/USCODE-2013-title12/pdf/USCODE-2013-title12-chap30.pdf

14 Joseph Fishkin and William E. Forbath, *The Anti-Oligarchy Constitution: Reconstructing the Economic Foundations of American Democracy* (Cambridge, Massachusetts: Harvard University Press, 2022) 9-12.

15 Joseph E. Stiglitz, *The Great Divide: Unequal Societies and What We Can do About Them* (New York, W.W. Norton and Company, 2015) 13.

16 Stiglitz, *Great Divide*, 23, 50-54.

17 NCRC Research, CRA Qualified Lending 2009-2020, https://public.tableau.com/app/profile/ncrc.research/viz/CRAQualifiedLending2009-2020/Dashboard1

18 Author's calculations using the CRA ratings database available via the Federal Financial Institutions Examination Council (FFIEC) website at https://www.ffiec.gov/craratings/default.aspx

19   Jason Richardson, Bruce Mitchell, Jad Edlebi, *Gentrification and Disinvestment 2020*, (Washington, D.C., NCRC 2020), https://ncrc.org/gentrification20/; Bill Bradley, "Small-Town America Is Facing Big-City Problems," *Next City* February 29, 2016, https://nextcity.org/features/traverse-city-small-cities-growth-planning.

20   Community Reinvestment Act (CRA), Code of Federal Regulations (CFR), Title 12, Chapter 30, § 2903(b), 1433, https://www.govinfo.gov/content/pkg/USCODE-2013-title12/pdf/USCODE-2013-title12-chap30.pdf

21   Immergluck, 114-118; Tamara Jayasundera, Joshua Silver, Katrin Anacker, Denitza Mantcheva, "Foreclosure in the Nation's Capital: How Unfair and Reckless Lending Undermines Homeownership," (Washington, D.C.: NCRC, April 2010), 3, https://ncrc.org/foreclosure-in-the-nations-capital-how-unfair-and-reckless-lending-undermines-homeownership/; Debbie Gruenstein Bocian, Keith S. Ernst, and Wei Li, "Race, ethnicity and subprime home loan pricing," *Journal of Economics and Business* 60 (2008): 121, https://www.responsiblelending.org/sites/default/files/nodes/files/research-publication/jeb-60-2008-110124-bocian-ernst-li.pdf

22   National Commission on the Causes of the Financial and Economic Crisis in the United Sates, *The Financial Crisis Inquiry Report: Final Report of the National Commission on the Causes of the Financial and Economic Crisis in the United States* (New York: Public Affairs, 2011), xvii-xxiv, 7, 70, 75, 79.

23   Testimony of John Taylor, President and CEO, NCRC, on behalf of NCRC, the National Consumer Law Center, and Rainbow/Push, Before the House Financial Services Committee, October 24, 2007, https://ncrc.org/wp-content/uploads/2007/10/ncrctestimonyfinal.doc%20%5B1%5D-1.pdf

24   Neil Bhutta and Daniel Ringo, "Assessing the Community Reinvestment Act's Role in the Financial Crisis," Feds Notes, posted May 2015 on the website of the Federal Reserve System, https://www.federalreserve.gov/econresdata/notes/feds-notes/2015/assessing-the-community-reinvestment-acts-role-in-the-financial-crisis-20150526.html

25   Chapter 2 describes that CRA exams provide an option for banks not to include their mortgage lending affiliates on their exams and how a Department of Justice settlement involved Suntrust's mortgage company which was not included on its CRA exam. See Federal Reserve Bank of Atlanta, CRA Exam of Suntrust Bank, March 2013, 2, https://www.frbatlanta.org/-/media/Documents/banking/cra_pes/2013/675332.pdf

26   Alique G. Berberian, David J. X. Gonzalez, and Lara J. Cushing, "Racial Disparities in Climate Change-Related Health Effects in the United States," Current Environmental Health Reports (May 2022), https://www.ncbi.nlm.nih.gov/pmc/articles/PMC9363288/

27   Federal Deposit Insurance Corporation, "FDIC Seeks Public Comment on Proposed Revisions to its Statement of Policy on Bank Merger Transactions," PR-17-2024, March 21, 2024, https://www.fdic.gov/news/press-releases/2024/pr24017.html; FDIC webpage section regarding the Federal Deposit Insurance Act, specifically Section 18(c)(5)(B) via https://www.fdic.gov/regulations/laws/rules/1000-2000.html

28   National Community Reinvestment Coalition, "Community Benefit Agreements: How Banks Ensure They Meet Local Needs," https://ncrc.org/cba/

29   Urban Institute, Housing Finance Policy Center, "Bank lending outside CRA assessment areas," (PowerPoint presentation, National Association of Affordable Housing Lenders webinar series, Washington DC, January 26, 2022) 5, https://naahl.org/wp-content/uploads/2022/01/Urban-CRA_Project-CRA-Assessment-Areas-v12.pdf

30   National Information Center, "Large Holding Companies," https://www.ffiec.gov/npw/Institution/TopHoldings and FDIC, "BankFind Suite: Find Annual Historical Bank Data," https://banks.data.fdic.gov/bankfind-suite/historical

31   NCRC, "About NCRC," https://ncrc.org/about/

Chapter 1

32   Harold Holzer and Norton Garfinkle, *A Just and Generous Nation: Abraham Lincoln and the Fight for American Opportunity* (Philadelphia: Basic Books, 2015) 71.

33   Derek Hyra, *Slow and Sudden Violence: Why and When Uprisings Occur* (Oakland: University of California Press, 2024) 38-39, 133.

34   Kevin Rector, "Administrative case wraps up for Baltimore officer who drove Freddie Gray," *Washington Post*, November 6, 2017, https://www.washingtonpost.com/local/public-safety/disciplinary-board-begins-to-consider-case-of-officer-who-drove-freddie-gray/2017/11/06/27d8eb8e-c32e-11e7-aae0-cb18a8c29c65_story.html

35   Keith L. Alexander and Dana Hedgpeth, "Baltimore city officials approve $6.4 million settlement for family of Freddie Gray," *Washington Post*, September 9, 2015, https://www.washingtonpost.com/local/crime/baltimore-city-officials-approve-64-million-settlement-for-family-of-freddie-gray/2015/09/09/9e00c112-56eb-11e5-abe9-27d53f250b11_story.html

36   Janell Ross, "Why you should know what happened in Freddie Gray's life — long before his death," *Washington Post*, December 19, 2015, https://www.washingtonpost.com/news/the-fix/wp/2015/12/19/why-you-should-know-what-happened-in-freddie-grays-life-long-before-his-death/

37   Peter Hermann, "Friends and neighbors remember Freddie Gray: He 'was our family," *Washington Post*, April 24, 2015, https://www.washingtonpost.com/local/crime/freddie-was-our-family/2015/04/24/662956a2-e9d4-11e4-9a6a-c1ab95a0600b_story.html?itid=lk_inline_manual_12

38   Federal Financial Institutions Examination Council, Geocoder/Mapping System, last accessed January 24, 2023. https://geomap.ffiec.gov/FFIECGeocMap/GeocodeMap1.aspx

39   Hermann, "Friends and neighbors remember."

40   Bruce Mitchell PhD., Senior Research Analyst and Juan Franco, Senior GIS Specialist, *HOLC "Redlining" Maps: The Persistent Structure Of Segregation And Economic Inequality*, (Washington, D.C., NCRC, March 2018). https://ncrc.org/holc/

41   Kristen B. Crossney and David W. Bartelt, "The Legacy of the Home Owners' Loan Corporation," *Housing Policy Debate*, Fannie Mae Foundation, Issues 3 and 4, Volume 16, (2005), 551 https://web.archive.org/web/20080414023817/http://www.mi.vt.edu/data/files/hpd%20vol.16%20issues%203%20and%204/articles/hpd6(3,4)%20crossney.pdf

42   Price Fishback, Jonathan Rose, Ken Snowden, and Thomas Storrs, "New Evidence on Redlining by Federal Housing Programs in the 1930s," WP 2022-01, Federal Reserve Bank of Chicago, Chicago, January 3, 2022: 3, https://doi.org/10.21033/wp-2022-01

43   Todd M. Michney, "How and Why the Home Owners' Loan Corporation Made Its Redlining Maps," Mapping Inequality: Redlining in New Deal America, accessed on January 24, 2023, https://dsl.richmond.edu/panorama/redlining/howandwhy

44   Jason Richardson, Director, Research & Evaluation, NCRC Bruce C. Mitchell PhD., Senior Research Analyst, NCRC, Helen C.S. Meier, PhD, MPH, Assistant Professor of Epidemiology, University of Wisconsin – Milwaukee,

Emily Lynch, MPH, Graduate Student Research Assistant, University of Wisconsin – Milwaukee, and Jad Edlebi, GIS Specialist, NCRC, *Redlining and Neighborhood Health*, (Washington, D.C., NCRC 2020). https://ncrc.org/holc-health/

45   Dan Immergluck, *Credit to the Community: Community Reinvestment and Fair Lending Policy in the United States* (Armonk: M.E. Sharpe, 2004) 93. Also, Todd M. Michney, "How and Why the Home Owner's Loan Corporation Made its Redlining Maps."

46   Immpergluck, 94-95.

47   Fishback and Price, 11.

48   Immergluck, 95.

49   Fishback and Rose, 16.

50   Dalton Conley, *Being Black, Living in the Red: Race Wealth, and Social Policy in America* (Berkeley, California: University of California Press, 1999), 37 and David L. Kirp, John P. Dwyer, Larry A. Rosenthal, *Our Town, Race, Housing, and the Soul of Suburbia* (New Brunswick, New Jersey: Rutgers University Press, 1997), 7.

51   Federal Reserve Bank of St. Louis, "The Three C's of Credit," accessed January 17, 2024, https://www.stlouisfed.org/education/making-personal-finance-decisions-curriculum-unit/three-cs-of-credit

52   Munnell, Alicia H, Browne, Lynn E., McEneaney, James, and Geoffrey M. B. Tootell, "Mortgage Lending in Boston, Interpreting the HMDA Data" (Working Paper, No., 92-7, Federal Reserve Bank of Boston, October 1992), https://www.bostonfed.org/publications/research-department-working-paper/1992/mortgage-lending-in-boston-interpreting-hmda-data.aspx, 2, 27

53   "Justice Department Reaches Significant Milestone in Combating Redlining Initiative After Securing Over $107 Million in Relief for Communities of Color Nationwide" U.S. Department of Justice, Office of Public Affairs, accessed January 15, 2024, https://www.justice.gov/opa/pr/justice-department-reaches-significant-milestone-combating-redlining-initiative-after

54   Terri Friedline and Zibei Chen, "Digital redlining and the fintech marketplace: Evidence from US zip codes," *The Journal of Consumer Affairs* Volume 55, Issue2 (Summer 2021): https://doi.org/10.1111/joca.12297

55   Friedline and Chen.

56   Josh Silver, "SoFi, Not So Good: Is This Virtual Redlining?" *Shelterforce*, July 27, 2017, https://shelterforce.org/2017/07/27/sofi-not-good-virtual-redlining/

57   Richardson, Mitchell, Meier, Lynch and Edlebi, *Redlining and Neighborhood Health*.

58   Richard Rothstein, *The Color of Law: A Forgotten History of How Our Government Segregated America* (New York: Liveright Publishing Company, 2017)

59   Mitchell and Franco, Redlining Maps, 9.

60   Richardson, Mitchell, Meier, Lynch and Edlebi, *Redlining and Neighborhood Health*.

61   Richardson, et al., *Redlining and Neighborhood Health*.

62   Michela Zonta and Caius Z. Willingham, *A CRA To Meet the Challenge of Climate Change* (Washington, D.C, Center for American Progress, December 2020). https://www.americanprogress.org/article/cra-meet-challenge-climate-change/

63   Bruce Mitchell, PhD. and Josh Silver, *Adding Underserved Census Tracts As Criterion On CRA Exams* (Washington, D.C., NCRC, January 14, 2020) https://ncrc.org/adding-underserved-census-tracts-as-criterion-on-cra-exams/

64   Todd M. Michney, "How and Why the Home Owners' Loan Corporation Made Its Redlining Maps," *Digital Scholarship Lab*, 2023, https://dsl.richmond.edu/panorama/redlining/howandwhy

65   For a description of Not Even Past, the partnership between the Digital Lab and NCRC, see https://dsl.richmond.edu/socialvulnerability/. For the maps and statistics on Sandtown-Winchester, see https://dsl.richmond.edu/socialvulnerability/map/#loc=11/39.313/-76.633&city=baltimore-md&tract=24510140300

66   For a description of the SVI, see https://dsl.richmond.edu/socialvulnerability/ and https://ncrc.org/holc-health/

67   For maps of several cities, see https://ncrc.org/holc-health/ and scroll down towards the bottom. For a map and statistics of this community, see https://dsl.richmond.edu/socialvulnerability/map/#loc=11/33.523/-86.812&city=birmingham-al&tract=01073004200

68   David J. X. Gonzalez, Anthony Nardone, Andrew V. Nguyen, Rachel Morello-Frosch, and Joan A. Casey, "Historic redlining and the siting of oil and gas wells in the United States," *Journal of Exposure Science & Environmental Epidemiology,* 33 (January, 2023): 76–83, https://doi.org/10.1038/s41370-022-00434-9

69   Report of the National Advisory Commission on Civil Disorders, 1968, Summary, available for download from U.S. Department of Justice, Office of Justice Programs, https://www.ojp.gov/ncjrs/virtual-library/abstracts/national-advisory-commission-civil-disorders-report

70   Rebecca Marchiel, *After Redlining: The Urban Reinvestment Movement in the Era of Financial Deregulation* (Chicago: The University of Chicago Press, 2020) 56.

71   Marchiel, *After Redlining*, 51 and 57.

72   Marchiel, 57.

73   Marchiel, 65.

74   Marchiel, 92.

75   Marchiel, 50 and 79.

76   Marchiel, 62.

77   Department of Housing and Urban Development, "Housing Discrimination under the Fair Housing Act," https://www.hud.gov/program_offices/fair_housing_equal_opp/fair_housing_act_overview

78   Brian Kreiswirth and Anna-Marie Tabor, "What you need to know about the Equal Credit Opportunity Act and how it can help you: Why it was passed and what it is," (blog) *Consumer Financial Protection Bureau*, October 31, 2016, https://www.consumerfinance.gov/about-us/blog/what-you-need-know-about-equal-credit-opportunity-act-and-how-it-can-help-you-why-it-was-passed-and-what-it/

79   Marchiel, 114-119.

80   Marchiel, 143.

81   Wisconsin Historical Society, Senator William Proxmire Collection, "An oral history interview with Ken McLean," 63, accessed on January 23, 2024, https://content.wisconsinhistory.org/digital/collection/proxmire/id/1874/rec/3

82   Wisconsin Historical Society, Interview with Ken McLean, 66, 68.

83   Robert Kuttner (author and former Banking Committee staff person) in discussion with author, March 2023.

84   Sarah Mancini and Margot Saunders, "Land Installment Contracts: The Newest Wave of Predatory Home Lending Threatening Communities of Color," *Federal Reserve Bank of Boston*, April 2017, https://www.bostonfed.org/publications/communities-and-banking/2017/spring/land-installment-contracts-newest-wave-of-predatory-home-lending-threatening-communities-of-color.aspx

85   Community Reinvestment Act (CRA), Code of Federal Regulations (CFR), Title 12, Chapter 30, § 2901(a)(3), 1431, https://www.govinfo.gov/content/pkg/USCODE-2013-title12/pdf/USCODE-2013-title12-chap30.pdf

86   Federal Reserve Board's version of the regulation at 12 CFR § 228.21-228.24, §228.43, https://www.ecfr.gov/on/2024-01-28/title-12/chapter-II/subchapter-A/part-228?toc=1

87   Josh Silver, Seunghoon Oh, Annelise Osterberg, Jaclyn Tules, "The Financial Benefits of Homeownership: An Evaluation of a Nonprofit Housing Development Model (unpublished manuscript, May 2014)

88   Silver, et. al., "The Financial Benefits," 2.

89   Silver, et. al., 2 and 30.

90   Dalton Conley, *Being Black, Living in the Red: Race, Wealth, and Social Policy in America* (Berkeley, California, University of California Press, 1999) 47-51.

91   Dalton, 53.

92   Ruben Castaneda, *S Street Rising; Crack, Murder, and Redemption in D.C.* (New York: Bloomsbury, 2014) 49-51.

93   Manna, "100 Years of the Whitelaw," November 22, 2019, https://static1.squarespace.com/static/609b35920e3190766272da65/t/61aa39d0049b6f7d-ed6e1389/1638545873096/Whitelaw-press-release.pdf

94   Silver, et. al., 27 and 32.

95   Sarah Shoenfield, *Mapping Segregation in D.C.* (Washington, D.C: D.C. Policy Center, April 2019) https://www.dcpolicycenter.org/publications/mapping-segregation-fha/

96   Sabrina Walls (Manna homeowner) in discussion with the author, February 2023.

97   Sabrina Walls, February 2023.

98   Bob Dickerson (Executive Director, Birmingham Business Resource Center) in discussion with the author, February 2023.

99   Katherine Shaver, "Was your home once off-limits to non-Whites? These maps can tell you," *Washington Post*, December 19, 2022, https://www.washington-post.com/transportation/2022/12/17/racial-covenants-mapping/

100 Marchiel, 126-128 and 151-152.

101 Silver, et. al., 13.

Chapter 2

102 Peter Schweizer, "A Poisonous Cocktail," *Forbes*, October 5, 2009, https://www.forbes.com/2009/10/03/community-reinvestment-act-mortgages-housing-opinions-contributors-peter-schweizer.html?sh=5a0bbb63b907

103 Randall Kroszner, "The Community Reinvestment Act and the Recent Mortgage Crisis," in *Revisiting the CRA: Perspectives on the Future of the Community Reinvestment Act*, eds. Prabal Chakrabarti, David Erickson, Ren S. Essene, Ian Galloway, and John Olson (Federal Reserve Banks of Boston and San Francisco, February 2009), 8, https://www.frbsf.org/community-development/wp-content/uploads/sites/3/cra_recent_mortgage_crisis1.pdf

104 Community Reinvestment Act (CRA), Code of Federal Regulations (CFR), Title 12, Chapter 30, § 2901, 1431, https://www.govinfo.gov/content/pkg/USCODE-2013-title12/pdf/USCODE-2013-title12-chap30.pdf

105 CRA, § 2902(3), § 2903(a), 1432-1433.

106 CRA, § 2906(b)(2), 1434.

107 CRA, § 2906(d)(1), 1434-1435.

108 CRA, § 2906(d)(3), 1435.

109 Board of Governors of the Federal Reserve System (Board); Federal Deposit Insurance Corporation (FDIC), *Community Reinvestment Act Regulations Asset-Size Thresholds*, Vol. 88, No. 243 (Washington, D.C: Federal Register, Wednesday, December 20, 2023), https://www.federalregister.gov/d/2023--27934/p-15

110 Federal Reserve Board's version of the regulation at 12 CFR § 228.21-228.24, https://www.ecfr.gov/on/2024-01-28/title-12/chapter-II/subchapter-A/part-228?toc=1

111 Federal Reserve, CRA regulation, 12 CFR 228.22, https://www.ecfr.gov/on/2024-01-28/title-12/section-228.22

112 Office of the Comptroller of the Currency, Federal Reserve System, Federal Deposit Insurance Corporation, *Community Reinvestment Act; Interagency Questions and Answers Regarding Community Reinvestment*, Vol. 81, No. 142 (Washington, D.C: Federal Register, Monday, July 25, 2016), Q&A § _12(h), 48528, https://www.govinfo.gov/content/pkg/FR-2016-07-25/pdf/2016-16693.pdf

113 Federal Reserve, CRA regulation, 12 CFR 228.23, https://www.ecfr.gov/
on/2024-01-28/title-12/section-228.23

114 Office of the Comptroller of the Currency, Federal Reserve System, Federal
Deposit Insurance Corporation, *Community Reinvestment Act; Interagency
Questions and Answers Regarding Community Reinvestment*, Q&A § _12(t)—4,
48523, https://www.govinfo.gov/content/pkg/FR-2016-07-25/pdf/2016-16693.
pdf

115 Federal Reserve, CRA regulation, 12 CFR 228.24, https://www.ecfr.gov/
on/2024-01-28/title-12/section-228.24

116 Office of the Comptroller of the Currency, Federal Reserve System, Federal
Deposit Insurance Corporation, *Community Reinvestment Act; Interagency
Questions and Answers Regarding Community Reinvestment*, Q&A §_.12(i)—3,
48530-48531, https://www.govinfo.gov/content/pkg/FR-2016-07-25/pd-
f/2016-16693.pdf

117 FDIC Consumer Compliance Examination Manual, September 2015, XI–4.9,
https://www.fdic.gov/resources/supervision-and-examinations/consumer-
compliance-examination-manual/documents/11/xi-4-1.pdf

118 Board of Governors of the Federal Reserve System (Board); Federal Deposit
Insurance Corporation (FDIC), *Community Reinvestment Act Regulations
Asset-Size Thresholds,* https://www.federalregister.gov/d/2023-27934/p-15

119 Federal Reserve, CRA regulation, 12 CFR 228.26(b), https://www.ecfr.gov/on/
2024-01-28/title-12/part-228/section-228.26#p-228.26(b)

120 Federal Reserve, CRA regulation, 12 CFR 228.26(c), https://www.ecfr.gov/on/
2024-01-28/title-12/part-228/section-228.26#p-228.26(c)

121 Federal Reserve, CRA regulation, 12 CFR 228.26(a), https://www.ecfr.gov/on/
2024-01-28/title-12/part-228/section-228.26#p-228.26(a)(1)

122 Federal Reserve, CRA regulation, 12 CFR Appendix-A-to-Part-228(d)(1)(i)(D),
https://www.ecfr.gov/on/2024-01-28/title-12/appendix-Appendix%20A%20to
%20Part%20228#p-Appendix-A-to-Part-228(d)(1)(i)(D)

123 Federal Reserve, CRA regulation, 12 CFR 228.25, https://www.ecfr.gov/on/
2024-01-28/title-12/section-228.25

124 Federal Reserve, CRA regulation, 12 CFR 228.27(f), https://www.ecfr.gov/on/
2024-01-28/title-12/part-228/section-228.27#p-228.27(f)

125 Federal Reserve, CRA regulation, 12 CFR 228.27(d), https://www.ecfr.gov/on/
2024-01-28/title-12/part-228/section-228.27#p-228.27(d)

126 Federal Reserve, CRA regulation, 12 CFR 228.28(c), https://www.ecfr.gov/on/
2024-01-28/title-12/part-228/section-228.28#p-228.28(c)

127 See the search engine for CRA exams and ratings at https://www.ffiec.gov/
craratings/default.aspx

128 Federal Reserve, CRA regulation, 12 CFR 228.42, https://www.ecfr.gov/on/
2024-01-28/title-12/section-228.42

129 CRA, Title 12, Chapter 30, § 2908, 1436.

130 Testimony of John Taylor, President and CEO, NCRC, *Examination of the
Gramm-Leach-Bliley Act Five Years After its Passage*, Before the Senate Committee on Banking, Housing and Urban Affairs, July 13, 2004, 5-6, https://www.
banking.senate.gov/imo/media/doc/ACF3BD.pdf

131 Office of the Comptroller of the Currency, Office of Thrift Supervision, Federal
Reserve System, Federal Deposit Insurance Corporation, "Submission for
OMB Review," Federal Register, May 28, 1999 (Volume 64, Number 103),
29084, https://www.govinfo.gov/content/pkg/FR-1999-05-28/pdf/99-13567.
pdf

132 Josh Silver, "MAP: Here's Where Changes To CRA Asset Thresholds Will
Undermine Community Reinvestment," (blog), *NCRC*, June 30, 2022, https://
ncrc.org/map-heres-where-changes-to-cra-asset-thresholds-will-undermine-
community-reinvestment/

133 Josh Silver, "The Community Reinvestment Act and Geography: How Well Do
CRA Exams Cover the Geographical Areas that Banks Serve?" (Washington
D.C.: NCRC, April 2017), 5, https://ncrc.org/wp-content/uploads/2017/05/
cra_geography_paper_050517.pdf

134 Federal Reserve, CRA regulation, 12 CFR 228.41, https://www.ecfr.gov/
on/2024-01-28/title-12/section-228.41

135 Federal Reserve, CRA regulation, 12 CFR 228.22(c), https://www.ecfr.
gov/on/2024-01-28/title-12/part-228/section-228.22#p-228.22(c); 12 CFR
228.23(c), https://www.ecfr.gov/on/2024-01-28/title-12/part-228/section-
228.23#p-228.23(c); 12 CFR 228.24(c); https://www.ecfr.gov/on/2024-01-28/
title-12/part-228/section-228.24#p-228.24(c)

136 Federal Reserve, CRA regulation, 12 CFR 228.29, https://www.ecfr.gov/
on/2024-01-28/title-12/section-228.29

137 FDIC webpage section regarding the Federal Deposit Insurance Act, specifically Section 18(c)(5)(B) via https://www.fdic.gov/regulations/laws/
rules/1000-2000.html

138 Author's calculations using the CRA ratings database available via the Federal
Financial Institutions Examination Council (FFIEC) website at https://www.ffiec.
gov/craratings/default.aspx

139 Stephen M. Cross (former Deputy Comptroller for Compliance: OCC) in discussion with the author, April 2023.

140 Author's calculations using the CRA ratings database from the FFIEC website.

141 Richard Hunt and Stephen Congdon, Comment letter of the Consumer Bankers Association, Community Reinvestment Act, Docket No. R-1723, RIN 7100-AF94, February 16, 2021, 23, https://www.federalreserve.gov/SECRS/2021/May/20210517/R-1723/R-1723_021621_137975_409513790319_1.pdf

142 Testimony of John Taylor, President and CEO of NCRC, Presented at the Community Reinvestment Act Hearings at the FDIC's William Seidman Center, July 19, 2010, https://www.fdic.gov/resources/regulations/federal-register-publications/2010/10c04ad60.pdf

143 FDIC website, "Statistics at a Glance," September 2022, https://www.fdic.gov/analysis/quarterly-banking-profile/statistics-at-a-glance/2022sep/industry.pdf

144 Letter of Jerome H. Powell, Chairman, Board of Governors of the Federal Reserve System, May 10, 2018 to Senator Elizabeth Warren, https://www.warren.senate.gov/imo/media/doc/Powell%20Response%20re%20Mergers.pdf

145 Board of Governors of Federal Reserve System, "Banking Applications Activity, Semiannual Report, January 1–June 30, 2022," Vol. 9, No. 2, December 2022, 1-2, https://www.federalreserve.gov/publications/files/semiannual-report-on-banking-applications-20221221.pdf

146 Federal Reserve System, Semiannual Report, December 2022, 2-3.

147 The date and outcome of the FDIC's decision can be retrieved via https://www.fdic.gov/regulations/applications/actions.html. The agency did not make its approval order widely available to the public, but NCRC obtained a copy and the author has a copy available upon request.

148 Michael S. Barr, "Credit Where It Counts: The Community Reinvestment Act and Its Critics," *75 New York University Law Review*, no. 103 (April 2005), 121-123, available via University of Michigan Law School, https://repository.law.umich.edu/law_econ_archive/art43/

149 Joint Center for Housing Studies of Harvard University, *The 25th Anniversary of the Community Reinvestment Act: Access to Capital in an Evolving Financial Services System* (Cambridge, March 2002), 65, http://www.jchs.harvard.edu/research/publications/25th-anniversary-community-reinvestment-act-access-capital-evolving-financial

150 Joint Center for Housing Studies of Harvard University, *The 25th Anniversary*, 70.

151 Daniel Ringo, *Mortgage Lending, Default and the Community Reinvestment Act* (December 14, 2017), 4 and 13, Available at SSRN: https://ssrn.com/abstract=2585215 or http://dx.doi.org/10.2139/ssrn.2585215

152 Lei Ding and Leonard Nakamura, *Don't Know What You Got Till It's Gone: The Community Reinvestment Act in a Changing Financial Landscape*, Working Paper No. 20-18 (Philadelphia: Federal Reserve Bank of Philadelphia, February 2020), 23, https://www.philadelphiafed.org/community-development/housing-and-neighborhoods/dont-know-what-you-got-till-its-gone

153 Lei Ding, Raphael Bostic, and Hyojung Lee, *Effects of CRA on Small Business Lending,* Working Paper 18-27 (Philadelphia: Federal Reserve Bank of Philadelphia, December 2018) 1, https://www.philadelphiafed.org/community-development/credit-and-capital/effects-of-the-community-reinvestment-act-cra-on-small-business-lending or https://doi.org/10.21799/frbp.wp.2018.27

154 Ding, Bostic, Lee, 14.

155 Ding, Bostic, Lee, 15.

156 Federal Reserve Board publishes Community Reinvestment Act Analytics Data Tables, March 6, 2020, https://www.federalreserve.gov/newsevents/pressreleases/bcreg20200306a.htm.

157 Josh Silver and Jason Richardson, *Do CRA Ratings Reflect Differences In Performance: An Examination Using Federal Reserve Data* (Washington, D.C., NCRC, May 2020) https://ncrc.org/do-cra-ratings-reflect-differences-in-performance-an-examination-using-federal-reserve-data/

158 Paul Calem, Lauren Lambie-Hanson, and Susan Wachter, *Is the CRA Still Relevant to Mortgage Lending?* (Philadelphia: Penn Institute for Urban Research, September 2019), 6, https://penniur.upenn.edu/uploads/media/Calem_Lambie-Hanson_Wachter.pdf

159 Calem, Lambie-Hanson, Wachter, See Figures 4 through 7, 12-15

160 Silver and Richardson, *Do CRA Ratings Reflect Differences*

161 Daniel Ringo, *"Revitalize or Stabilize": Does Community Development Financing Work?,* Finance and Economics Discussion Series 2020-029 (Washington, D.C: Board of Governors of the Federal Reserve System, 2020), 19-22, https://doi.org/10.17016/FEDS.2020.029.

162 Ringo, 22.

163 Lei Ding and Carolina K. Reid, *The Community Reinvestment Act (CRA) and Bank Branching Patterns,* Working Paper, 19-36 (Philadelphia: Federal Reserve Bank of Philadelphia, September 2019), 8, https://www.philadelphiafed.org/-/media/frbp/assets/working-papers/2019/wp19-36.pdf or https://doi.org/10.21799/frbp.wp.2019.36

164 Ding and Reid, 12.

165 Ding and Reid, 14.

166 Ding and Reid, 16-17.

167 Bruce C. Mitchell, PhD, Jason Richardson, and Zo Amani, *Relationships Matter: Small Business and Bank Branch Locations* (Washington, D.C: NCRC, March 2021) https://ncrc.org/relationships-matter-small-business-and-bank-branch-locations/

168 Marchiel, 176-177.

169 NCRC, "CRA commitments" (unpublished, 2007) available upon request from the author.

170 Alexandria Robinson, "Explainer: How NCRC Brings Banks And Local Leaders Together For Community Benefits Agreements," (blog), NCRC, updated January 2024, https://ncrc.org/explainer-how-ncrc-brings-banks-and-local-leaders-together-for-community-benefits-agreements/

171 NCRC comment to Federal Reserve Board on the Notice and Application filed by Capital One Bank, NA to acquire HSBC Bank, Nevada, NA, November 2011, https://ncrc.org/wp-content/uploads/2011/10/ncrc%20final%20comment%20letter_capital%20one_10122011.pdf

172 Raphael W. Bostic and Breck L. Robinson, "What Makes CRA Agreements Work? A Study of Lender Responses to CRA Agreements," 14. Paper prepared for the Federal Reserve System's third biennial research conference titled "Sustainable Community Development: What Works, What Doesn't and Why," February 2003. https://www.federalreserve.gov/communityaffairs/national/CA_Conf_SusCommDev/pdf/bosticraphael.pdf.

173 Bostic and Robinson, 15.

174 Bostic and Robinson, 18-19.

175 Bostic and Robinson, 20.

176 Raphael W. Bostic and Breck L. Robinson, "Do CRA Agreements Influence Lending Patterns?" *Real Estate Economics*, released ahead of print, August 2002, 10-11.

177 Bostic and Robinson, 23-25.

178 Bostic and Robinson, 26.

179 Colleen Casey, Joseph Farhat, Gregory Cartwright, "Community Reinvestment Act and Local Governance Contexts: Advancing the Future of Community Reinvestment?" *Cityscape: A Journal of Policy Development and Research*, Volume 19 Number 2 (Washington, D.C: U.S. Department of Housing and Urban Development, Office of Policy Development and Research 2017), 146, https://www.jstor.org/stable/26328333

180 Casey, Farhat, Cartwright, 151.

181 Casey, Farhat, Cartwright, 154.

182 Diego Zuluaga, "The Community Reinvestment Act in the Age of Fintech and Bank Competition" *Policy Analysis*, Number 875 (Washington, D.C: Cato Institute, July 10, 2019), 9, https://www.cato.org/sites/cato.org/files/pubs/pdf/pa-875-updated.pdf

183 Elizabeth Laderman and Carolina Reid, "CRA Lending during the Subprime Meltdown" in *Revisiting the CRA: Perspectives on the Future of the Community Reinvestment Act*, 122.

184 Neil Bhutta and Daniel Ringo, "Assessing the Community Reinvestment Act's Role in the Financial Crisis," Feds Notes, posted May 2015 on the website of the Federal Reserve System, https://www.federalreserve.gov/econresdata/notes/feds-notes/2015/assessing-the-community-reinvestment-acts-role-in-the-financial-crisis-20150526.html

185 The Financial Crisis Inquiry Report, *Final Report of the National Commission on the Causes of the Financial and Economic Crisis in the United States*, xxvii, http://fcic-static.law.stanford.edu/cdn_media/fcic-reports/fcic_final_report_full.pdf

186 Department of Justice, "Federal Government and State Attorneys General Reach Nearly $1 Billion Agreement with SunTrust to Address Mortgage Loan Origination as Well as Servicing and Foreclosure Abuses," June 2014, https://www.justice.gov/opa/pr/federal-government-and-state-attorneys-general-reach-nearly-1-billion-agreement-suntrust

187 Department of Justice.

188 Federal Reserve Bank of Atlanta, CRA Exam of Suntrust Bank, March 2013, 2, https://www.frbatlanta.org/-/media/Documents/banking/cra_pes/2013/675332.pdf

189 John Dunbar and David Donald, "The roots of the financial crisis: Who is to blame?," Center for Public Integrity, May 6, 2009, https://publicintegrity.org/inequality-poverty-opportunity/the-roots-of-the-financial-crisis-who-is-to-blame/

190 Zuluaga, 10.

191 Report by the Board of Governors of the Federal Reserve System, submitted to the Congress pursuant to section 713 of the Gramm-Leach-Bliley Act of 1999, *The Performance and Profitability of CRA-Related Lending*, July 17, 2000, 45, https://www.federalreserve.gov/boarddocs/surveys/craloansurvey/cratext.pdf

192 Report by the Board of Governors, 46.

193 Report by the Board of Governors, 48.

194 Report by the Board of Governors, 45.

195 Report by the Board of Governors, 50.

196 Report by the Board of Governors, 64 and Table 8 in https://www.federalreserve.gov/boarddocs/surveys/craloansurvey/cratables.pdf

197 NCRC Comment Letter Regarding the Community Reinvestment Act Proposed Rulemaking [87 FR 33884], August 3, 2022, 126, https://ncrc.org/ncrcs-full-public-comment-letter-on-community-reinvestment-act-interagency-rulemaking/

198   Consumer Financial Protection Bureau (CFPB), *Data Point: 2020 Mortgage Market Activity and Trends* (Washington, D.C.: CFPB August 2021) Table 2, 18, https://files.consumerfinance.gov/f/documents/cfpb_2020-mortgage-market-activity-trends_report_2021-08.pdf

199   David Krechevsky, "Independent Mortgage Bank Profits On Loans Fell Nearly 58% In 4Q 2021," *National Mortgage Professional*, March 2022, https://nationalmortgageprofessional.com/news/independent-mortgage-bank-profits-loans-fell-nearly-58-4q-2021#:~:text=Independent%20mortgage%20banks%20(IMBs)%20and,MBA)%20Quarterly%20Mortgage%20Bankers%20Performance

200   Diego Zuluaga, "A tool meant to help minorities buy homes is instead speeding up gentrification in D.C.," Washington Post, August 9, 2019, https://www.washingtonpost.com/opinions/local-opinions/a-tool-that-helps-minorities-buy-homes-is-speeding-up-gentrification-in-the-district/2019/08/09/10c08366-a744-11e9-9214-246e594de5d5_story.html

201   Ding and Nakamura, 27-28; Bostic and Robinson, 2002, 23-25.

202   Jacob Conway, Jack N. Glaser, Matthew C. Plosser, *Does the Community Reinvestment Act Improve Consumers' Access to Credit?,* Federal Reserve Bank of New York Staff Reports, No. 1048, January 2023, 2-3, https://www.newyorkfed.org/medialibrary/media/research/staff_reports/sr1048.pdf

203   Conway, Glaser, Plosser, 11-12.

204   Conway, Glaser, Plosser, 21.

Chapter 3

205   Marchiel, 176-177

206   Kevin Hill (Senior Policy Advisor, National Community Reinvestment Coalition (NCRC)) in discussion with the author, January 2023.

207   Alexandria Robinson, "Explainer: How NCRC Brings Banks and Local Leaders Together For Community Benefits Agreements," (blog), NCRC, November 2022, https://ncrc.org/explainer-how-ncrc-brings-banks-and-local-leaders-together-for-community-benefits-agreements/

208   Kevin Hill, January 2023.

209   Kevin Hill, January 2023.

210   Catherine Petrusz (Senior CRA Analyst, NCRC) in discussion with the author, January 2023.

211   Kevin Hill, January 2023.

212   Kevin Hill, January 2023 and a list of NCRC CBAs are on the NCRC website at https://ncrc.org/cba/ last accessed on February 5, 2024.

213   Kevin Hill, January 2023.

214 Application of PNC Bank, National Association, Wilmington, Delaware, to Acquire BBVA USA, submitted to Office of the Comptroller of the Currency, December 29, 2020, 56.

215 Kevin Hill, January 2023.

216 Josh Silver, Archana Pradhan. and Spencer Cowan, *Access to Capital and Credit in Appalachia and the Impact of the Financial Crisis and Recession on Commercial Lending and Finance in the Region* (Washington, D.C: Appalachian Regional Commission, 2013), 215-222. https://www.ncrc.org/access-to-capital-and-credit-in-appalachia-and-the-impact-of-the-financial-crisis-and-recession-on-commercial-lending-and-finance-in-the-region/

217 Memorandum by Demetria L. McCain for the Office of Fair Housing and Equal Opportunity, Fair Housing Assistance Program Agencies, Fair Housing Initiative Program Grantees, "FHEO's Statement by HUD's Office of Fair Housing and Equal Opportunity on Special Purpose Credit Programs as a Remedy for Disparities in Access to Homeownership," December 2021, https://www.hud.gov/sites/dfiles/FHEO/documents/FHEO_Statement_on_Fair_Housing_and_Special_Purpose_Programs_FINAL.pdf

218 Kevin Hill, January 2023.

219 Office of the Comptroller of the Currency, Federal Reserve System, Federal Deposit Insurance Corporation, *Community Reinvestment Act, Final Rule* (October 24, 2023), 1111 https://www.fdic.gov/news/board-matters/2023/2023-10-24-notice-dis-a-fr.pdf

220 Kevin Hill, January 2023.

221 Office of the Comptroller of the Currency, Federal Reserve System, Federal Deposit Insurance Corporation, *Community Reinvestment Act; Interagency Questions and Answers Regarding Community Reinvestment*, Vol. 81, No. 142 (Washington, D.C: Federal Register, Monday, July 25, 2016), Q&A § .28−1, 48539, https://www.govinfo.gov/content/pkg/FR-2016-07-25/pdf/2016-16693.pdf

222 NCRC, "NCRC Announces Expanded Community Benefits Agreement With First Merchants Bank," November 11, 2022, https://ncrc.org/ncrc-announces-expanded-community-benefits-agreement-with-first-merchants-bank/

223 Scott McKee (SVP/Director, Corporate Social Responsibility: First Merchants Bank) in discussion with the author, February 2023. For information about the racial and ethnic composition in the United States in 20 years, see, William H. Frey, "The U.S. will become 'minority white' in 2045, Census Projects," *Brookings* (commentary), March 14, 2018, https://www.brookings.edu/articles/the-us-will-become-minority-white-in-2045-census-projects/

224 Scott McKee, February 2023.

225 Kevin Hill, January 2023.

226 Scott McKee, February 2023.

227 NCRC Announces Expanded Community Benefits Agreement with First Merchants Bank

228 Website of First Merchants Bank, "Dreaming of Buying a Home," https://www.firstmerchants.com/personal-banking/mortgage/next-horizon-mortgage

229 Scott McKee, February 2023.

230 Website of the Cities for Financial Empowerment Fund and its Bank On program: https://cfefund.org/ and https://joinbankon.org/

231 Scott McKee, February 2023.

232 NCRC Announces Expanded Community Benefits Agreement with First Merchants Bank

233 NCRC, "NCRC Announces $40 Billion Community Benefits Plan With BMO Harris Bank," November 28, 2022, https://ncrc.org/ncrc-announces-40-billion-community-benefits-plan-with-bmo-harris-bank/

234 NCRC, "U.S. Bancorp, NCRC, CRC Announce $100 Billion Community Benefits Plan," May 9, 2022, https://ncrc.org/u-s-bancorp-ncrc-crc-announce-100-billion-community-benefits-plan/

235 NCRC, "NCRC And KeyBank Announce Landmark $16.5 Billion Community Benefits Agreement," March 18, 2016, https://ncrc.org/ncrc-and-keybank-announce-landmark-165-billion-community-benefits-agreement/

236 Jesse Van Tol, "Why We're Breaking Up With KeyBank," *NCRC* (blog), December 13, 2022, https://ncrc.org/why-were-breaking-up-with-keybank/

237 Van Tol, "Why we are breaking up with KeyBank"

238 Kevin Hill, January 2023.

239 NCRC, "NCRC And KeyBank To Renew Their Relationship," April 3, 2024, https://ncrc.org/ncrc-and-keybank-to-renew-their-relationship/

240 Jesse Van Tol, "NCRC Comment on 2022 OCC CRA Exam of Citizens Bank," (unpublished, September 30, 2022), 3.

241 Van Tol, NCRC Comment on CRA Exam of Citizens, 7.

242 Office of the Comptroller of the Currency, Community Reinvestment Act Performance Evaluation: Woodforest National Bank (Houston: Office of the Comptroller of the Currency, 2012), 2, https://occ.gov/static/cra/craeval/dec13/16892.pdf

243 Office of the Comptroller of the Currency, Community Reinvestment Act Performance Evaluation: Woodforest National Bank (Houston: Office of the Comptroller of the Currency, 2015), 1, https://occ.gov/static/cra/craeval/oct16/16892.pdf

244 Office of the Comptroller of the Currency, Community Reinvestment Act Performance Evaluation: Woodforest National Bank (Houston: Office of the Comptroller of the Currency, 2019), 13-14, https://occ.gov/static/cra/craeval/nov19/16892.pdf

245 Office of the Comptroller of the Currency, CRA Evaluation, 2019, 18

246 Office of the Comptroller of the Currency, Community Reinvestment Act Per-
     formance Evaluation: Woodforest National Bank (Houston: Office of the Comp-
     troller of the Currency, 2023) https://occ.gov/static/cra/craeval/Oct23/16892.
     pdf

247 Federal Reserve Bank of Atlanta, Community Reinvestment Act Performance
     Evaluation: Banco Bilbao Vizcaya Argentaria Compass Bank (Atlanta: Federal
     Reserve Bank of Atlanta, 2013) 1, https://www.federalreserve.gov/apps/CRA-
     PubWeb/CRA/BankRating

248 Federal Reserve Bank of Atlanta, Community Reinvestment Act Performance
     Evaluation: Compass Bank (Atlanta: Federal Reserve Bank of Atlanta, 2018), 1,
     https://www.federalreserve.gov/apps/CRAPubWeb/CRA/BankRating

249 Federal Deposit Insurance Corporation, Community Reinvestment Act Evalua-
     tion, Transportation Alliance Bank, Inc., d/b/a TAB Bank (San Francisco: FDIC
     San Francisco Regional Office, April 13, 2022), 1, https://crapes.fdic.gov/pub-
     lish/2022/34781_220413.PDF

250 NCRC, "40 Groups Urge FDIC To Downgrade TAB Bank," June 30, 2022,
     https://ncrc.org/40-groups-urge-fdic-to-downgrade-tab-bank/

251 NCRC, "40 Groups Urge FDIC To Downgrade TAB Bank."

252 Adam Rust (Senior Policy Advisor, National Community Reinvestment Coalition
     (NCRC)) in discussion with the author, February 2023.

253 Kevin Hill, January 2023.

254 Kevin Hill, January 2023.

255 For example, see Federal Deposit Insurance Corporation (FDIC), Division
     of Depositor and Consumer Protection, Kansas City Regional Office, Com-
     munity Reinvestment Act Evaluation, Security Bank of Kansas City (Kansas
     City, Missouri: FDIC, November 2023) 17, https://crapes.fdic.gov/pub-
     lish/2023/4705_231128.PDF

256 Office of the Comptroller of the Currency, Community Reinvestment Act Eval-
     uation, Wells Fargo Bank, National Association (Washington D.C: Office of the
     Comptroller of the Currency, 2012) 13-14, https://occ.gov/static/cra/craeval/
     apr17/1.pdf

257 Bob Dickerson (Executive Director, Birmingham Business Resource Center
     (BBRC)) in discussion with the author, February 2023.

258 Bob Dickerson, February 2023.

259 Bob Dickerson, February 2023.

260 Bob Dickerson, February 2023.

261 Dan Immergluck, *Red Hot City: Housing, Race, and Exclusion in Twenty-First
     Century Atlanta* (Oakland: University of California Press, 2022) 77-80.

262 Namoch Sokhom (Director of Loan Services, Vermont-Slauson Economic Development Corporation) in discussion with the author, January 2024.

263 Namoch Sokhom, January 2024.

264 Namoch Sokhom, January 2024.

265 Namoch Sokhom, January 2024.

266 Namoch Sokhom, January 2024.

267 Maria Elena Guerra (Meg) (Executive Director, Farmworker Housing Development Corporation) in discussion with the author, February 2024.

268 Meg Guerra, February 2024.

269 Meg Guerra, February 2024.

270 Meg Guerra, February 2024.

271 Meg Guerra, February 2024.

272 Oregon IDA Initiative, (website), accessed February 4, 2024, https://oregonidainitiative.org/

273 Peter Hainley, email message to author, February 2, 2024.

274 Dave Castillo (Chief Executive Officer, Native Community Capital) in discussion with the author, February 2024.

275 Dave Castillo, February 2024.

276 Dave Castillo, Bruce C. Mitchell, PhD, Jason Richardson, Jad Edlebi, *Redlining the Reservation: The Brutal Cost Of Financial Services Inaccessibility In Native Communities* (Washington DC: NCRC, December 2023), https://ncrc.org/redlining-the-reservation-the-brutal-cost-of-financial-services-inaccessibility-in-native-communities/

277 Office of the Comptroller of the Currency, Federal Reserve System, Federal Deposit Insurance Corporation, Community Reinvestment Act, Final Rule, Vol. 89, No. 22 (Washington, D.C.: October 24, 2023), 6699, https://www.federal-register.gov/documents/2024/02/01/2023-25797/community-reinvestment-act.

278 Redlining the Reservation

279 Dave Castillo, February 2024.

280 Dave Castillo, February 2024.

281 Dave Castillo, February 2024.

282 CRA Final Rule, 6699.

283 Dave Castillo, February 2024.

284 Dave Castillo, February 2024.

285 Dave Castillo, February 2024.

286 Denise Rodriguez (Executive Director, Washington Homeownership Resource Center) in discussion with the author, February 2024.

287 Denise Rodriguez, February 2024.

288 Denise Rodriguez, February 2024.

289 Black Home Initiative (website) accessed February 7, 2024, https://www.
homeownership-wa.org/services/bhi

290 Denise Rodriguez, February 2024.

291 Denise Rodriguez, February 2024.

292 Islamic Finance Foundation (website) accessed December 2, 2024,
https://www.sukuk.com/education/muslims-reject-interest-riba-
274/#/?playlistId=0&videoId=0

293 Denise Rodriguez, February 2024.

294 Denise Rodriguez, February 2024.

295 Denise Rodriguez, February 2024.

296 Kevin Stein (Chief of Legal and Strategy, California Reinvestment Coalition) in
discussion with the author, February 2023.

297 Kevin Stein, February 2023.

298 Community Benefits Agreement between Banc of California, N.A. and the
Greenlining Institute and the California Reinvestment Coalition, signed by CEO of
Banc of California, CEO, the Greenlining Institute, and Executive Director, the
California Reinvestment Coalition, 3, 2021, https://calreinvest.org/wp-content/
uploads/2021/10/BANC-of-California_CBA_-2021.pdf

299 $40 Billion BMO Harris Bank Community Benefits Plan, December 2022,
https://calreinvest.org/publications/bank-agreements/

300 California Reinvestment Coalition, Anti-Displacement Code of Conduct: How
Banks, Private Equity and Wall Street Can Stop Contributing to Displacement,
https://calreinvest.org/about/code-of-conduct/

301 Jaime Weisberg, "New York State to Lenders: You ARE Accountable for
Multifamily Displacement Lending," ANHD, October 10, 2018, https://anhd.org/
blog/new-york-state-lenders-you-are-accountable-multifamily-displacement-
lending

302 Jaime Weisberg, "The Banking and Legal Systems That Support the City's
Worst Evictors," ANHD, October 22, 2019, https://anhd.org/blog/banking-
legal-systems-support-citys-worst-evictors

303 Kevin Stein, February 2023.

304 CRA Final Rule, 6648.

305 Kevin Hill, January 2023.

306 Federal Reserve System, H.2A: Notice of Formation and Mergers of, and
Acquisitions by, Bank Holding Companies or Savings and Loan Holding Companies; Change in Bank Control, https://www.federalreserve.gov/apps/h2a/
h2aindex.aspx

307   Office of the Comptroller of the Currency, FOIA Library, https://foia-pal.occ. gov/App/ReadingRoom.aspx, Corporate Applications Search, https://apps. occ.gov/CAAS_CATS/CAAS_Details.aspx?FilingTypeID=13&FilingID=327439&- FilingSubtypeID=1080

308   FDIC, Applications In Process Subject to the CRA, https://cra.fdic.gov/, OCC Licensing Office Contacts, https://www.occ.gov/topics/charters-and-licensing/ licensing-office-contacts.html

309   FDIC, CRA Examination Schedule, https://www.fdic.gov/resources/bankers/ community-reinvestment-act/examination-schedule/, Federal Reserve System, Search Exam Schedules and Submit CRA Comments, https://www.federalre- serve.gov/apps/CRAPubWeb/Schedule/DistrictSchedule, OCC, Community Reinvestment Act (CRA) Evaluations Coming Due, https://occ.gov/topics/ consumers-and-communities/cra/exam-schedule/index-cra-evaluations- coming-due.html

310   FDIC, Applications In Process Subject to the CRA Report Selection Options, https://cra.fdic.gov/; Federal Reserve System, Search Exam Schedules & Submit CRA Comments, https://www.federalreserve.gov/apps/CRAPubWeb/ Schedule/DistrictSchedule, last accessed April 2024.

311   OCC, Organization, Comptroller's Office, Department, and Offices, https://occ. gov/about/who-we-are/organizations/index-organization.html

312   For example, see Federal Reserve System, Order Approving the Acquisition of a Bank Holding Company and the Merger of Bank Holding Companies, Bank of Montreal, of Montreal, Canada, and BMO Financial Corp., of Wilmington, Delaware, to acquire BancWest Holding Inc., January 17, 2023, 16-20, https:// www.federalreserve.gov/newsevents/pressreleases/files/orders20230117a1. pdf

313   Federal Reserve Bank of Richmond, Community Reinvestment Act Perfor- mance Evaluation of Sandy Spring Bank (Richmond, Federal Reserve Bank of Richmond: October 12, 2021), 7, https://www.federalreserve.gov/apps/CRA- PubWeb/CRA/BankRating

314   Josh Silver, *CRA Performance Context: Why it is Important for Community Development and How to Improve It* (Washington D.C: National Commu- nity Reinvestment Coalition, April 2016), https://ncrc.org/ncrc-makes- recommendations-to-improve-performance-context-analysis-in-community- reinvestment-act-exams/

315   Community Reinvestment Act (CRA), Code of Federal Regulations (CFR), Title 12, Chapter 30, § 2906(c), 1434, https://www.govinfo.gov/content/pkg/ USCODE-2013-title12/pdf/USCODE-2013-title12-chap30.pdf

316   CRA Final Rule, 6782-6784.

317   John Taylor (Founder and former President and CEO, National Community Reinvestment Coalition (NCRC)) in discussion with the author, February 2023.

318 HMDA & PMIC Data Products, https://www.ffiec.gov/hmda/hmdaproducts. htm, this was the data that the Federal Reserve Board collected and made available over the FFIEC webpage until 2016.

319 Consumer Financial Protection Bureau, "HMDA Dataset Filtering," last accessed on April 15, 2024, https://ffiec.cfpb.gov/data-browser/data/2022?category=states

320 Josh Silver, Data Disclosure Laws Lose Power If the CFPB Makes Data Hard To Use (blog), *NCRC*, December 20, 2022, https://ncrc.org/data-disclosure-laws-lose-power-if-the-cfpb-makes-data-hard-to-use/

321 John Taylor, February 2023.

322 Acting Comptroller of the Currency Michael J. Hsu, Remarks at Brookings "Bank Mergers and Industry Resiliency," May 9, 2022, 8, https://www.occ.gov/news-issuances/speeches/2022/pub-speech-2022-49.pdf

323 Office of the Comptroller of the Currency, Final Rule: Business Combinations under the Bank Merger Act, Federal Register, Vol. 89, No. 186 (Washington D.C.: September 25, 2024), 78220, https://www.govinfo.gov/content/pkg/FR-2024-09-25/pdf/2024-21560.pdf)

324 Federal Deposit Insurance Corporation, Final Statement of Policy on Bank Merger Transactions, Federal Register, Vol. 89, No. 186 (Washington D.C: September 27, 2024), 79138, https://www.govinfo.gov/content/pkg/FR-2024-09-27/pdf/2024-22189.pdf

325 Marchiel, 143.

326 Interview with NCRC members, June 2022.

327 Federal Reserve System, Order Approving the Acquisition of a Bank Holding Company and the Merger of Bank Holding Companies, Bank of Montreal, of Montreal, Canada, and BMO Financial Corp., of Wilmington, Delaware, to acquire BancWest Holding Inc., January 17, 2023, 20, https://www.federalreserve.gov/newsevents/pressreleases/files/orders20230117a1.pdf

328 "Streamlined Business Combination Application," Office of the Comptroller of the Currency, last accessed March 19, 2024, 3, https://www.occ.treas.gov/static/licensing/form-business-combo-app-streamlined-v2.pdf

329 Office of the Comptroller of the Currency, "OCC Announces Conditional Approval of U.S. Bank, National Association – MUFG Union Bank, National Association Merger," NR 2022-128, October 14, 2022, https://occ.gov/news-issuances/news-releases/2022/nr-occ-2022-128.html, OCC Decision Letter to Conditionally Approve Bank Merger Act Application from U.S. Bank National Association, 8-9, https://occ.gov/news-issuances/news-releases/2022/nr-occ-2022-128a.pdf

330 Federal Deposit Insurance Corporation, Final Statement of Policy on Bank Merger Transactions, 79138.

331 Federal Deposit Insurance Corporation, Final Statement of Policy on Bank Merger Transactions, 79132.

332 NCRC, Letter To Federal Reserve On Capital One Acquisition, August 16, 2011, 6-7, https://ncrc.org/letter-to-federal-reserve-on-capital-one-acquisition/ and NCRC's Final Comment To Federal Reserve On Capital One ING Acquisition, October 13, 2011, 48-52, https://ncrc.org/final-comment-to-federal-reserve-on-capital-one-ing-acquisition/

Chapter 4

333 Significant parts of the discussion of the CRA hearings are from Josh Silver, *The Purpose And Design Of The Community Reinvestment Act (CRA): An Examination Of The 1977 Hearings And Passage Of The CRA* (Washington D.C: NCRC, June 2019), https://ncrc.org/the-purpose-and-design-of-the-community-reinvestment-act-cra-an-examination-of-the-1977-hearings-and-passage-of-the-cra/. A version of this article first appeared in Conference of Consumer Finance Law, Quarterly Report, Vol. 72, No. 4.

334 *Community Credit Needs: Hearings on S. 406 Before the S. Comm. on Banking, Housing, and Urban Affairs*, 95th Cong. 9 (1977) (statement of Sen. William Proxmire, Chairman, S. Comm. on Banking, Housing, and Urban Affairs) [hereinafter *Banking Hearings*].

335 123 Cong. Rec. 17630 (June 6, 1977).

336 *Banking Hearings*, 323.

337 Marchiel, 143.

338 *Banking Hearings,* 2.

339 *Banking Hearings,* 11.

340 *Banking Hearings*, 9.

341 *Banking Hearings*, 9.

342 *Banking Hearings,* 10.

343 *Banking Hearings*, 9.

344 Marchiel, 135.

345 Marchiel, 135.

346 Robert Kuttner (author and former Banking Committee staff person) in discussion with author, March 2023.

347 Marchiel, 138, 142.

348 Wisconsin Historical Society, Senator William Proxmire Collection, "An oral history interview with Robert L. Kuttner," 30, accessed on January 24, 2024, https://content.wisconsinhistory.org/digital/collection/proxmire/id/3398/rec/34

349 Calvin Bradford (Senior Research Fellow at the Woodstock Institute) in discussion with author, January 2024.

350 *Banking Hearings,* 44.

351 *Banking Hearings,* 48.

352 *Banking Hearings,* 50–51.

353 *Banking Hearings,* 58–59.

354 *Banking Hearings,* 136.

355 123 CONG. REC. 17630 (June 6, 1977).

356 123 CONG. REC. 17630.

357 123 Cong. Rec. 17630.

358 *Banking Hearings,* 193.

359 123 CONG. REC. 17630.

360 *Banking Hearings,* 297.

361 *Banking Hearings,* 308.

362 *Banking Hearings,* 305–06.

363 *Banking Hearings,* 299.

364 *Banking Hearings,* 166

365 *Banking Hearings,* 168.

366 *Banking Hearings,* 177.

367 *Banking Hearings,* 177.

368 *Banking Hearings,* 12.

369 *Banking Hearings,* 13.

370 *Banking Hearings,* 13.

371 *Banking Hearings,* 15.

372 *Banking Hearings,* 14.

373 *Banking Hearings,* 315.

374 *Banking Hearings,* 324.

375 *Banking Hearings,* 330.

376 123 CONG. REC. 17604 (June 6, 1977).

377 Kuttner, March 2023.

378 Bradford, January 2024.

379 Bradford, January 2024.

380 *Banking Hearings,* 6-7 (providing the text of the draft CRA bill).

381 *Banking Hearings,* 3-8.

382 Housing and Community Development Act of 1977, Pub. L. No. 95-128, 91 Stat. 1147 (1977), Title VIII Community Reinvestment, https://www.congress.gov/bill/95th-congress/house-bill/6655/text

383 Warren L. Dennis, "The Community Reinvestment Act of 1977, Its Legislative History and Its Impact on Applications for Changes I n Structure Made by Depository Institutions to the Four Federal Financial Supervisory Agencies," (working paper No. 24, Credit Research Center, Purdue University, 1978) 19, https://docplayer.net/47347583-The-community-re-investment-act-of-1977.html.

384 Marchiel, *After Redlining,* 145.

385 Wisconsin Historical Society, Senator William Proxmire Collection, "An oral history interview with Ken McLean," 67, accessed on January 23, 2024, https://content.wisconsinhistory.org/digital/collection/proxmire/id/1874/rec/3

386 Congress.gov, "H.R.6655 - Housing and Community Development Act," accessed on January 23, 2024, https://www.congress.gov/bill/95th-congress/house-bill/6655/actions

387 An oral history interview with Ken McLean.

388 123 CONG. REC. 17632 (June 6, 1977). During a discussion, Senator Proxmire confirmed that reporting requirements were deleted.

389 *Banking Hearings*, 2.

390 123 CONG. REC. 31888 (October 1, 1977).

391 Warren Dennis, "The Community Reinvestment Act of 1977," 7.

392 Dennis, 9.

393 *Banking Hearings*, 291.

394 Immergluck, *Credit to the Community*, 147.

395 Kuttner, March 2023.

396 Bradford, January 2024.

397 Brandford, January 2024.

398 Community Reinvestment Act of 1977 Proposed by National People's Action (unpublished), 6.

399 NPA CRA proposal (unpublished), 7.

400 Bradford, January 2024.

401 Kuttner, March 2023.

402 Dennis, original version of bill in Appendix A compared to passed version in Appendix C

403 Kuttner, March 2023.

404 Marchiel, 136-137.

405 Immergluck, 155-157

406 Marchiel, 174-175

407 Immergluck, 157.

408 Immergluck, 160

409 John Taylor (Founder and former President and CEO, National Community Reinvestment Coalition (NCRC)) in discussion with the author, February 2023.

410 John Taylor, February 2023.

411 John Taylor, February 2023.

412 John Taylor, February 2023.

413 Financial Institutions Reform, Recovery, and Enforcement Act (FIRREA), Pub. L. No. 101-73, 1991, 103 Stat. 527 (1989), https://www.congress.gov/bill/101st-congress/house-bill/1278/text

414 To view the specific CRA amendment of FIRREA, see http://uscode.house.gov/statviewer.htm?volume=103&page=527

415 Federal Deposit Insurance Corporation Improvement Act of 1991, Pub. L. No. 102-242, 105 Stat. 2306 (1991), Sec. 222 – Discussion of Lending Data, https://www.congress.gov/bill/102nd-congress/senate-bill/543/text

416 Patrick Mulloy, *The Riegle-Neal Interstate Banking and Branching Efficiency Act of 1994: Responding to Global Competition*, 21 J. Legis. 255, 258, 269–71 (1995), https://scholarship.law.nd.edu/jleg/vol21/iss2/8

417 *Banking Hearings*, 11.

418 Riegle-Neal Interstate Banking and Branching Efficiency Act, Pub. L. No. 103-328, 108 Stat. 2364 (1994) § 110, Community Reinvestment Act evaluation of banks with interstate branches, https://www.congress.gov/bill/103rd-congress/house-bill/3841/text

419 *Interstate Banking and Branching Hearing Before the Subcommittee on Financial Institutions Supervision, Regulation, and Deposit Insurance of the Committee on Banking, Finance and Urban Affairs, House of Representatives*, 103th Congress, First Session (October 26, 1993), 16.

420 *Interstate Banking and Branching Hearing Before the Subcommittee on Financial Institutions Supervision, Regulation, and Deposit Insurance of the Committee on Banking, Finance and Urban Affairs, House of Representatives*, 103th Congress, First Session (July 29, 1993), 19, 22, 99. *Interstate Banking Efficiency Act, Conference Report, House of Representatives,* 103th Congress, Second Session (August 2, 1994), 52, 62, 63.

421 Housing and Community Development Act of 1992, Pub. L. No. 102-550, 106 Stat. 3874 (1992), Sec. 909, Community Reinvestment Act of 1977, https://www.congress.gov/bill/102nd-congress/house-bill/5334/text

422 Resolution Trust Corporation, Refinancing, Restructuring, and Improvement Act of 1991, Pub. L. No. 102-233, 105 Stat. 1775 (1991), Sec 402. Operation of Branch Facilities by Minorities and Women, https://www.congress.gov/102/statute/STATUTE-105/STATUTE-105-Pg1761.pdf

Chapter 5

423 The White House, Office of the Press Secretary, "Remarks by The President in Announcement of Community Lending Initiative," July 15, 1993, https://web.archive.org/web/20110608074710/http://clinton6.nara.gov/1993/07/1993-07-15-presidents-remarks-on-community-development.html

424 John Taylor, former President and CEO, NCRC, February 2023.

425 Office of the Comptroller of the Currency, Federal Reserve System, Federal Deposit Insurance Corporation, Office of Thrift Supervision, *Community Reinvestment Act Regulations: Joint Final Rule*, Vol. 60, No. 86 (Washington, D.C: Federal Register, Thursday, May 4, 1995), 22158.

426 John Taylor, former President and CEO, NCRC, February 2023.

427 1995 final rule, 22157.

428 Office of the Comptroller of the Currency, Federal Reserve System, Federal Deposit Insurance Corporation, Office of Thrift Supervision, *Community Reinvestment Act Regulations: Joint Notice of Proposed Rulemaking*, Vol. 58, No. 243 (Washington, D.C: Federal Register, Tuesday, December 21, 1993), 67467.

429 1993 proposed rule, 67470.

430 1993 proposed rule, 67484.

431 Office of the Comptroller of the Currency, Federal Reserve System, Federal Deposit Insurance Corporation, Office of Thrift Supervision, *Community Reinvestment Act Regulations: Joint Notice of Proposed Rulemaking*, Vol. 59, No. 194 (Washington, D.C: Federal Register, Friday, October 7, 1994), 51242.

432 1994 proposed rule, 51242.

433 Stephen M. Cross (former Deputy Comptroller for Compliance: OCC) in discussion with the author, April 2023.

434 Stephen Cross, April 2023.

435 Office of the Comptroller of the Currency, Federal Reserve System, Federal Deposit Insurance Corporation, *Interagency Questions and Answers Regarding Community Reinvestment,* Vol. 81, No. 142 (Washington, D.C: Federal Register, Monday, July 25, 2016), Q&A §__.22(b)(5)−1, 48539

436 1994 proposed rule, 51234.

437 1994 proposed rule, 51270.

438 1993 proposed rule, 67474.

439 1994 proposed rule, 51245.

440 1995 final rule, 22170.

441 1993 proposed rule, 67480.

442 1994 proposed rule, 51235.

443 1994 proposed rule, 51253.

444 Stephen Cross, April 2023.

445 1995 final rule, 22209.

446 Stephen Cross, April 2023.

447 Stephen Cross, April 2023.

448 Stephen Cross, April 2023.

449 1994 proposed rule, 51235.

450 1993 proposed rule, 67470.

451 1994 proposed rule, 51238.

452 Office of the Comptroller of the Currency, Community Reinvestment Act Performance Evaluation: U.S. Bank, National Association (Washington D.C: OCC Large Bank Supervision, January 18, 2022), 20, https://occ.gov/static/cra/craeval/Feb23/24.pdf, and Federal Deposit Insurance Corporation, Community Reinvestment Act Performance Evaluation: Eastern Bank (New York City: FDIC, March 22, 2021), 14, https://crapes.fdic.gov/publish/2021/32773_210322.PDF

453 1994 proposed rule, 51235.

454 1995 final rule, 22165

455 1995 Final Rule, 22173

456 National Community Reinvestment Coalition, "Home Loans to Minorities and Low- and Moderate-Income Borrowers Increase in the 1990s, but then Fall in 2001: A Review of National Data Trends from 1993 to 2001," unpublished report, available from author upon request.

457 Federal Reserve Bank of Richmond, Community Reinvestment Act Performance Evaluation: Signet Bank (Richmond, VA: Federal Reserve Bank of Richmond, January 15, 1996) 18, https://www.federalreserve.gov/dcca/cra/1996/460024.pdf

458 Stephen Cross, April 2023.

459 1993 proposed rule, 67469.

460 1995 final rule, 22170.

461 1993 proposed rule, 67469. The agencies cited their authority to terminate insurance under 12 U.S.C. 1818, which can be found here: https://www.law.cornell.edu/uscode/text/12/1818

462 1995 final rule, 22158

Chapter 6

463 Federal Reserve History, "Banking Act of 1933 (Glass-Steagall)," https://www.federalreservehistory.org/essays/glass-steagall-act#:~:text=The%20Glass%2DSteagall%20Act%20effectively,Roosevelt%20in%20June%201933.

464 Early in 1999 during the mark-up of an early version of the bill in the House Banking Committee, Rep. Luis Gutierrez introduced his amendment that would expand CRA to all affiliates of holding companies. Co-sponsored by Waters, Sanders, and Capuano, the amendment would apply CRA to mortgage companies, securities firms, insurance companies, and all other affiliates and subsidiaries. The amendment lost 17-39 in committee. In the House Commerce Committee, Rep. Thomas Barrett (D-WI) expanded upon the original Gutierrez amendment which required insurance company affiliates of banks to report the income, race, and census tract of their policyholders. Barrett expanded the amendment to all insurance companies including those not affiliated with banks. The amendment was defeated 17 to 28. Source: Author's notes.

465 Gramm-Leach-Bliley Act, Pub. L. No. 106-102, 113 Stat. 1466-1469 (1999), https://www.congress.gov/bill/106th-congress/senate-bill/900

466 Bloomberg, "What Does Giving Away Cash Have to do with Community Lending?," *Investment News,* May 10, 1999, https://www.investmentnews.com/what-does-giving-away-cash-have-to-do-with-community-lending-1803

467 Howard Husock, "The Trillion-Dollar Bank Shakedown That Bodes Ill for Cities," *City Journal*, Winter 200, https://www.city-journal.org/html/trillion-dollar-bank-shakedown-bodes-ill-cities-12096.html

468 Gramm-Leach-Bliley Act, Pub. L. No. 106-102 (1999), 113 Stat. 1466 -1469, Sec. 711: CRA Sunshine Requirements.

469 NAACP v. Button, 371 U.S. 415 (1963), decision available in FindLaw, https://caselaw.findlaw.com/court/us-supreme-court/371/415.html

470 Josh Silver, "CRA Sunshine Reveals Benefits of Bank-Community Group Partnerships," (NCRC, Washington D.C., September 2002), 3, available upon request from author.

471 Kenneth H. Thomas, "There's a surprising risk lurking in the details of bank mergers," *American Banker*, January 30, 2023, https://www.americanbanker.com/opinion/theres-a-surprising-risk-lurking-in-the-details-of-bank-mergers

472 Office of the Comptroller of the Currency, Federal Reserve System, Federal Deposit Insurance Corporation, Community Reinvestment Act, Final Rule, Vol. 89, No. 22 (Washington, D.C.: October 24, 2023), 7133-7134, https://www.federalregister.gov/documents/2024/02/01/2023-25797/community-reinvestment-act.

473 Gramm-Leach-Bliley Act, Pub. L. No. 106-102 (1999), 113 Stat. 1469, Sec. 712: Small Bank Regulatory Relief.

474 Gramm-Leach-Bliley Act, Pub. L. No. 106-102 (1999), 113 Stat. 1347.

475 Community Reinvestment Modernization Act of 2000, H.R.4893, 106th Congress (2000), https://www.congress.gov/bill/106th-congress/house-bill/4893/cosponsors?s=2&r=2

476 Introduction of the Community Reinvestment Modernization Act of 20001, Extension of Remarks, March 6, 2001, 147 Cong. Rec. (2001). https://www.congress.gov/congressional-record/volume-147/issue-28/extensions-of-remarks-section/article/E290-2

477 Robert Kuttner in discussion with the author, March 2023.

478 Jesse Van Tol (President and CEO, National Community Reinvestment Coalition (NCRC)) in discussion with the author, March 2023.

479 Liz Cohen and Rosalia Agresti, "Expanding the CRA to All Financial Institutions," in *Revisiting the CRA: Perspectives on the Future of the Community Reinvestment Act*, eds. Prabal Chakrabarti, David Erickson, Ren S. Essene, Ian Galloway, and John Olson (Federal Reserve Banks of Boston and San Francisco, February 2009), 134-137, https://www.frbsf.org/community-development/files/revisiting_cra.pdf

480 Brendan Pedersen, "Societal upheaval strengthens case to expand CRA to nonbanks: Ludwig," *American Banker*, June 22, 2020, https://www.americanbanker.com/news/societal-upheaval-strengthens-case-to-expand-cra-to-nonbanks-ludwig

481 "Louis D. Brandeis, Other People's Money," Louis D. Brandeis School of Law Library, https://louisville.edu/law/library/special-collections/the-louis-d.-brandeis-collection/other-peoples-money-by-louis-d.-brandeis

482 Gregory D. Squires, "Insurance Redlining: Still Fact, Not Fiction," *Shelterforce*, January 1, 1995, https://shelterforce.org/1995/01/01/insurance-redlining-still-fact-not-fiction/

483 Julia Angwin, Jeff Larson, Lauren Kirchner and Surya Mattu, "Minority Neighborhoods Pay Higher Car Insurance Premiums Than White Areas With the Same Risk," *ProPublica and Consumer Reports*, April 5, 2017, https://www.propublica.org/article/minority-neighborhoods-higher-car-insurance-premiums-white-areas-same-risk

484 Emily Flitter, *The White Wall: How Big Finance Bankrupts Black America*, (New York, New York: One Signal Publishers, 2022), 148-156.

485 "Nine Charts about Wealth Inequality in America (Updated)," Urban Institute, last updated October 5, 2017, https://apps.urban.org/features/wealth-inequality-charts/

486 Kim Parker and Richard Fry, "More than half of U.S. households have some investment in the stock," *Pew Research Center*, March 25, 2020, markethttps://www.pewresearch.org/fact-tank/2020/03/25/more-than-half-of-u-s-households-have-some-investment-in-the-stock-market/

487 Eugene A. Ludwig, "Remarks of Eugene A. Ludwig Comptroller of the Currency before the National Urban League," (News Release 1997-78, August 5, 1997), https://www.occ.treas.gov/news-issuances/news-releases/1997/nr-occ-1997-78.html

488 DBRS,"DBRS Publishes "DBRS: Out of the Shadows – Drivers of Global Growth in FSB's Shadow Banking," April 9, 2019, https://www.dbrsmorning-star.com/research/343310/dbrs-publishes-dbrs-out-of-the-shadows-drivers-of-global-growth-in-fsbs-shadow-banking

489 "Facts + Statistics: Industry overview," Insurance Information Institute, last updated 2023, https://www.iii.org/fact-statistic/facts-statistics-industry-overview#:~:text=The%20U.S.%20insurance%20industry%20em-ployed,and%20reinsurers%20(28%2C500%20workers)

490 Investment Company Institute (ICI), "Chapter 3, U.S. Mutual Funds," in *2022 Investment Company Factbook* (Washington, D.C: ICI, 2022), 45, https://www.icifactbook.org/pdf/2022_factbook_ch3.pdf

491 Jason Richardson, "2018 HMDA overview: Banks fell further behind, non-banks dominated home lending," *NCRC*, https://ncrc.org/2018-hmda-overview-banks-fell-further-behind-non-banks-dominated-home-lending/

492 Community Reinvestment Modernization Act of 2000, H.R.4893, 106th Cong. (2000), Sec. 102, https://www.congress.gov/bill/106th-congress/house-bill/4893/text?s=2&r=2

493 H.R. 4893, Sec. 103.

494 H.R. 4893, Sec. 307.

495 H.R. 4893, Sec. 221.

496 Dodd-Frank Wall Street Reform and Consumer Protection Act, Pub. L. No: 111-203, 124 Stat. 2056 (2010), Sec. 1071 and Sec. 1094, https://www.congress.gov/bill/111th-congress/house-bill/4173/text

497 H.R. 4893, Sec. 101.

498 H.R. 4893, Sec. 102.

499 H.R. 4893, Sec. 102.

500 H.R. 4893, Sec. 304 & 305.

501 H.R. 4893, Sec. 105.

502 H.R. 4893, Sec. 105.

503 H.R. 4893, Sec. 106 & 104.

504 Liz Cohen and Rosalia Agresti, *Expanding the CRA to All Financial Institutions*, 136.

505 H.R. 4893, Sec. 201-215.

506 Gregory D. Squires, Sally O' Connor, Josh Silver, "The Unavailability of Information on Insurance Unavailability: Insurance Redlining and the Absence of Geocoded Disclosure Data," *Housing Policy Debate*, Vol. 12, Issue 2 (Fannie Mae Foundation: 2001), http://www.colodnyfass.com/uploads/1975_Insurance%20Data%20Article.pdf

507 California Organized Investment Network – COIN, https://www.insurance.ca.gov/0250-insurers/0700-coin/

508 H.R. 4893, Sec. 302.

509 H.R. 4893, Co-sponsors, https://www.congress.gov/bill/111th-congress/house-bill/1479/cosponsors?s=1&r=40

510 Community Reinvestment Modernization Act of 2009, H.R.1479, 111th Cong. (2009), https://www.congress.gov/bill/111th-congress/house-bill/1479/text?r=40&s=1

511 H.R. 1479, Section 308, https://www.congress.gov/bill/111th-congress/house-bill/1479/text?r=40&s=1#toc-HF306790DB1D3480BA3C21E6DD9668D9

512 NCRC, "Restoring Accountability in the Financial System," March 12, 2009, https://ncrc.org/restoring-accountability-in-the-financial-system/

513 H.R. 1479, Sec. 111, https://www.congress.gov/bill/111th-congress/house-bill/1479/text?r=40&s=1#H3660B07B90834381811D4E698F5EC84D

514 Mass.gov, "The Community Reinvestment Act (CRA) for banks and credit unions," https://www.mass.gov/info-details/the-community-reinvestment-act-cra-for-banks-and-credit-unions

515 Hearings of the United States House of Representatives Committee on Financial Services on Community and Consumer Advocates' Perspectives on the Obama Administration's Financial Regulatory Reform Proposals, July 16, 2009 (Testimony of John Taylor, President and CEO, NCRC), 15, https://ncrc.org/wp-content/uploads/2009/07/ncrc%20taylor%20hfsc%20community%20perspectives%2071609.pdf

516 American Housing and Economic Mobility Act of 2021, S.1368, 117th Cong. (2021), https://www.congress.gov/bill/117th-congress/senate-bill/1368?s=4&r=68

517 S. 1368, Sec. 203, https://www.congress.gov/bill/115th-congress/senate-bill/3503/text?s=2&r=4#id9776A6A6B22440FAA453A3358CEC3EC2

518 S. 1368, Sec. 203, https://www.congress.gov/bill/117th-congress/senate-bill/1368/text?s=4&r=68#id130F72D5B91E4714849E69CE50F8BD42

519 S. 1368, Sec. 203, https://www.congress.gov/bill/117th-congress/senate-bill/1368/text?s=4&r=68#id80BE805A0B2E44CFA7B8FC1AD8C152E5

520 S. 1368, Sec. 203, https://www.congress.gov/bill/115th-congress/senate-bill/3503/text?s=2&r=4#id37946D8C0A5440CC9045674841AA119E

521 Bruce Mitchell, PhD. and Josh Silver, "Adding Underserved Census Tracts As Criterion On CRA Exams," (NCRC, Washington, DC, January 2020), NCRC, https://ncrc.org/adding-underserved-census-tracts-as-criterion-on-cra-exams/

522 S. 1368, https://www.congress.gov/bill/115th-congress/senate-bill/3503/text?s=2&r=4#id6CDF0D62E898407A94715FA3FD900D2B

523 S. 4824, https://www.congress.gov/bill/118th-congress/senate-bill/4824/text?s=3&r=7#id4A940B60A6E54611B7552890E464E48E

524 S. 1368, https://www.congress.gov/bill/115th-congress/senate-bill/3503/text?s=2&r=4#id864D82C48D6C49358B72880F8DAF1D12

525 S. 1368, https://www.congress.gov/bill/115th-congress/senate-bill/3503/text?s=2&r=4#idB0242AD2957A45318E978D8518123285

526 Making Communities Stronger through the Community Reinvestment Act, H.R.8833, 117th Cong. (2022), Sec. 6, https://www.congress.gov/bill/117th-congress/house-bill/8833/text?s=5&r=1&q=%7B%22search%22%3A%5B%22hr+8833%22%5D%7D#H0587DF6F212C49598EAEE144331D3A78

527 H.R. 8833, Sec. 5, https://www.congress.gov/bill/117th-congress/house-bill/8833/text?s=5&r=1&q=%7B%22search%22%3A%5B%22hr+8833%22%5D%7D#H9D4BC91DE68A43C3A760F699D450C8AD

Chapter 7

528 Office of the Comptroller of the Currency, Federal Reserve System, Federal Deposit Insurance Corporation, Community Reinvestment Act Regulations: Joint Final Rule, Vol. 70, No. 147 (Washington, D.C: Federal Register, Thursday August 2, 2005), https://www.federalregister.gov/d/05-15227/p-3 in https://www.federalregister.gov/documents/2005/08/02/05-15227/community-reinvestment-act-regulations

529 NCRC comment letter on proposed CRA rule, May 6, 2005, 6, unpublished available from author upon request.

530 NCRC comment letter, 3.

531 Josh Silver and Richard Marsico, "An Analysis of the Implementation and Impact of the 2004-2005 Amendments to the Community Reinvestment Act Regulations: The Continuing Importance of the CRA Examination Process," *The New York Law School Law Review*, 2008-2009, Volume 53, Number 2, 286, https://digitalcommons.nyls.edu/nyls_law_review/vol53/iss2/5/

532 Deposit Market Share Reports, https://www.fdic.gov/resources/data-tools/

533 NCRC comment letter, 8.

534 Office of Thrift Supervision, Community Reinvestment Act Regulations: Final Rule, Vol. 69, No. 159 (Washington D.C.: Federal Register, August 18, 2004), 51157, https://www.federalregister.gov/documents/2004/08/18/04-18863/community-reinvestment-act-regulations

535 Office of Thrift Supervision, Final Rule, https://www.federalregister.gov/d/05--4016/p-71

536 Silver and Marsico, An Analysis, 280-281.

537 Office of Thrift Supervision, Community Reinvestment Act-Interagency Uniformity, Vol. 72, No. 55 (Washington D.C.: Federal Register, Thursday, March 22, 2007), https://www.federalregister.gov/documents/2007/03/22/E7-5188/community-reinvestment-act-interagency-uniformity

538 Summaries of Comptroller Calls with Bank CEOs, April 8, 2020, Posted by the Comptroller of the Currency on Regulations.gov, https://www.regulations.gov/document/OCC-2018-0008-2668

539 Office of the Comptroller of the Currency, Community Reinvestment Act Regulations, Final Rule, Vol. 85, No. 10 (Washington D.C.: Federal Register, Friday, June 5, 2020), https://www.federalregister.gov/d/2020-11220/p-61

540 NCRC, "Analysis of the OCC's Final CRA Rule" (NCRC: Washington, D.C.: June 2020), https://ncrc.org/analysis-of-the-occs-final-cra-rule/

541 Richard Hunt and Stephen Congdon, "Comment Letter on proposed Community Reinvestment Act Regulations, Docket ID OCC-2018-0008," (Consumer Bankers Association: Washington, D.C., April 8, 2020), 3, https://www.consumerbankers.com/sites/default/files/CBA%20Comments%20to%20OCC%20and%20FDIC%20CRA%20NPR_0.pdf

542 Lilly Thomas, "Comment Letter on proposed Community Reinvestment Act Regulations, Docket ID OCC-2018-0008," (Independent Community Bankers of America: Washington, D.C., April 8, 2020), 2, https://www.regulations.gov/document/OCC-2018-0008-2953

543 Lilly Thomas, "Comment Letter," 16-17.

544 Office of the Comptroller of the Currency (OCC), Final Rule, Community Reinvestment Act Regulations, 34794, https://www.federalregister.gov/documents/2020/06/05/2020-11220/community-reinvestment-act-regulations

545 OCC, Final Rule, 34794.

546 OCC, Final Rule, 34795.

547 OCC Final Rule, 34775 and 34802.

548 12 CFR 25.43(a)(1), https://www.ecfr.gov/current/title-12/chapter-I/part-25#p-25.43(a)

549 National Community Reinvestment Coalition (NCRC) and California Reinvestment Coalition (CRC) v. Office of the Comptroller of the Currency (OCC) and Brian Brooks acting in his official capacity as Acting Comptroller of the Currency filed in the United States District Court, Northern District of California, San Francisco Division, June 25, 2020, 2, https://democracyforward.org/wp-content/uploads/2020/06/CRA-Complaint-06.25.20.pdf

550 NCRC and CRC v. OCC, 2.

551 NCRC and CRC v. OCC, 16-17.

552 NCRC and CRC v. OCC, 17.

553 NCRC and CRC v. OCC, Order Denying Motion to Dismiss, Case 4:20-cv-04186-KAW, January 29, 2021, 4, https://democracyforward.org/wp-content/uploads/2021/02/NCRC-et-al-v.-OCC-Ruling-1.29.21.pdf

554 NCRC and CRC v. OCC, January 2021, 5.

555 NCRC and CRC v. OCC, January 2021, 5.

556 NCRC and CRC v. OCC, January 2021, 12.

557 Office of the Comptroller of the Currency (OCC), "OCC Issues Final Rule to Rescind its 2020 Community Reinvestment Act Rule," News Release 2021-133, December 14, 2021, https://www.occ.gov/news-issuances/news-releases/2021/nr-occ-2021-133.html

Chapter 8

558 Federal Reserve Board, "Federal Reserve Board issues Advance Notice of Proposed Rulemaking on an approach to modernize regulations that implement the Community Reinvestment Act," September 21, 2020, https://www.federalreserve.gov/newsevents/pressreleases/bcreg20200921a.htm

559 Joint Press Release of Board of Governors of the Federal Reserve System, Federal Deposit Insurance Corporation, Office of the Comptroller of the Currency, "Agencies issue joint proposal to strengthen and modernize Community Reinvestment Act Regulations," May 5, 2022, https://www.federalreserve.gov/newsevents/pressreleases/bcreg20220505a.htm

560 Statement by Martin J. Gruenberg, Chairman, FDIC, Final Rule on Community Reinvestment Act Regulations, October 24, 2023, https://www.fdic.gov/news/speeches/2023/spoct2423.html

561 Statement by Vice Chairman Travis Hill on the Final Rule on Community Reinvestment Act Regulations, October 24, 2023, https://www.fdic.gov/news/speeches/2023/spoct2423c.html

562 Office of the Comptroller of the Currency, Federal Reserve System, Federal Deposit Insurance Corporation, Community Reinvestment Act, Final Rule, Federal Register, Vol. 89, No. 22 (Washington, D.C.: February 1, 2024), 6769, https://www.federalregister.gov/documents/2024/02/01/2023-25797/community-reinvestment-act.

563 CRA Final Rule, 6770, 6771.

564 CRA Final Rule, 7044.

565 CRA Final Rule, 6773.

566 CRA Final Rule, 6775.

567 CRA Final Rule, 6774.

568   CRA Final Rule, 6596. Office of the Comptroller of the Currency, "Community Reinvestment Act: Revision of Small and Intermediate Small Bank and Savings Association Asset Thresholds," OCC Bulletin 2022-28, December 29, 2022, https://www.occ.gov/news-issuances/bulletins/2022/bulletin-2022-28.html

569   CRA Final Rule, 6596.

570   Josh Silver, " MAP: Here's Where Changes To CRA Asset Thresholds Will Undermine Community Reinvestment," *NCRC*, June 30, 2022, https://ncrc.org/map-heres-where-changes-to-cra-asset-thresholds-will-undermine-community-reinvestment/

571   Josh Silver, "MAP".

572   CRA Final Rule, 6596.

573   CRA Final Rule, 7048, 7049.

574   CRA Final Rule, 7126-7129.

575   CRA Final Rule, 7049.

576   CRA Final Rule, 6587-6588.

577   CRA Final Rule, 7081.

578   Jason Richardson, Joshua Devine, Jamie Buell, and Dedrick Asante-Muhammad, "NCRC 2020 Home Mortgage Report: Examining Shifts During COVID-19" (National Community Reinvestment Coalition (NCRC), Washington DC, January 2022), https://ncrc.org/ncrc-2020-home-mortgage-report-examining-shifts-during-covid/

579   Richardson, et al., NCRC, January 2022.

580   Feng Liu, Young Jo, and Noah Cohen-Harding, "Data Point: 2022 Mortgage Market Activity and Trends," (Consumer Financial Protection Bureau, Washington DC, September 2023), 6, https://files.consumerfinance.gov/f/documents/cfpb_data-point-mortgage-market-activity-trends_report_2023-09.pdf

581   Illinois Department of Financial and Professional Regulation, Second Notice, Proposed Rulemaking, Banking Community Reinvestment (Springfield, Illinois: September 25, 2023) https://idfpr.illinois.gov/

582   Kevin Hill (Senior Policy Advisor, National Community Reinvestment Coalition (NCRC)) in discussion with the author, November 2023.

583   Public Act 103-0959, Illinois General Assembly, https://www.ilga.gov/legislation/BillStatus.asp?DocNum=3235&GAID=17&DocTypeID=SB&LegId=152543&SessionID=112&GA=103

584   42 U.S. Code § 3608, https://www.law.cornell.edu/uscode/text/42/3608

585   CRA Final Rule, 6588-6590, 6850, 6852.

586   Federal Financial Institution Examination Council (FFIEC), Community Reinvestment Act: Distressed and Underserved Tracts, Regulatory Background, accessed November 2023, https://www.ffiec.gov/cra/distressed.htm

587 CRA Final Rule, 6905.

588 Bruce Mitchell, PhD. and Josh Silver, "Adding Underserved Census Tracts As Criterion On CRA Exams," (NCRC, Washington DC, January 2020), https://ncrc.org/adding-underserved-census-tracts-as-criterion-on-cra-exams/

589 CRA Final Rule, 6588.

590 CRA Final Rule, 6588.

591 CRA Final Rule, 6942.

592 Board, FDIC, NCUA, OCC, CFPB, HUD, U.S. Dept of Justice, Federal Housing Finance Agency, "Interagency Statement on Special Purpose Credit Programs Under the Equal Credit Opportunity Act and Regulation B," Feb. 22, 2022, https://www.fdic.gov/news/financial-institution-letters/2022/fil22008.html

593 CRA Final Rule, 6590.

594 Students for Fair Admissions, Inc. v. President and Fellows of Harvard College, 600 U.S. 181 (2023), 184, https://www.supremecourt.gov/opinions/22pd-f/600us1r53_4g15.pdf

595 Glenn Schlactus (Partner, Relman Colfax) in discussion with the author August 2023.

596 Students for Fair Admissions, 600 U.S. 181 (2023), 215.

597 Glenn Schlactus, August 2023.

598 Laura Meckler, *Dream Town: Shaker Heights and the Quest for Racial Equity* (New York: Henry Holt and Company, 2023), 53.

599 Richard and Leah Rothstein, *Just Action: How to Challenge Segregation Enacted Under the Color of Law* (New York: Liveright Publishing Corporation, 2023), 222.

600 Tracy Hadden Loh, Christopher Coes, and Becca Buthe, "Separate and unequal: Persistent residential segregation is sustaining racial and economic injustice in the U.S" (Washington DC: Brookings, December 16, 2020), https://www.brookings.edu/articles/trend-1-separate-and-unequal-neighborhoods-are-sustaining-racial-and-economic-injustice-in-the-us/

601 Antwan Jones, Gregory Squires, and Carolynn Nixon, "Ecological Associations Between Inclusionary Zoning Policies and Cardiovascular Disease Risk Prevalence: An Observational Study," *Cardiovascular Quality and Outcomes* 14, no. 9 (September 8, 2021), https://www.ahajournals.org/doi/10.1161/CIRCOUTCOMES.120.007807

602 Josh Silver, "CRA Could Do a Better Job Promoting Integration," in *Housing Finance: A Series on New Directions* (Washington DC: Poverty and Race Research Action Council (PRRAC), May 2021), 66-68, https://prrac.org/pdf/racial-justice-in-housing-finance-series-2021.pdf

603 U.S. Department of Housing and Urban Development, Affirmatively Furthering Fair Housing, https://www.hud.gov/AFFH

604 CRA Final Rule, 6722.

605 CRA Final Rule, 6643, 6646.

606 CRA Final Rule, 6869.

607 CRA Final Rule, 6884.

608 CRA Final Rule, 6886-6887.

609 CRA Final Rule, 6886-6887.

610 CRA Final Rule 6898, 7119.

611 CRA Final Rule, 6864, 6854.

612 CRA Final Rule, 6894.

613 CRA Final Rule, 6908.

614 CRA Final Rule, 6914.

615 CRA Final Rule, 7163.

616 Statement by Vice Chairman Travis Hill on the Final Rule on Community Reinvestment Act Regulations

617 CRA Final Rule, 6927-6928, 7120.

618 Federal Reserve Board's version of the regulation at 12 CFR Appendix-A-to-Part-228(b)(3)(i) (Jan. 28, 2024), https://www.ecfr.gov/on/2024-01-28/title-12/appendix-Appendix%20A%20to%20Part%20228#p-Appendix-A-to-Part-228(b)(3)(i)

619 CRA Final Rule, 6933, 7120.

620 CRA Final Rule, 6925.

621 CRA Final Rule, 7121.

622 CRA Final Rule, 7120.

623 CRA Final Rule, 6934-6935.

624 CRA Final Rule, 6941, 7121.

625 CRA Final Rule, 6944.

626 FDIC CRA exam of Republic Bank (New York: FDIC New York Regional Office, April 24, 2023) 12, ratio uses assets, https://crapes.fdic.gov/publish/2023/27332_230424.PDF, OCC CRA exam of Bank of America, N.A. (Washington, DC: OCC, January 3, 2022), 23, ratio uses Tier I capital, https://occ.gov/static/cra/craeval/Jul23/13044.pdf

627 CRA Final Rule, 6967, 6971.

628 CRA Final Rule, 6973.

629 CRA Final Rule, 6958.

630 CRA Final Rule, 6715.

631 CRA Final Rule, 6977.

632   NCRC, "NCRC's Full Public Comment Letter On Community Reinvestment Act Interagency Rulemaking," August 2022, https://ncrc.org/ncrcs-full-public-comment-letter-on-community-reinvestment-act-interagency-rulemaking/

633   Josh Silver, "How To Evaluate Community Development Financing And Services Under CRA," *NCRC*, December 10, 2019, https://ncrc.org/how-to-evaluate-community-development-financing-and-services-under-cra/

634   Calvin Bradford (Senior Research Fellow at the Woodstock Institute) in discussion with author, January 2024.

635   CRA Final Rule, 6704, 6992.

636   CRA Final Rule, 6992-6996, 7124.

637   CRA Final Rule, 7113; Scholastica (Gay) Cororaton, "Distribution of Housing Wealth Across Income Groups from 2010–2020," *National Association of Realtors*, March 11, 2022, https://www.nar.realtor/blogs/economists-outlook/distribution-of-housing-wealth-across-income-groups-from-2010-2020; FDIC, *2021 FDIC National Survey of Unbanked and Underbanked Households* (Washington DC: FDIC, July 2023), 75, https://www.fdic.gov/analysis/household-survey/2021report.pdf

638   CRA Final Rule, 6774.

639   CRA Final Rule, 7126.

640   CRA Final Rule, 6634.

641   CRA Final Rule, 6715-6718.

642   CRA Final Rule, 6931.

643   CRA Final Rule, 6628-6629.

644   CRA Final Rule, 6693.

645   CRA Final Rule, 6684.

646   CRA Final Rule, 6686.

647   CRA final Rule, 7112.

648   CRA Final Rule, 6671.

649   CRA Final Rule, 6675.

650   CRA Final Rule, 6677.

651   CRA Final Rule, 6677.

652   CRA Final Rule, 6704.

653   CRA Final Rule, 6726.

654   CRA Final Rule, 7123.

655   Urban Institute, Housing Finance Policy Center, "Bank lending outside CRA assessment areas," (PowerPoint presentation, National Association of Affordable Housing Lenders webinar series, Washington DC, January 26, 2022) 5, https://naahl.org/wp-content/uploads/2022/01/Urban-CRA_Project-CRA-Assessment-Areas-v12.pdf

656 Josh Silver, "The Community Reinvestment Act and Geography: How Well Do CRA Exams Cover the Geographical Areas that Banks Serve?" (NCRC, Washington DC, April 2017), https://ncrc.org/wp-content/uploads/2017/05/cra_geography_paper_050517.pdf

657 Josh Silver, "The Community Reinvestment Act and Geography".

658 CRA Final Rule, 6744, 6750-6751, 7115.

659 CRA Final Rule, 6744-6747.

660 Office of the Comptroller of the Currency, Federal Reserve System, Federal Deposit Insurance Corporation, Community Reinvestment Act: Joint notice of proposed rulemaking; request for comment, (Washington DC: Issued Version, Federal Register Notice, May 5, 2023), 134, https://www.federalreserve.gov/consumerscommunities/files/cra-npr-fr-notice-20220505.pdf

661 CRA Final Rule, 6742.

662 CRA Final Rule, 6738.

663 CRA Final Rule, 6735.

664 CRA Final Rule, 6909.

665 CRA Final Rule, 6878, 6910.

666 CRA Final Rule, 6761.

667 Josh Silver, "The Community Reinvestment Act and Geography".

668 CRA Final Rule, 7030.

669 CRA Final Rule, 7088-7089.

670 CRA Final Rule, 7088.

671 CRA Final Rule, 7084-7085.

672 CRA Final Rule, 7132-7136.

673 CRA Final Rule, 7135-7136.

674 CRA Final Rule, 7136.

675 CRA Final Rule, 7081.

676 American Bankers Association, "Trade Associations Sue Regulators for Exceeding Statutory Authority in New Community Reinvestment Act Rules," February 5, 2024, https://www.aba.com/about-us/press-room/press-releases/cra-joint-trades-lawsuit

677 Texas Bankers Association, Amarillo Chamber of Commerce, American Bankers Association, Chamber of Commerce of the United States of America, Longview Chamber of Commerce, Independent Community Bankers of America, Independent Bankers Association of Texas, "Complaint for Declaratory and Injunctive Relief, in the United States District Court for the Northern District of Texas, Amarillo Division," 5, 26, 29. https://www.aba.com/advocacy/policy-analysis/trade-associations-sue-regulators-cra Complaint.

678 Community Reinvestment, 12 U.S.C., 30, Section 2901(a)(1), 1431, https://www.govinfo.gov/content/pkg/USCODE-2013-title12/pdf/USCODE-2013-title12-chap30.pdf

679 Community Reinvestment, Section 2902(3)(A), 1432.

680 Community Reinvestment, Section 2903, 1433.

681 Texas Bankers Association, "Complaint for Declaratory and Injunctive Relief," 30.

682 Stephen Breyer, *Reading the Constitution: Why I Chose Pragmatism, Not Textualism* (New York: Simon and Schuster, 2024) 107.

683 Texas Bankers Association, "Complaint for Declaratory and Injunctive Relief," 44.

684 Texas Bankers Association, "Complaint for Declaratory and Injunctive Relief," 42.

685 Brad Blower, "The Banking Lobby's Cynical And Hollow Challenge To The Community Reinvestment Act Rule," *NCRC*, February 15, 2024, https://ncrc.org/the-banking-lobbys-cynical-and-hollow-challenge-to-the-community-reinvestment-act-rule/

686 Texas Bankers Association, "Complaint for Declaratory and Injunctive Relief," 46.

687 Texas Bankers Association, "Complaint for Declaratory and Injunctive Relief," 45, 46.

688 Defendants Consolidated Brief in Opposition to Plaintiff's Motion for a Preliminary Injunction, filed in the United States District Court for the Northern District of Texas, Amarillo Division, Civil NO. 2:24-cv-00025-Z-BR, 34.

689 Josh Silver, "NCRC Initial Analysis Of Federal Reserve's ANPR On The Community Reinvestment Act: A Step Forward But Needs To Be More Rigorous," *NCRC*, October 2020, https://www.ncrc.org/ncrc-initial-analysis-of-federal-reserves-anpr-on-the-community-reinvestment-act-a-step-forward-but-needs-to-be-more-rigorous/

690 Texas Bankers Association, "Complaint for Declaratory and Injunctive Relief," 38.

691 Texas Bankers Association, "Complaint for Declaratory and Injunctive Relief," 40, 41.

692 Texas Bankers Association, "Complaint for Declaratory and Injunctive Relief," 53, 54.

693 "GOP uses ACORN's woes to try to repeal bank law," *The Columbus Dispatch*, October 13, 2009, https://www.dispatch.com/story/news/2009/10/13/gop-uses-acorn-s-woes/24105404007/

694 CRA Final Rule, 7137-7138.

695 Kevin Hill, "Don't Fear The Data: Why The Lawsuit To Repeal Section 1071 Is Wrong," NCRC, June 2023, https://ncrc.org/dont-fear-the-data-why-the-lawsuit-to-repeal-section-1071-is-wrong/

696 Nate Raymond, "US lenders lose court battle over CFPB rule to collect small business data," *Reuters*, August 26, 2024, https://www.reuters.com/legal/banking-industry-loses-challenge-cfpb-small-business-loan-rule-2024-08-26/

Chapter 9

697 John Taylor, (former President and CEO of NCRC) in discussion with the author, February 2023.

698 Consumer Financial Protection Bureau (CFPB), "State Community Reinvestment Acts," (CFPB, Washington DC, 2023), https://www.consumerfinance.gov/data-research/research-reports/state-community-reinvestment-acts-summary-of-state-laws/

699 Marchiel, 143.

700 Federal Housing Finance Agency, *Single-Family and 2022 Multifamily Enterprise Housing Goals, 12 CFR Part 1282 RIN 2590-AB12, 2022-2024*, Vol. 86, No. 246 (Washington, D.C: Federal Register, Tuesday, December 28, 2021), 73641 – 73658, https://www.fhfa.gov/SupervisionRegulation/Rules/Pages/2022-2024-Enterprise-Housing-Goals-Final-Rule.aspx

701 NCRC comment letter on FHFA affordable housing goals, October 25, 2021, https://ncrc.org/ncrc-comment-letter-on-fhfa-affordable-housing-goals/

702 Jesse Van Tol, (President and CEO of NCRC) in discussion with the author, March 2023.

703 Joseph Fishkin and William E. Forbath, *The Anti-Oligarchy Constitution: Reconstructing the Economic Foundations of American Democracy* (Cambridge, Massachusetts: Harvard University Press, 2022), 478-479.

704 Internal Revenue Service, Community Health Needs Assessment for Charitable Hospital Organizations - Section 501(r)(3), https://www.irs.gov/charities-non-profits/community-health-needs-assessment-for-charitable-hospital-organizations-section-501r3

705 American Hospital Association, ProMedica Approaches Hunger as a Health Issue, https://www.aha.org/case-studies/2013-05-06-promedica-approaches-hunger-health-issue

706 American Hospital Association, Making Health Care Accessible Via a Volunteer Driven Transportation Program, https://www.aha.org/case-studies/2014-06-03-making-health-care-accessible-volunteer-driven-transportation-program

707 Lown Institute Hospital Index, 2023 Results - Fair Share Spending, https://lownhospitalsindex.org/2023-fair-share-spending/

708 Julian Gross, Greg LeRoy and Madeline Janis-Aparicio, *Community Benefit Agreements: Making Development Projects Accountable* (Good Jobs First and the California Partnership for Working Families, 2005), 10, https://juliangross.net/docs/CBA_Handbook.pdf

709 PowerSwitch Action, Community Benefit Agreements, https://www.power-switchaction.org/resources/community-benefits-agreements

710 PowerSwitch, *Common Challenges in Negotiating Community Benefits Agreements – And How to Avoid Them* (January 2016), 5-7 https://www.datocms-assets.com/64990/1657040054-effective-cbas.pdf

711 Department of Housing and Urban Development, Affirmatively Furthering Fair Housing, https://www.hud.gov/AFFH

712 NCRC comment letter on the District- Maryland-Virginia Regional Fair Housing Plan, April 10, 2023, https://ncrc.org/ncrc-comment-letter-on-the-district-maryland-virginia-regional-fair-housing-plan/

www.ingramcontent.com/pod-product-compliance
Lightning Source LLC
Chambersburg PA
CBHW021829190326
41518CB00007B/798